PRAISE FOR *GAP Y...*

"Having worked with the author of *Gap Ye...* ...
that she would be so courageous as to sell all her worldly possessions
and begin an amazing adventure traveling through Europe. Her
memo... ...e but
also a... ...it their
jobs t... ...

—... Collins

"... a...

—... *Magazine*

"For t... ...g up
the 'r... ...a
daydr... ...y and
planr... ...ws
(the i... ...usband
retra...

—...it Travel

"Don'... ...e world?
Mari... ...ets of
colle... ...rget
their...

—...EverPub

"I live... ...of
getti... ...aris
mara... ...ent's raw
emo...

—...arathoner

"*Gap*... ...time
you... ...also that
you'...

—John Ray Hoke, Jr., FAIA, former Publisher, AIA Press

"... an inspiring travelogue that shares insights on and off the
beaten path, the author's raw emotions while experiencing what she
dreamed of for years, and the realities of life in cultures previously
unknown. *Gap Year Girl* is an open book, not afraid to share and filled
with passion for history, food, wine and her travel partner."

—A. Edward, Volunteer Alumnus, Cross-Cultural Solutions

"To all my friends in book clubs . . . a perfect read to inspire all to live our dreams!"

—Lynn Arndt, Deputy Director,
Community Ministries of Rockville

"*Gap Year Girl* goes well beyond travel literature: it's a fascinating story of the author and her husband's journey, full of insights into what goes into intense travel. The author's sincere and open voice gives the reader an honest view of the realities of travel by presenting rich illustrations of the highs and lows, the exhilaration and tedium, that are necessary parts of extensive travel. This book was hard to put down, and I was sorry to see it end."

—Chris Darby, Film Editor, Univision

"I really enjoyed making the journey with the author. The book has a real sense of place, is beautifully written, and provides insights on so many different cultures."

—— Caroline Fallon, Bali Adventure Travel

"*Gap Year Girl* is a wonderfully written account of the author's travels with her high school sweetheart husband. Much more than a memoir, the book knits details of the trip with memories gone by and hopes for what's to come. If you yearn to be an independent traveler, you'll totally enjoy this book."

—Nancy McKeown-Brand, Vice President, Sun & Fun

"Marianne Bohr did what all of us dream of doing: she visited the exotic places of her youth with a lifetime's worth of experience to sharpen the view. With humor and candor and an enormous amount of appreciation, *Gap Year Girl* gives us back the excitement of travel and the charm of European life."

—Trish O'Hare, Publisher, GemmaMedia

"*Gap Year Girl* gives delicious descriptions of the many places on three continents that Bohr visited with her husband. And like the best of the genre, it leaves the reader feeling more than a bit jealous of both the journey and her ability to effortlessly write about it in such an illuminating way."

—Chuck Dresner, Publishing Consultant

GAP YEAR GIRL

GAP YEAR GIRL

A
Baby Boomer
Adventure
Across
21
Countries

Marianne C. Bohr

SHE WRITES PRESS

Published 2015
Printed in the United States of America
ISBN: 978-1-63152-820-0
Library of Congress Control Number: 2015936357
Map by Mike Morgenfeld

For information, address:
She Writes Press
1563 Solano Ave #546
Berkeley, CA 94707

She Writes Press is a division of SparkPoint Studio, LLC.

Portions of this book appeared previously in Bethesda magazine.

DEDICATION

~

For Joe

Contents

FOREWORD

◦∼◦

DURING THE MOST PROLIFIC (and frenzied) years of our involvement as the chief writers in the crafting and compilation of Frommer's guides, we aimed our writing at an archetypal consumer whom we imagined as bright, savvy, experimental, adventurous, and rigorously opposed to domination by a tour operator. Our ideal reader would almost certainly have been Marianne Bohr, who seems, with the release of this memoir, to have found travel wings of her own. A wide-eyed and alert "empty nester" in need of adventures abroad, this good-looking, spunky blonde from Washington, DC, relays why and how she and her husband decided to take off and fly in this appealing read.

In its idiosyncratic, personalized, and sometimes quirky way, her memoir has redefined both the craft of travel writing and the post-Internet art of travel itself. Its sense of giddy curiosity (and triumph) comes from insights Marianne adapted from a laptop-generated blog that she crafted during the course of her year abroad. The result is an absorbing rundown of a cultural odyssey bursting with insights and quiet truths, which she absorbed, way out there, without a guide, and often intuitively—some might even say through her pores.

Marianne exemplifies the best of the Internet age's new breed of traveler. Worldly and tech-savvy, she was motivated to extend her perspective beyond the barriers of the home and corporate career she had successfully forged and then (temporarily) abandoned. After intense soul searching, she did the unthinkable: she sold the house, sold the car, sold the furniture, said a temporary au revoir to her workaday nine-to-five, and took off, persuading her husband, Joe, whom no one plays for a fool, to hang on for the ride as muse, bodyguard, and travel companion. Evoking the envy of many of her workaday colleagues, she rebirthed herself and turned her midlife crisis into a dream. The memoir that emerged is the living manifestation of how she did it.

That Marianne has penned such an iconoclastic book comes as no surprise to those who have watched her evolve into a potent new breed of travel journalist. Even her first name seems to fit: In the late eighteenth century, Jacques-Louis David depicted her as a nubile maiden, an athletic female incarnation of the French Enlightenment storming the trenches of the ancien régime. Today, this Gap Year Girl, despite her hip, modern-day sense of fashion, might best be imagined as waving a symbolic torch across the previously jaded trenches of travel journalism—a field sorely in need of rebirth.

Thanks to Gap Year Girl, Ms. Bohr's travel universe and the way it's recorded are an inspiration to thousands of baby boomers who are coming to realize that it's possible not only to dream Don Quixote's Impossible Dream, but to make it come true. *Vive la Révolution!*

DARWIN PORTER AND DANFORTH PRINCE
are coauthors of many dozens of editions of the
best-selling travel references, the Frommer's guides.

Go confidently in the direction of your dreams.

Live the life you've imagined.

—HENRY DAVID THOREAU

INTRODUCTION

⁓

THE SEEDS OF A GAP YEAR ABROAD—the age-old British tradition of spending time far from home—were sown when I was twenty-two and doing graduate work in France's Loire Valley. It was 1978, and my time abroad ignited a love affair with France and all things French and uncovered a wanderlust that compelled me to travel the Continent.

But, truth be told, my remarkable year was marred by that particular brand of isolation that comes with knowing few people in a foreign land. I was on my own, unaffiliated with an American program, and making friends was difficult for a to-her-core introvert. I so yearned to share my experiences with Joe, the high school sweetheart I would later marry. I promised myself I would return to Europe one day for an encore year when I was older and wiser, this time with my partner beside me.

From early in our marriage, Joe and I discussed our future gap year with joint imaginings that soon took on a definite shape. I'm a person who thrives on making things happen, so, as time went by, I became borderline obsessive about fleshing out the details of our sabbatical, pushing aside what we should do and replacing it with what we wanted to do at every juncture.

I was the driving force behind making the dream a reality, but Joe is as passionate about travel as I am and needed a break from work as much as I did. I was burned out from a career in book publishing, and Joe from his job as a marine engineer. He bought into my gap year vision with gusto and added specifics of his own. Our code word for taking leave of the United States was "2011," a reference to the year we would shake off the weighty string of bills for our children's education. Our son, Chris, would graduate from college in 2007 and our daughter, Caroline, in 2010. We contemplated life after tuition and planned how we would drastically reduce our financial footprint (sell the house, along with the cars, and divest ourselves of the belongings accumulated from raising children), thereby freeing the funds for our "senior year" abroad. Internet sales, a variety of charities, and our children would help us unload half our belongings, and the rest would go into storage.

Even so, our impending departure never seemed quite real. After so many years of planning and imagining, we found it difficult to believe that the pictures in our minds would actually become our life for a year.

The moniker Gap Year Girl made its appearance about six years prior to our departure. One hazy summer afternoon, while sitting behind my office desk, gazing out the window at the suburban parking lot below, my mind wandering beyond the budgets and strategic plan in front of me, I had an existential moment. I needed the prospect of an escape, and I needed to give it a name. In my mind's eye, I was no longer senior vice president of a book distribution company; I was Gap Year Girl, an expat living in Europe—my new alter ego.

This paradigm shift of how I viewed myself changed everything. From that point forward, I focused on making our gap year a reality. And I decided then and there to leave the world of business I'd inhabited for a quarter of a century. I saw my future as clear as day: I was going to make a midlife, post–gap year change and follow my bliss.

By the end of the week, I'd registered for a master's degree program in secondary education and was on my way to becoming a middle school French teacher.

Fast-forward to September 2011: our children had college degrees and were gainfully employed, and our bank account was fattened as a result of our having sold most of our worldly possessions. Armed with spreadsheets that meticulously detailed our projected daily and monthly budgets, we took our cue from adventurous youth who leave their lives behind to hit the road. Joe and I quit our jobs, said goodbye to the United States at the ripe old age of fifty-five, and set off on our long-awaited, long-intended gap year. We left with no notion of where we would settle upon our return and recognized that extended and likely frustrating job searches would ensue once our year abroad concluded. But we looked forward to the change, the demarcation between the earlier and later stages of our lives. And the psychological weightlessness of financial freedom, albeit temporary, was priceless; we knew the rewards would be well worth the risks.

Family and close friends were hardly surprised; we'd been talking about our intentions for years. But colleagues deemed us either incredibly brave or absurdly foolish. The truth was likely somewhere in between. "Please, take me with you," some implored. "You're my hero for just walking away." Others weren't shy about sharing their negativity. "Are you serious?" they asked. "What about your house? Making money? Chris and Caroline?"

Did we worry about leaving our children, jettisoning everything, and moving to Europe without a home, a car, or jobs? Without a doubt. Were we nervous about living out of a couple of duffels, blissfully unaware of the difficulties we might encounter as we created our itinerary as we went along? Absolutely. It was a terrifying venture, but we knew it felt right deep down inside and that if we yielded to our fears, backed down, and decided not to go, we would regret it for the rest of our lives.

That doesn't mean spending a gap year in Europe and points beyond is everyone's cup of tea. Others fantasize about twelve months of ocean breezes on a tropical island, at an ethereal artist's colony far from civilization, or as a volunteer in the wilds of Africa. But our personal dream was to wander through our destinations in search of local color, history, architecture, drink, and food.

Other than that, we had no grand strategy for our year, no fleshed-out, burnished blueprint. We wanted it to unfold organically, without too much definition, so that we would have the flexibility to take advantage of possibilities and change our plans according to how we felt. And thus we left plenty of room for the spontaneity, flights of fancy, and reflection our spirits would require. We did have a skeletal framework, a tentative list of countries, a budget, and a few ground rules—one of which was that we would spend many months in my beloved France—but all we knew for sure was that we would start with a month in Paris, our favorite city, where previous weeklong stays had always left us wanting more, and end with a farewell in the City of Light eleven months later. We mapped out an approximate itinerary and booked our accommodations online along the way.

Budget-conscious throughout, we stuck mostly to inexpensive, often out-of-the-way lodgings and ate modest meals. But there were occasional splurges: staying in a château in Provence, skiing in the Dolomites, enjoying

a spectacular riad in Morocco, and dining in multiple-
starred restaurants. Our trek included some European
Grand Tour destinations, but we added visits to lesser-
known places such as Carcassonne, the fortified town
in southern France; Andorra, the Catalan principality
perched high in the Pyrenees; Agrigento, Sicily, with its
honey-colored Greek temples lining the ridge; Lipica,
Slovenia, where Lipizzaner stallions are bred; and Butrint,
Albania, one of the most spectacular archaeological
sites on the Mediterranean. We savored the rich food of
southwestern France, sipped the wines of Italy, smelled
the blooms of Holland's Keukenhof, and scrambled over
ruins in Turkey.

But enough with the summaries. Grab your backpack, curl up in a chair, and come along to the continent
with Gap Year Girl and her faithful mate, Joe. Be sure to
pack your appetite, a map, and a healthy sense of adventure.
I do hope you enjoy the journey with us.

I. Anticipation

THE COUNTDOWN BEGINS: September 2010

LABOR DAY 2010 is behind us, and our gap year countdown begins. The departure for Europe we've planned for over a decade will be just after Labor Day 2011, less than twelve months away. My anticipation has built continuously, and I'm now ready to explode. The time for list writing, pile making, and counting down the days is finally here. May the serious plotting begin.

We'll have a full year in Europe, September through August, and the most obvious question is: Where shall we go?

What started as a straightforward picture (one month in Paris, three months in far-flung corners of *la belle France profonde*, two months in Spain, three months in Italy, and three months in Greece) has become muddled. After watching *Casablanca* late one night, we decide to take a ferry from Spain to Paul Bowles's Morocco for a week. We're not particularly interested in Germany but have always wanted to visit Berlin, so let's add that to the list. And while we're at it, why not stop in Prague, Budapest, and Vienna on the way? Dubrovnik is one of the world's up-and-coming destinations, so let's stay there for a week on our way to Greece.

The itinerary has fractured as our wanderlust has entered a tug-of-war with our desire to settle down and live in select places for months at a time. The dilemma: How to balance these natural adversaries, yet satisfy them both? We must continue to envision our trip as fluid, to be altered as needed along the way.

People often ask, when I tell them our plans, "Do you have any fears?"

Well, sure, I tell them. And the first of these involves our son and daughter. Anyone with children knows that going off and leaving them behind is difficult—even if they're young adults totally capable of taking care of themselves. At twenty-six and twenty-three, Chris and Caroline have been away from home, at college, and then on their own on the West Coast for several years now. But being in a foreign country with an ocean between us will feel so much farther than being on opposite sides of our own country. Yes, the children will visit us—if we're lucky, more than once—but still. Maybe the fact that we can actually go to Europe and leave them behind marks a separation milestone of sorts, and a bittersweet one at that. We've tried to raise our children to be independent, yet can we be independent of them?

But, as our children always do, they cheer us on. Excited for our adventure. Anxious to visit us in foreign lands. Our biggest advocates.

My only other nagging fear is something that an annoying little voice deep inside me keeps whispering: *Can you go back? Can you really go back?*

My first trip to Europe was in the summer of 1977, after my junior year of college. Like so many American youth, my college roommate, two friends, and I embarked on our coming-of-age adventure, armed with *Let's Go Europe* as our bible. We applied for passports, booked the cheapest charter flight available, bought Eurail passes, stuffed our backpacks till the seams almost burst, and headed off to London. We were on strict budgets but managed to visit ten countries in six weeks.

That first time in Europe, that inaugural experience of a world outside my own—of unfamiliar and extraordinary art and architecture; language; food and drink; smells, people, and landscapes—and the jaw-dropping nature of the trip can never be re-created. It was the wonder of Christmas morning every day, and while I may never again tingle with those exact feelings, I do expect to be seized by the sheer exhilaration and freedom of living abroad for 365 days as an unemployed, unencumbered adult.

I spent the year after college (1978–79) living in Tours, France, in the heart of the Loire Valley. Finances hadn't allowed for a junior year abroad, but I received a Rotary Fellowship that paved the way for graduate study in Europe. In addition to tuition, I was given a stipend for living expenses to spend as I pleased. I opted for renting a room in a retired woman's townhome in the city center, rather than going the more expensive route of living with a family and being fed three daily squares. I managed to eat on just a few dollars a day and saved the balance for traveling. And travel I did.

It was shoestring trekking at its best, and I wanted to go everywhere. I had lists of places to see—those I'd heard or read about over the years and those my landlady recommended. Almost every weekend I headed out of town and stretched my travel dollars as far as they would go, sleeping on trains, atop station benches, and in inexpensive guest rooms. I always managed to treat myself to one proper sit-down meal on each of my journeys— at one of the prix-fixe restaurants I'd found in *Let's Go*— where I would have a salad, an entrée, dessert, and *un pichet* of wine for $8. At these solo meals, I amused myself with people-watching and writing my weekly batch of postcards to friends and family back home.

While I relished the familiar routine of keeping in touch, long before the advent of the Internet, e-mail, and cell phones, I had a difficult time writing about the places I'd visited and adequately conveying the sense of adventure I experienced.

How could I explain seeing Mont Saint-Michel as it rose ominously out of the gloomy English Channel for the first time, or the briny smell of the fresh seafood proudly displayed along the narrow streets of Saint-Malo? What words could possibly capture the fear of being stranded in an unexpected snowstorm, slipping, sliding, and falling on the steep streets of Carcassonne on a Sunday night, all the inns I could afford full?

My writing never did justice to the story of the grandparents and grandson I met in Lourdes. The older couple had exhausted their life savings to travel from Iowa to bring the teenager afflicted with a serious case of cystic acne to the springs of Lourdes, hoping for a miraculous cure. To this day, I'm overcome with uneasy melancholy when I recall my time in Lourdes and the hundreds of people I passed in wheelchairs, on crutches, and being carried on their pilgrimage to the holy waters.

Most of my travels that year were solo. Few of my peers shared the depth of my desire to regularly leave town and explore corners of the country unknown. At times I was pleased to be by myself, following my own rhythm and determining my itinerary, but I had frequent bouts of loneliness as I yearned to share my exploits. It was during the months I spent studying abroad, far from my now husband, Joe, that we solidified our relationship— he sailing on merchant ships and I gallivanting through Europe. I promised myself that one day we would come back to explore Europe at length and create our own travelogue together. I'd had enough of unaccompanied jaunts and unsuccessful attempts to describe them. We've been back to France several times since my year in Tours, but only for a week or two at a time—hardly adequate for thorough exploration.

When we're young and curious, almost everything we do is an adventure—it's all brand-new and for the very first time. As we age and our risk-averse wiring takes over, it gets harder to keep adventure in our lives. In fact, many adults go to great lengths to eradicate any hint of the word from their worlds. They want their days scheduled, nights predictable, and meals familiar and would never think about embarking on something unless they knew the outcome. While a huge fan of schedules, organization, and checklists, I also crave adventure, and perhaps that's why I love to travel, especially to places I've never been. If more adults embraced adventure in their lives and—God forbid—actively sought it, perhaps they'd feel happier and younger and be open to more possibilities.

I'm determined to go fully back with my eyes, ears, and mind open to as many adventures as we can find. While some may fall in our path, others we'll seek out. And while nothing may ever be as raw and surprising as when I was twenty-one, I'll embrace this dream-made-reality with open arms and a racing heart. By acknowledging up front that this time will be different (and, who knows, maybe better), I know I can go back. Just as I had no idea what would happen when I headed to Europe in the '70s, I don't know what will await us when we leave next September.

So here we are, anticipating our gap year, ready to discover new places and revisit familiar haunts, together.

RESOLUTIONS: January 2011

I've never been a fan of January resolutions. For me, the Tuesday after Labor Day has always seemed more appropriate as the start of a new year. September is the time for new shoes and crisp new folders, blank paper and fresh ideas.

In the frigid, unconscious, gray days of January, I want to hunker down to the hard work of imagining, researching, and preparing. In the weeks after New Year's, my heart turns to filling in the details of our next escape. Over the years, it's become a ritual of the Martin Luther King Jr. holiday weekend: I make initial arrangements for our summer getaway. I've always said I work in order to travel and that I make a deposit in our vacation fund before I go to the grocery store. It's always been this way, and I suspect it will never change.

This January, more than ever, all I want to do is plan for and dream about leaving the country in September. As I observe the steely, oh-so-dismal frozen Maryland landscape through the shutters of my bedroom, my dewy-eyed imaginings of strolling through Granada, hiking in the Alps, and sunning by a fountain in Provence take over. What I'm looking at now is ashen, lifeless. What I see in my mind's eye is in Technicolor—filled with promise and potential. Such are the initiatives I focus on with my January resolutions.

Then, one day soon after, I wake and ask myself, *Are you crazy? Are we nuts? In this terrible economy, you're going to walk away from everything and expect to come back on your own terms after twelve full months?* I haven't had many, but I admit there have been a few of them—days of fear and self-doubt and thoughts of encroaching insanity. They creep up after I hear just-released economic statistics predicting continued doom and gloom, further unemployment, and ongoing malaise, or on the heels of a dismal story about middle-agers being unemployed for years. And years. My normal optimism turns to doubt, I convince myself that something will go horribly wrong, and I sit up in the middle of many a night in a cold sweat. *Can we actually afford to temporarily stop climbing the materialistic American ladder to leave the country? Will the European Union finally collapse under the weight of the mounting Greek debt? Did I underestimate the budget by inadvertently misplacing a decimal?*

My inner guilt complex scolds, *You're going to abandon secure incomes and expect to land not one but two jobs when you return? Who do you think you are?*

These marauding attacks of anxiety drive me straight to my gap year spreadsheets for numerical reassurance that we've saved enough, and that we have an adequate financial cushion and accurate budgets. Initially, I panic about going broke, moving in with our children, and becoming laughingstocks. But after I've fretted for several hours, my fear about being in the poorhouse turns into a very different terror that screams, *But we have to go, no matter what. We've anticipated this for so long!* My brave voice always surfaces and says, *You can do it, and you must do it. You will never, ever regret it*—and this is the voice that always wins. I've taken some leaps in my life after listening to the voices in my recesses, and in the end, they've always been right.

There's an episode of the TV series *The Love Boat* that has stayed with me. It featured a recently retired couple on a much-anticipated cruise. Shortly after the ship sets sail, the wife can hardly contain herself; she has a surprise for her husband. Over the course of their forty-five-year marriage, she reveals, she's built a substantial nest egg for traveling the world in their old age. Expecting to be greeted with cries of joy, she is crushed as he slowly absorbs what she tells him and becomes increasingly angry. He's furious that in order to save for the promise of future travel, she denied them trips during their working and child-rearing years—the years when they needed getaways the most. There were countless times, he shared, when there was nothing he wanted more than to go away with her. Why did she sacrifice adventure while they were young and healthy, he asks tearfully, for the promise of journeys when they were old and weary?

I was a young adult when I saw that episode, and, as hokey as this sounds, it taught me a lesson: You cannot wait for tomorrow. You must listen to your brave voices, tell the panicky ones to disappear, and jump into your dreams with both feet.

So why do I still have butterflies in my stomach? *It's excitement, not fear* becomes my daily mantra.

FILLING IN THE BLANKS: February 2011

As we inch closer to our anticipated departure, our gap year slowly comes into focus and starts to take shape. We've begun to pepper the calendar with specific dates and confirm some travel details. I remain in the throes of the tension between staying in a few places for several months at a time and moving around to experience as much as possible. We have yet to settle on a firm itinerary but have drafted a skeletal calendar and committed to a couple of anchor activities: New Year's Eve 2011 in Rome, and for 2012, the Paris Marathon in April and an Aix-en-Provence French course in August. We'll fill in the rest around these highlights.

When we began the twelve-month countdown in September 2010, we made a list of things that had to happen before we could leave. We've checked off items one by one over the past few months, but one big one lingers. Yet to be accomplished before we pack up and leave is the sale of our home—no small feat in the 2011 economy. We consider renting it but don't want the hassle of tenants in the place. Getting a call about a burst pipe as we wander down the Champs-Élysées would certainly break the mood. We can't leave for Europe as unemployed gap year travelers with no income and a mortgage on a vacant property. The proceeds from the sale will finance our leave-taking, so we cannot go away until we sell the house.

THE MASTER PLAN: March 2011

Student-teaching boot camp is consuming my spring. Our gap year will mark not only a personal milestone but a professional one as well: upon our return, I'll become a middle school French teacher—all part of our master plan.

The good news is that my formal training is almost over, the better news is that I'm surviving, and the best news is that I know I made the right choice by embarking on the French-teacher trail. When in Europe, I'll take every opportunity to loosen my jaw and rediscover the ease I had when speaking French as a resident. Upon our return, I'll launch a new career with the fresh scent of lavender and a whiff of goat cheese in my hair. And while we're away, Joe will determine whether to remain an engineer or pursue something new. Only time will tell.

THE HOUSE SELLS: April 2011

The day we anticipated for so long has arrived: we sold the house after it languished on the market for over a year. We have a signed contract and a closing date of June 30. Now the real fun begins: packing, sorting, figuring out where we'll live for the summer, and moving our finances online.

Last night I dreamed about hiking the Alps.

On my 1977 summer backpacking trip, I left my fellow travelers in Interlaken, Switzerland, and went hiking on my own. *Let's Go* recommended an all-day round-trip walk from Grindelwald up to the snow line at the Kleine Scheidegg pass at the base of the Jungfrau and Eiger peaks. I left the youth hostel at dawn, took the train to the trailhead, and headed for the snow. When I think back on that excursion, which introduced me to hiking, I realize just how poorly equipped I was, but at twenty-one I wanted only to experience climbing an alp.

We pencil in a visit to Switzerland. This time when I hike, I'll have all the proper gear and I'll know what I'm in for. My middle-aged body will slow the pace, and I'll no longer have to describe the experience to Joe. My partner will be with me.

FINALIZING THE DETAILS: May 2011

Every morning I wake up with a headache and a mixed bag of to-dos rattling in my brain. What needs to be done before we move out next month is even infiltrating my dreams. But by the end of each day, I've checked off several more items on the list. Order duffel bags: check. Complete change-of-address forms: check. Make dentist appointments: check. Locate our birth certificates for visa applications: check.

But whenever I delete one item from the list, three more appear.

While taking care of the logistics for our gap year is part of the whole experience, I can't forget to slow down every few days and devote myself to emotional preparation. While packing the scores of books, pictures, and knickknacks from our living room shelves, I sit down on the couch and read the Lawrence Durrell quote from *Bitter Lemons* that I had framed and used as a bookend for our travel-book collection years ago:

"Journeys, like artists, are born and not made. A thousand differing circumstances contribute to them, few of them willed or determined by the will—whatever we may think. They flower spontaneously out of the demands of our natures—and the best of them lead us not only outwards in space, but inwards as well. Travel can be one of the most rewarding forms of introspection. . . ."

Durrell is one of my favorite travel writers, and his prose has enriched my trips to the Mediterranean. What he expresses is why Joe and I have only a rough idea of where we'll travel for twelve months: our trip will unfold as "our natures" require.

I close my eyes for a few needed moments of

reflection, but there is much work to do. Time to get back online and cancel the newspaper.

This past weekend was an important one, since it led to writing an actual departure date—in pen—on the calendar. We booked our flights to Paris and signed a lease on an apartment for our first month abroad.

My daydreams always had us leaving for our gap year the day after Labor Day—the minute the postsummer airfares drop—and that's exactly what we'll do. A Tuesday, September 6, departure yields the best and cheapest one-way fare. Exactly when we return is a decision for the future. We'll wave goodbye to the United States from Washington Dulles and say hello to Europe at Paris Charles de Gaulle. Fingers crossed that we can make it through the visa appointment with one-way tickets in hand. The agents may indeed have cause to worry: Will we actually want to come home?

Joe and I spend multiple hours browsing the Paris apartment offerings on the Internet, imagining life in the various and very different properties, weighing the pros and cons of each. We pore over listing after listing: this one's too expensive; that one's in an ugly building (yes, there are some, even in Paris); that one has no Wi-Fi; this one's decorated all in red (we don't want to inhabit the Moulin Rouge for a month); that one's not available for our dates; this one's on a busy street; that one has only a pullout couch.

After sending countless e-mails to owners, we finally zero in on what we hope will be the perfect pied-à-terre in the 7th arrondissement, on the Avenue de Suffren, one block over from the Eiffel Tower. The studio is well within the budget, and it just feels right. It's on a tree-lined street on the ground level of a Haussmann-era building and opens on a small courtyard. Despite the fact that it's a tiny twenty-five square meters, the Eiffel Tower is in the backyard and the Seine down the street, so why complain about close quarters? Maybe it's the warm lighting in the pictures or the fact that its hardwood floors and beige and taupe decor make it look like a space I decorated myself. Whatever the reason, something about this flat reaches across the ocean and takes hold of us.

The Eiffel studio is now ours for our first month in Europe, and our misty reveries of living in Paris finally have a mise-en-scène.

We're officially over the hill. We're also now members of Hosteling International and have received our first-ever senior discounts. While I was thrilled to save on our annual fees because we're fifty-five, I was less than enthusiastic about the reason for the deductions.

Are we seniors? Really?

A friend suggested that rather than refer to our year away as a gap year, we call it our senior year abroad. It didn't grab me at first, especially since I was a youngster of fifty-four when he offered the comment. But the term is growing on me. Junior year abroad includes living in another country, meeting new people, exploring uncharted territory, experiencing adventure and ongoing learning—all things we'll embrace during our twelve months away. So maybe "senior year abroad" is indeed the better term. We'll be doing it at fifty-five, instead of twenty-one, and if we're lucky, there will be many more senior discounts in our future. I wonder if the luxurious

Relais & Châteaux hotels will offer us reduced rates.

Hostels may not always ooze local charm (Joe comments that if you add armed guards, some could be mistaken for prisons), but they're sanitary, safe, and cheap. Staying at hostels for a few nights a month will free up funds for treating ourselves to some magical castle hotels along the way.

HOMELESS VAGABONDS: June 2011
I expected to feel sad when we sold our home of nine years, and yes, the waves of melancholy come and go. But the sense of relief comes out of the blue.

As we leave the settlement office, the proceeds safely wired, I feel as if I'm untethered and now have the freedom no mortgage, no fixed address, and not a dollar of debt afford. We paid off our old gray mare of a Chrysler long ago, and if we can just add another two months to her useful life on top of the 212,000 miles she's already given us, we'll unload her and leave the country car-free as well. We'll soon be camping out in the home of dear friends until our departure.

In preparation for our move, we donate and sell whatever we can. Books have always been the hardest to relinquish, but this time we're ruthless, and even those go with little regret. I find myself astonished by what people will buy. That old antique chair with the missing seat cushion, the distressed copper planters from the front stoop, the oversize corkboard that displayed our children's artwork, the prehistoric laptops missing hard drives, and the stereo cabinet designed for a record player: all found homes with happy new owners.

It's a time-consuming, tedious process of sorting

all we own, making meticulous piles, and deciding what to do with every item in the house. We don't want to pay to store anything unnecessarily. We're left with only what we'll need for the summer and next year in tow. All else is shrink-wrapped, crated, and stored, not to be seen until we're back in the United States, some fourteen months from now. Our load is now quite light indeed.

THE RUBICON HAS BEEN CROSSED: July 2011

The die is cast. Joe and I gave notice at work. We leave for Europe in seven weeks. *C'est fait.*

We're both so used to defining ourselves with professional titles and daily routines, but I can already tell that Joe will take longer than I to get psychologically accustomed to having no permanent address, car, or job. I'm doing my best to encourage him to let go, but he readily admits, "Having these touchstones disappear is liberating but also frightening."

We make a much-anticipated visit to the French embassy in Georgetown to apply for long-stay visas, since France is the country in which we'll spend the most time. Procuring our paperwork is both a final hurdle to clear in the United States and our first confrontation with the notorious French bureaucracy. I devote hours to researching and preparing the requirements. I collect bank statements, write affidavits stating we don't intend to work in France, get passport-size photos taken, print the Paris apartment lease, draft our itinerary, and complete the applications. Good Catholic schoolgirl that I am, I follow directions well. I diligently prepare the necessary documents according to the exact instructions provided. In typical Marianne style, I fret about the requirements and my stress levels rise. What if I've missed a detail or something goes wrong? We've planned for years, are no longer employed, have surrendered our home, and are so emotionally invested in leaving the country that to be denied visas at this point would be devastating. We must secure those pieces of paper.

We arrive at the embassy gate primed for our interviews, ready for battle, and armed with our meticulously prepared paperwork. We make ourselves as comfortable as we can in the molded plastic chairs. After twenty minutes, it's apparent we're here for the duration when they call the young woman with a 9:00 a.m. appointment an hour late. So much for obsessing about getting here on time.

We sit back to listen to the travails of the applicants before us, and I conjure up the roadblocks the clerks will build for us. First comes the Bulgarian student accompanied by her father. Her plan to visit her country for two weeks prior to landing in Paris is causing a problem. And then come the two young women with Algerian passports, again escorted by their father. They present their story to the woman behind the glass in muffled tones. The exchange becomes heated as the patriarch takes over. "It's because we're Muslim, isn't it? Who is your supervisor? This is an outrage." And with that, father and daughters storm out. We now understand why the processors are behind protective glass. Emotions boil over quickly when stakes are high. The longer we wait, the more my nerves take over, and I realize my anxiety isn't just about our visas; it's mixed with insecurity about having quit our jobs, angst about leaving our children, and fear of what's ahead.

After an hour, they call our names. Part one of the process goes without a hitch. We present our identification to the woman at window 1. She fingerprints us electronically, asks a few questions, and snaps our pictures, and we retreat to our seats. So far, so good. I try to relax.

Twenty-five minutes later, we're called to window 2 and find that our luck has suddenly changed. A not-so-dashing Inspector Clouseau who speaks English with a thick Marseille accent has an attitude from the start.

"No, these are the wrong applications—these are 2009 versions. Fill out these new ones." He throws the forms at us.

"Your last three pay stubs." (When I protest that pay stubs aren't on the list, he rudely fires back that he'll print the requirements from the website—extended pause—"madame.")

"Proof that you live in Washington, DC." (This wasn't on the list either.)

"Show me where this letter says you have health coverage in France." (We highlight the sentence that says "outside the US," and he tosses it back. "Inadequate.")

We retreat to our chairs, humiliated, after he scoffs one final time and dismisses us: "Sit and wait. You will be called."

On the verge of tears, I want to strangle the man. Does he not know that I am Gap Year Girl and that he is the only thing standing between me and my dream? Lucky for him, there is that protective window. Yes, emotions do run over. We dutifully complete the "new" forms he gave us, which are exactly the same bloody forms, except that the "2009" printed in five-point type in the lower-right corner of our forms says "2011" on his. I sit and fume, reviewing the requirements I printed from the website: it says nothing about residency proof and pay stubs. I stifle a scream.

In the end, we leave the embassy after an audience at window 3. The sympathetic young man gives us a to-do checklist and graciously explains the three items we still need to provide: a one-page narrative about what we will do for a year; an explanation of how we sold our Maryland home and are living with friends, our friends' driver's licenses, and a utility bill proving their DC residency; and a revised letter from our health insurance provider with specific language about coverage in France. His parting suggestion leaves us deflated: you may have to find a new insurance company. Really? Why does health insurance always have to be so hard?

Time is ticking, and still no health insurance letter. We receive a gracious communication from the embassy stating that our file is "approximately" complete. We should present ourselves in person, no appointment needed, once we have the precious documentation in hand. Our insurance company's customer care office assures us the letter is coming, but I won't believe they've handled it correctly until I have the paperwork in hand. I'm trusting by nature, and I want to believe we won't have to resort to Insurance Plan B. But I can't help but ask, are we waiting for Godot?

Why does one country fascinate me and another leave me cold? Why does my heart flutter at the mention of anything French, my spirit light up at the thought of a Greek isle, my muscles relax and my mouth water at the sight of an Italian taverna, but I feel little enthusiasm for discussing our upcoming visits to Berlin or Budapest? Is it because I know so much more about France, Greece, and Italy than I do about Eastern Europe? Is it because I speak French? But wait—I speak no Greek, yet all things Hellenic appeal to my every sense. And while I can get by in an Italian restaurant, I don't speak Italian.

I try to pinpoint what it was that initially piqued my interest in France. It wasn't simply that I learned the language. I took Spanish years before I started studying French, and while I liked *mis clases de español*, once I walked into my very first high school French class, I was smitten. Mesmerized. Committed.

I consider the possibility that I was a French peasant in a former life because of my innate appreciation for all things French. I'm sure I wasn't royal; the flamboyant French court is definitely not my style. It's amusing to think about, especially when I connect some of my avocations to the life of a peasant: my love of gardening, getting my hands dirty, and making a plot of land my own; my affinity for the countryside and uncharted walkabouts; my powerful need to retreat from crowds and the sounds of the city to revel in the landscape and go inward. I can spend hours in a museum taking in French medieval tapestries and learning about the stories behind them, not because I'd like to hang them in my home but because I'm fascinated by the people who made them.

So I'm left with the question of why France? Why Greece? And why the other countries that take hold of me and won't let go? Why do these places and their possibilities make me feel incomplete without them? Perhaps I'll discover there are other countries, territories, and cultures that seize my heart with their pleasures and treasures. Morocco? Turkey? The Czech Republic? Spain? I can't wait to find out.

With only six weeks until our departure date, I have to work very, very hard to relax.

My to-do lists give structure to my days, whether I'm working, going to school, or hanging around the house. They've served me well for fifty-five years and helped me accomplish much. However, one of my goals for our year abroad is to simply relax, make room for quiet, reflective space, and consciously take in and appreciate my surroundings.

There's a Pascal quote that says something about how all men's miseries derive from not being able to sit in a quiet room alone. Well, I want to make sure that such suffering has no place in our gap year. We'll build in plenty of lazy expanses of unscheduled time to simply sit quietly and look around, whether in a rustic *gîte* or a comfortable inn, on a mountaintop or a park bench. While it may go against my get-it-done grain, I'm determined to slow down and resist the fast pace of our life stateside, and not to worry if we miss a few must-see sights. It will be more important to take in, absorb, and remember those we do see. The big question is: Will I be able to accept that relaxing is indeed an accomplishment?

THE FINAL COUNTDOWN: August 2011
We leave for Paris four weeks from today.

The last countdown I recognized was in September 2010, when we had twelve months to go until departure. We can now start counting the days. Our packing dress rehearsal shows us that all we plan to take will indeed fit in our bags (a rolling duffel, an overnight bag, and a backpack each), so we're almost ready to go.

Thirty-three years ago this month, I left for Europe to study in France. My parents drove a terrified me from our home on Long Island to the sleek, futuristic TWA terminal at JFK and waved goodbye as I boarded. I was keenly aware at that moment of departure just how alone I was, heading for a year in a foreign country where I knew not a soul.

This time around, I'll leave from Dulles (another winged, Saarinen-designed terminal) with Joe at my side, and terror will not be an issue. Anticipating our impending departure has me thinking about the differences between my young-adult persona and my fifty-five-year-old self.

On the epicurean side, when I arrived in Tours, France, wine was of no consequence to me. Little did I know that where I chose to study would lead to a fervent French palate for wine. Crisp, citrusy sauvignon blancs from the Loire quickly became my wines of choice and remain my favorites. Living in the Loire Valley, the Garden of France, also turned me into quite the foodie. It opened my eyes and alerted my taste buds to French cheeses, pâtés, rillettes, and savory galettes, all of which I could afford on my grad-student budget. I first arrived in France a food and wine neophyte, and I now return an aficionado.

I also crave more creature comforts than I did at twenty-two, although I can still rough it with the youth. While I look forward to our hostel stays for nostalgia's sake and the funds they'll free up for fine dining, I doubt Joe and I will camp out in railway stations or on overnight train floors, as I did so often as a student. The aches and pains that come with being fifty-five and the time it would take to physically recover from sleeping on a park bench will hold us hostage to having a proper mattress beneath us every night.

On a deeper level, I'm going back to Europe with a more fully developed personal core. I now know what's important and what I want from our year abroad, and for the most part, I know how to get it. Understanding my own needs, how I'll react in a variety of situations and to different stimuli, and being able to listen to my inner voices are gifts that have come with the years. Such insight was nowhere to be found in my twenties.

When I left for France the first time, my uncertainty about what I would return to was a source of great anxiety, especially during the last months of my year abroad. I was like so many liberal arts graduates: clueless about what to do professionally and desperate to retrieve my self-confidence from a ditch. How do you pursue a job, no less a career, when you have no idea what you're looking for? This time when I return, the objective will be clear: securing a position as a French teacher. There's great comfort in knowing what you want and having a goal, neither of which I had in 1979.

Finally, the biggest difference between leaving then and leaving now is that this departure will leave a hole in my heart for Chris and Caroline. Thirty-three years ago, I had no idea of the unyielding heartstrings that would bind me to my children. And while I'll ache for them physically, having them anchor me to this world is such a blessing. At twenty-two, I had no such tethers, so I'll be thankful every day that I have them to miss while we're gone.

Getting a revised insurance letter is making me crazy. Repeated calls finally yield a supervisor who shares that repatriation expenses, one of the embassy requirements, are not paid under our plan. Emergency health care is covered, but they won't bring our bodies home if we fall off an alp or are flattened by a Vespa. Lovely.

So, off to the supplemental-travel-insurance market we go for a repatriation policy. Not a happy thought, but over the past two weeks we've had to deal with possible death abroad as it relates to health insurance, our bank accounts, and other assets. Necessary, yes. Pleasant, no.

The day after I receive the new policy, we return to the embassy. I fear that, just as the Wizard of Oz instructs Dorothy to bring him the Wicked Witch of the West's broom before he'll send her home, we'll be told there's yet something else we need for our visas. We hand over our paperwork, try to look confident (can the clerk see I'm shaking?), cross our fingers, and wait an agonizing forty minutes while the officials review our file. "Voilà, your visas" are the sweetest words I've heard in a very long time. After weeks of my gnashing teeth and biting nails, the embassy gods have cooperated and our prized French visas are in our very grateful hands. The final obstacle has been removed. We can make our way to the gap year starting blocks.

I've fallen prey to anticipatory madness.

Is it possible that all the years of planning are down to seven days? One week from today, we'll be on a jet plane to Paris for a year in Europe. What will it be like to transition from expectation to fruition?

Anticipation is such a delicious mix of future pleasure and anxious pain, and I have always been its slave. When something I look forward to is on the horizon—a trip, a reunion with my children, a dinner out, a well-researched hike—my imaginings take over to prolong the pleasure of the experience itself. I once read that to appreciate life, you need to believe time is a *promising* medium in which to do pleasurable things. According to that dictum, I'm thoroughly enjoying my every day. Depending on the moment, I smile uncontrollably like a madwoman, go through the motions in a trance, or frown, appearing to be ill.

ALMOST THERE: September 2011

September 4

My nerves have made their appearance. I've kept them at bay for as long as possible, but now it's only two days before our departure, and this morning, as I try to place my belongings in my duffel, I just can't do it. Some function well under stress. I, on the other hand, break down and my brain goes blank when time is tight and a deadline looms. And so today, with final packing to be accomplished, I can't get myself to proceed. The thought of at long last filling my bags with what I have so painstakingly and lovingly gathered over the past year and possibly forgetting something critical—like phone numbers or bank account passwords or my leather date book—leaves me frozen.

I should be nervous about things most people fear when going abroad, like pickpockets, lost luggage, or being cheated, attacked, or swindled, but these possibilities rarely concern me. I could probably use a healthy dose of fear about such things, but my last-minute nerves are internally generated. I don't want something that goes wrong to be the result of my forgetfulness, carelessness, or lack of foresight. Joe's in charge of electronics—our chargers, phones, converters, anything with a plug—so none of that concerns me. Joe appears not nervous in the least and packed his bags with no hesitation. The tangible results of my planning—books, maps, articles, documents, clothes, hiking boots, and toiletries—are strewn across the bedroom. All has come down to the final step of putting what I've collected in my luggage. I finally remind myself I have two days to review my checklists and to pack and repack as needed—we aren't leaving in a matter of hours, after all—and this spurs me to action. Once I've accomplished the task of filling my bags, the trick will be remembering into which bag I put what, and where I stored the passwords.

September 5
Today we sold our car, and with the sale said goodbye to our final key. As departure has approached, we've had fewer and fewer keys, and as each one disappears, the more free we feel. The first to go was the key to our second car last spring, then the keys to our home in June, and, finally, the key to our Chrysler. Homeless, carless, carefree. It feels good. We have no more keys. It's time to go.

II. Paris, Beginnings
September 2011

WE SAIL THROUGH PASSPORT CONTROL on a stopover in Reykjavik, Iceland, no questions asked and no attention paid to our hard-earned visas. We reboard the plane for the two-and-a-half-hour flight to Paris.

For the first time since I flew into this same airport as a student, we arrive at the original CDG Terminal I. While not completely refreshed, we're in pretty good shape as we're ushered onto the moving walkway inside the clear plastic tubes that crisscross the center of the terminal. Unlike my arrival in 1978, when I was sincerely and naively amazed to hear French spoken all around me, I savor the language's soft sounds surrounding me now.

Our many pounds of bags arrive with little delay, and we dutifully head for the customs and passport windows. We look forward to telling passport control, "We'll both be here for a year," but before we know it, we're whisked through sliding glass doors and out onto the sidewalk to join the taxi queue, no passport check needed. The cursory glance at our documents by the official in Reykjavik got us into Europe for a year.

Once outside in the fresh French air, we look at each other in amazement. Why *did* we go through the trauma of getting *long-séjour* visas? We feel as if we've pulled an all-nighter studying for an exam that never happened. We anxiously anticipated proudly flashing the paperwork that would grant us a year's stay in Europe. Could we have skipped all the hassle and simply walked into France with no documentation? Apparently.

We pile into a taxi with a down-to-earth driver not just willing but eager to help with our heavy bags (why is it people say the French are rude?). The City of Light is under gray skies on the morning of September 7 as we make our way into town. Rather than jumping up and down, shouting, "Bonjour, Paris!" and doing a happy dance, we quietly enter the city and gently glide into our gap year. We exchange frequent silent smiles; in fact, we can't stop grinning. We continually ask each other, "Are we really, actually here?" and grip each other's hands when not wrangling our luggage. Perhaps when we arrive in cities brand new to us—Granada, Sorrento, Berlin—the reality of our year abroad will feel more incredible. But for now, knowing we'll be in Paris for a month is comfortable and pleasantly exciting and, as always, magical. It feels like home. We belong here.

To acclimate ourselves to the continent and deal with jet lag, we spend the first three nights in a Marais hotel before moving into our apartment. On past visits, knowing our days were limited, we never had the luxury of spending hours sleeping to adjust to the new time zone. Now, however, we feel no rush at all. We stay in bed past noon (*on fait la grasse matinée*, as the French say), take leisurely walks to research dinner venues, and allow ourselves time to settle in. There are international phones and various electronics to sort out, and we make great strides, even posting the first pictures to our website.

On day four, we move into our lovely little studio at 49 Avenue de Suffren, in the shadow of the Eiffel Tower in the 7th arrondissement. After a full afternoon of unpacking and organizing, we food-shop, explore our new neighborhood, and toast our arrival.

OUR PARIS APARTMENT

All is *magnifique* in Paris, despite gloomy weather. We love our cozy pied-à-terre, as well as our neighborhood. I'm in Francophone heaven: I love this country, I love this city, and my daily doings will become part of its incomparable fabric. I was meant to live in Paris.

Our studio, where we'll remain until we head for the southwest of France in four weeks, is small but sweet and is a marvel of efficient design, with a larger-than-expected bathroom, three meters of kitchen space next to the entry, and ample storage for our belongings. I think back to my college days, when all my earthly possessions fit in the back of a station wagon, and now I've come full circle here in Paris, with everything we need for a year packed in an armoire. The twenty-year-old Marianne and the woman I am now are not that far apart in some ways: I didn't need much then and I don't need much now, other than living in this city with Joe.

The neighborhood is quiet, on the western, nontouristy side of the Tour Eiffel, but close-by *boulangeries*, cafés, *supermarchés*, and the Motte-Picquet metro stop ensure plenty of residential activity. Right around the corner is the Champs de Mars, the vast public garden that connects the Tour Eiffel and the *École Militaire*. No, we have no panorama over the rooftops of Paris, but the convenience of being on the *rez-de-chaussée* (ground floor) and the fact that the Tour Eiffel is in our backyard outweigh the lack of a view.

Since we moved in, we keep pinching ourselves and asking, "Is this really our home for a full month?" "Are we actually Parisians, at least temporarily?" If this were a "normal" vacation visit, we would be packing up to head home already, since we arrived a week ago today. Seven nights in a row is the longest we've ever stayed in Paris, but now we have lots of time to go and plenty of ideas for filling those twenty-eight days. Not having to rush to fit in all we want to see and do in and around Paris is such a gift. We breathe deeply many times a day to savor the reality of being here. Our general approach to traveling is "eating purposefully and wandering aimlessly," and so far, this attitude has continued to serve us well.

We spend much of our days researching where to eat, traveling to the places we've chosen, eating, and then discussing what we ate, until we're masters of this simple agenda. Tender green salads with *la sauce vinaigrette* become daily necessities. Joe says no one does simple salads better than the French, and he is right. We discover flawlessly grilled *steak frites*, served with a "secret sauce," at le Relais de Venise near Porte Maillot and return multiple times. I indulge my urges for the unique sweetness of *les crêpes à la crème de marron* (chestnut cream) at takeaway stands, and Joe embarks on a tasting quest for the ultimate éclair (he finds several).

In an effort to enhance our appreciation of the local color, we've taken to watching relevant movies online well into the night. So far, we've seen *Charade* and the original *Breathless*, and they've definitely added to our experience. We resolve to watch pertinent films as we make our way through Europe, and Joe starts a list on his iPad.

Little things help us feel like true residents of Paris.

I receive an e-mail from Groupon Paris inviting me to join, we get our loyalty discount card for Monoprix (the French version of Safeway), and we start running with the locals every other day. But despite our gratitude for the time we have in this city, we also have moments when the prospect of eventually having to leave gets the best of us. When flashes of melancholy threaten our mood, we snap out of them quickly with a leisurely walk around "our" neighborhood.

We embrace getting a late start to the day, and even Joe is getting accustomed to the lack of a schedule. I'm typically an early-morning person, but I can't seem to get myself out from under the cozy white duvet at my usual 6:30 a.m. We're lucky if we're up and out the door by noon. I shouldn't criticize these late starts, though, since our mornings in the studio include catching up on e-mails, reading the news, eating breakfast, and doing household chores.

Anyone who has spent a morning with me in the past twenty years knows my breakfast of choice is coffee yogurt mixed with All-Bran. On previous trips to Europe, we always stayed in a hotel, so I never even considered having my regular healthy breakfast instead of a buttery pastry. But because we now have our own mini-kitchen, we can make our meals as we choose. I am almost in tears when we find a Monoprix stocked with my treasured morning staples. They add a touch of the familiar to my day, but there's room for modification, too—this morning, I sent Joe out for fresh croissants.

LITERARY PARIS

Yesterday was a glorious, sunny, literary day. Paris of the 1920s fascinates me, and we do our best to pretend we were there with the Prohibition-refugee expat writers, artists, and composers. We wander for hours and visit Hemingway's haunts in Montparnasse—Le Select, La Coupole, and Le Dôme cafés—and stop at 10 Rue Delambre, around the corner from Le Dôme, where he first met F. Scott Fitzgerald. Previously the Dingo Bar (a play on the word *dingue*, French for "crazy"), number 10 is now an Italian restaurant, L'Auberge de Venise. We have lunch at another of Hemingway's favorite cafés, on the corner of Boulevards Montparnasse and Raspail: La Rotonde. The red velvet–upholstered place is packed, our goat cheese and Niçoise salads are delicious, and we hear not a word of English. A perfect lunch in Paris.

We recently observed two very different back-to-back dining experiences with Americans here for long stays. The first was when we sat next to an older married couple from Reno, Nevada, who had been coming to Paris for six weeks at the end of every summer for many years. The second was sitting across from a middle-aged man and woman from parts unknown (although her accent gave her away as coming from the Deep South). He teaches something somewhere in Paris, and she stated indignantly that she could "not take another year over here—one year was enough." Everyone has a story.

Some of their background they shared with us, and some we overheard. What absolutely amazed us—in fact, made us wince—was that none of these four Americans even attempted to speak French to the servers. I totally understand not knowing a language (just wait till we get to Greece!), but all these people had spent significant time in France. Would it have been so difficult to read off the menu and say *la salade* and *le poulet,* instead of "the salad" and "the chicken"? Could the guy who's been teaching here a year at least have learned to say *L'addition, s'il vous plaît,* instead of "The bill, please"? I'm sympathetic toward tourists here for a brief visit, but after six weeks every year and a full twelve months, people simply have no excuse.

After lunch with Ernest, we head down the Boulevard Montparnasse past the lilac- and wisteria-covered Closeries de Lilas (another favorite hangout of Hemingway, Picasso, and other notables). We make our way to the Boulevard Saint-Germain with a leisurely stroll through *le Jardin de Luxembourg.* I love the flowers in this park, more English than French in their natural style. Exploring Paris is the never-ending peeling of an onion: each layer offers something new to discover. We've walked these gardens on dozens of occasions over the years, but for the first time we come upon the Medici Fountain in a green grotto to the east of the Luxembourg Palace. In the cool shade of a canopy of trees, the surprising Italianate fountain and its long, narrow pool have a completely different feel from the rest of the park.

We cross the Boulevard Saint-Germain to the maze of streets that border the Seine and make our way to the quiet elegance of the difficult-to-find Place Furstenberg, which some writers have deemed an "ideal place for a kiss." We eagerly follow their recommendation and take advantage of the peace of the small, shaded square in the middle of the otherwise bustling quartier. Next up is a walk along the rue Jacob and rue de Seine to the former residences of Colette and George Sand. I have little difficulty imagining them writing in the nineteenth and early twentieth centuries behind the ashen walls and white shutters of the age-old buildings.

We return home after our peripatetic day to take care of mundane chores. Our first experiment with the compact washer-dryer combo in the bathroom has its problems, since the nature of these appliances is unforgiving. A complete cycle takes four hours, makes as much noise as if soup cans were in the drum, and leaves permanent wrinkles if clothes aren't removed the very second drying is complete. The water heats to the point of boiling and destroys the personality of any fabric it soaks. My crisp pink-and-white-striped pajamas are now dingy shades of rose and gray more fitting as prison garb in *Papillon* than for evenings in Paris.

From Ernest Hemingway to Colette to Henri Charrière, and all in the space of just one day.

ODE TO ÉPOISSES

The first time I succumbed to the pleasures of exquisite, runny *époisses* cheese was in a small country inn outside Amboise in the Loire Valley. The Auberge de la Croix Blanche in Veuves was not far from the *gîte* we rented with Chris and Caroline for a week one summer. At the end of our dinner at the auberge, the waitress presented the always-welcome cheese platter. We each made our selections, and mine included what the server called époisses.

As advised, I saved the époisses for last, savoring the milder goat and sheep cheeses first. There are few initial tastes that have startled my palate such that my eyes close and I'm left yearning for more, but my first encounter with this cheese was one of them. Époisses is indeed a "smelly" cheese, in only the best sense of the word, that runs on your plate and begs to be eaten on crusty bread, and whose distinctive flavor and creamy richness stay on your tongue for a long time. A soft cow's-milk cheese, it has its own *appellation*, much like the government-controlled labels for wine. One of forty-three cheeses of about four hundred French cheeses total with the AOP (Appellation d'Origine Protegée) designation, it was originally made by Cistercian monks in the small Burgundy town of Époisses.

Joe and I walk down the narrow, boutique-rich main artery that runs the length of the Île Saint-Louis, one of two islands in the Seine in the center of Paris. We're doing some *lèche-vitrine* (licking the windows—French for "window shopping") when we come across a particularly fragrant cheese shop, la Ferme Saint-Aubin. We step into the *crèmerie* after "licking the windows" for several minutes, and, lo and behold, there sits a pungent round of époisses just waiting for me to choose it. The balsa wood cheese box elicits a gasp of pleasure and brings tears to my eyes. I found époisses only once in the States, at a gourmet market at Christmastime, and to discover it again during our early days in Paris is a gastronomic surprise. We purchase $35 worth of cheese and sausage, including my beloved époisses, paying a premium, I'm sure, at the fashionable shop.

The cheese sits on our kitchen counter at room temperature for two days, ripening into a runny, soft wheel. Along with sweet butter, a very thin baguette called a *ficelle*, paper-thin slices of salami, and a bottle of Touraine sauvignon blanc, our *époisses* is the centerpiece of a memorable meal.

LUNCH IN FRAGONARD'S CHAIR

"I have very simple tastes—the very best satisfies me every time."

—*OSCAR WILDE*

I've never seen Paris so gorgeous. It shimmers, no matter the light, and today is a glorious, sunny day. We're lunching at le Grand Véfour, one of the city's most storied restaurants. A prix-fixe dinner at 282 euros each is out of the question, but we can justify lunch at 96. It will be our only meal of the day, after all, and we'll eat bread and cheese for a couple of days to get the budget back on track—hardly a sacrifice when the bread is a crusty baguette and the cheese is French.

This is our second visit to this monument to French history, art, and cuisine in the gilded northwest corner of the Palais Royale. We first lunched here on our twenty-fifth-anniversary trip to Paris five years ago and promised ourselves we would return, as it was one of the best dining experiences we'd ever had. Not only was every bite and sip delectable, but the grace of the orchestrated service was the impeccable combination of professionalism and warmth.

The bus leaves us by the Seine in front of the Louvre, and we walk across the sandy museum courtyard, past the I. M. Pei pyramid, through the Passage Richelieu arch, to the Rue de Rivoli. We anticipate the meal ahead as we cross in front of the Comédie Française and head into the Palais Royale. We breeze past the low black-and-white-striped pedestals in the south courtyard. I've never warmed to the abstract effect and pretend I don't see them. The symmetrically columned arcade of the final dénouement in one of our favorite films—*Charade*, with Audrey Hepburn and Cary Grant—is to our right.

The palace gardens are toward the end of their

summer brilliance, and the colors are somewhat muted, giving the flower beds the softness of a Monet painting. We wander the gardens until just before our 1:00 p.m. reservation and then head for the distinctive black-and-gold painted glass entryway of Le Grand Véfour.

Our experience begins before we enter. A uniformed attendant opens the heavy glass door, and, after passing through burgundy drapery into the foyer, we're greeted warmly by four gracious staff, one of whom takes us to our table. There are two small dining rooms, one behind the other, and we're seated in the front room. Behind the plush red benches are small brass plates inscribed with famous patrons' names. A tuxedoed gentleman proudly informs us that we are in the favorite seats of the French artist Fragonard, a painter and sculptor who worked in the start of the nineteenth century. For our first meal at Le Grand Véfour, we sat at Napoleon and Josephine's preferred table—quite a lucky draw for first-time diners. We settle in, order two kirs, and discreetly survey our fellow diners.

We're next to a single French gentleman of a certain age who we decide is on a business trip and treating himself to a fine lunch. The two French businessmen on our other side are sparing no expense. The man in his forties is paying and insists that his older companion have the finest of everything on the menu, including a huge lobster tail. No set-price menu for this duo. They appear to have just closed a deal, and a big one at that.

Several couples arrive in succession after we're seated. There are two American couples—three of the individuals about our age, and one gentleman close to eighty—sitting across from us. Next to them are two more couples, both of them British. An Eastern European man and woman, not dressed for the sumptuous surroundings, are seated diagonally. And that's as far as our sleuthing goes. We make selections from the prix-fixe menu, and our lunch officially begins.

We toast the magic of being together at Le Grand Véfour and our treasured daughter, Caroline, who turns twenty-four today. *Bon anniversaire*, Caroline. How we wish you and your brother could be seated next to us on the upholstered banquette, channeling the spirit of its favorite patron, Jean Cocteau.

Perhaps it's the kir, perhaps it's the sun filtering through the beveled glass windows, or perhaps it's every little thing about this dreamy afternoon, but I'm suddenly overcome with emotion, and the tears spill over. When Joe takes my hand, I recover quickly—and our food is starting to arrive.

I dab my tears with my linen napkin as the amuse-bouches appear with quiet ceremony. Each time a course or a special little something is presented, we're told in great detail about its contents. No fewer than six gentlemen serve us (there is one lone female among the staff), and despite the fact that they all speak English (albeit heavily accented), I do my best to continue in French. They follow my lead and present their descriptions *en français*. While Joe is hesitant to use the French he knows, his ear miraculously understands the explanations from waiters whenever the subject is food.

The amuse-bouche, the chef's complimentary hors d'oeuvre, is a miniature vegetable spring roll bursting with grassy flavors and a demitasse of cold yellow-tomato soup dotted with tiny, garlicky croutons. A delicious start. I always judge a restaurant by its bread, and I cannot wait to sample Le Grand Véfour's offerings. We're given the choice of whole wheat or white mini-baguettes with crisp, twisted ends. As expected, they are perfect: crusty on the outside and chewy in the middle.

The bottle of Chablis we select arrives, and the waiter proceeds with the graceful ritual of presenting the label, opening the bottle, and then allowing us a taste. Joe does the honors and gives the nod that the wine is *bon*, and the *serveur* puts our bottle on ice, waiting to pour initial glasses when we finish our kirs.

We've both ordered foie gras as our appetizer; it arrives atop pulled duck mixed with various herbs and spices and pressed into a thin rectangular cube. All sits on a dainty slice of vinegary radish. We remind ourselves to take our time and to breathe. We have all afternoon to make this experience last as long as possible. The remarkably creamy texture of the foie gras is nicely juxtaposed with the coarser duck, and we savor every bite. A chunk of baguette, a sliver of butter, and a slice of foie—is there a more delectable mouthful in all the world?

Our main dishes arrive next. I have the monkfish, and Joe has the veal. My fish is set on a large, delicate white dish. The presentation is an edible work of modern art in a palette of vivid red, orange, and yellow. The chunk of white monkfish is draped with a flaming red-pepper coulis, with broad strokes of orange, tomato, and yellow fennel sauces painting the plate. Joe's veal looks perfect: three medallions surrounded by a russet sauce flavored with capers, coriander, and anise. We trade bites, "hmmms," and "aaahs" and try not to disturb the other diners with our audible delight.

Next up is *La Table de Fromages de France*. The "cheese waiter" rolls the chariot in our direction and up against our table. The dozens of choices are arranged in descending order of size, from huge wedges of hard Alpine cheese to little rolls of goat cheese from the Lot. Hearing the waiter describe the selections reminds me of our visit here five years ago. Joe understood our accented server to have said something about "cheap cheese," and Joe said with a smile, "No cheap cheese for me." "*Non, monsieur,*" replied the waiter with a laugh, articulating as best he could, "these are sheep cheeses." We each make four selections, knowing this is the polite maximum, although it would have been easy to say, "One of each, *s'il vous plaît.*"

We've been at our table for over three hours now, and it's finally time for dessert. We receive two little cups of pureed fruits and a refreshing citrus granita. Our palates are now cleansed and ready for some serious sweets. We both order the chocolate hazelnut–caramel option. While milk chocolate is always good, and this is indeed delicious, I have a close-my-eyes-and-savor-the-moment experience when I taste the quenelle of salted caramel ice cream. It's simply the best ice cream that's ever passed my lips. I'm a borderline salt addict and will almost always choose a savory option over a sweet one, but this frozen delicacy has the best of both: sweet and salty in one delicious, melting mouthful.

As we finish our desserts, we're presented with two long trays of petits fours: mini-macaroons, lemon tarts, cream puffs, and madeleines. When our Eastern European neighbors are given their petits fours just after us, the woman takes a look at the additional sweets and asks the waiter in accented English, "Are you trying to kill me?" But dessert is not yet over.

We next receive rectangular grapefruit and strawberry sugared jelly cubes. Once again, I need a superlative.

While the *fraises* are juicy and sweet, the grapefruit jellies are incomparable. The combination of grapefruit tartness with the sugary crystals on the surface is perfection. We each let several melt in our mouths. The dining room is now down to a handful of staff charged with delivering new bits of *après-dessert*, each with the potential of sending diners into hyperglycemic shock. The penultimate offering is a tray of chocolates (we each choose a mint-flavored square), and the final presentation is a variety of nougats. Faithful and courageous till the bittersweet end, we each take a caramel and a nougat and manage to put them in our mouths. Joe orders coffee, the thick, strong French kind served without milk, to finish his meal properly. I'm happy for the opportunity to just sit and digest, although I'm looking forward to a postlunch stroll around the Palais Royale.

Still savoring the culinary glories of our midday meal and conscious of our newly rounded bellies, we do one more circuit of the gardens before heading home. We debate which dishes were our favorites (mine was the foie gras and Joe's was dessert) and do our best to aid digestion by forcing our wine-addled legs to carry us as far as we can before getting on a bus. As we doze off for decadent afternoon siestas, we promise to run an extra few miles the next morning. We'll go all the way along the Seine to the Louvre and the Palais Royal and then give a nod as we cruise right by Le Grand Véfour.

REAR WINDOW

Every morning we awaken to the muted banter of our next-door neighbors. We have yet to meet them, but we hear the daily conversations emanating from their apartment. Our one window and their kitchen window are just feet apart on perpendicular walls in the apartment building's courtyard corner. The weather has been balmy, so most windows, including ours, have remained open all day and through the night. We imagine our neighbors as an older French couple as we hear them discussing the weather, their breakfast, and plans for the day. It's a comforting start to our mornings. At the end of most days, we hear them preparing a typically late French dinner when we're climbing into bed and discussing the day's events.

The rectangular courtyard is small and practical, perhaps thirty by fifty feet. Our studio is on the ground level of the shorter wall, so we have a good view of what goes on behind most windows. Like Jimmy Stewart in *Rear Window*, I try to deduce the other tenants' stories. Unfortunately for Joe, there's been no sighting of a Miss Torso dancer or anyone who remotely resembles her. There is a Mr. Lonely Heart, however: a thirtysomething Asian man I often see looking out his window, always alone.

There's also the young guy who brings out a black plastic garbage bag every afternoon at five, and the older woman with the tubercular cough who periodically comes down to the garbage shed and whom we often hear hacking through her upper-level window. If she's home, she's coughing. We've heard children speaking American English scurry past our door and up the stairs, but we never hear them otherwise. There is one apartment from which the sounds and smells of cooking radiate most evenings; we see the shadows of whoever must be the cook, but we've never seen a face. Our noses tell us, however, whether s/he is having bouillabaisse, *steak frites*, or *poulet au curry*. On occasion, we hear a heated conversation from a kitty-corner window above. It's difficult to decipher the specifics of what they're debating and even harder to tell whether they're arguing angrily or simply discussing. The French love to debate almost any subject imaginable—the weather, the corner *boulangerie*, or the latest political scandal—purely for the pleasure of a lively exchange. It's a national trait that has kept the café culture vibrant for many years.

On one memorable morning, the sustained female cries of lovemaking drift from a floor above and echo through the courtyard. Are they aware their window is open and that their private pleasure is now communal? And if they do know, do they care? Which of our neighbors might they be? We'll have to observe those we pass in the hallway more closely from now on. Well, this is France, where love is everywhere and often a community business. Public displays of affection are abundant, and it's not just among the pretty young things. Young couples and old, glamorous and bohemian—all share kisses and embraces in public, many of them passionate: on the metro, on street corners, on park benches, and in cafés. Ardent romance is for everyone, everywhere. Perhaps it's because everything, including love, is better in Paris.

MERDE, ALORS!

Paris is a dog's city. They are everywhere. And not just the little froufrou, fit-in-a-purse, powder-puff variety you'd expect. There are plenty of Yorkies, dachshunds, and papillons, to be sure, but there are also shepherds and Labs, boxers and bulldogs, golden retrievers, and all variety of mutt. And the famous dog tales of Paris are all true: beloved pooches are indeed allowed in restaurants, some sitting on chairs, and there are doggie droppings soiling the sidewalks at every turn.

Joe and I have been diligent about exercising to work off the delicious calories we've consumed. We registered for the April 15, 2012, Paris Marathon—a heroic or foolish decision, depending on how you look at it. Our penciled-in itinerary has us somewhere in Greece next April, but dirt-cheap intra-Europe fares on discount carriers will make it easy for us to fly back to Paris for the race. It will be Joe's third and my first marathon—if I manage to make it through the training.

Staying motivated to run in Paris is not difficult, though. As Joe often asserts, "It's the most beautiful man-made landscape in the world." The Eiffel Tower is around the corner, so our runs begin with a circuit of the expansive Champs de Mars. From there, we continue along the Seine, past the Quai Branly and the Pont de l'Alma, and then over the ornate Pont Alexandre III, with its gilded statues and glistening sculptural details. Next up is the Place de la Concorde, former home of the guillotine, and then the broad entry to the sandy Jardin des Tuileries.

France has spent piles of money to make its crown jewel sparkle: Paris's flower beds are manicured to precision and bursting with multicolored blooms, the sandblasted buildings and bridges are a creamy French vanilla, and the work of the Propreté de Paris (the keep-Paris-clean squad sporting kelly-green trucks, barrels, aprons, garbage bags, and bins) is evident. With so much to look at and so much beauty to absorb while running, I can almost forget my sore knees and wheezing lungs. I do my best to avoid pavement and stay on sand or dirt walkways to lessen the shock of every step, but on occasion I find myself on cobblestones—high on charm but hard on my feet. At this time of year, the *châtaigniers* have dropped most of their chestnuts, so running on the garden paths can be dodgy as well, as I try to avoid the hard brown gumballs and prevent a twisted ankle. But, these hazards aside, the views and the people-watching are priceless.

Yes, Paris can be a runner's paradise. If only they could keep the *merde* off the sidewalks.

THIS AIN'T BOOT CAMP

We're doing a good job of maintaining a leisurely pace in Paris, knowing we have adequate time to explore and channel the spirit of my sister-in-law as we plan our time. Several days into her postnuptial trip, as my well-meaning brother purposefully dragged her across the capitals of Europe, she stopped, put her foot down midsprint along the Seine, and folded her arms defiantly. "Stop!" she demanded. "I did not sign up for honeymoon boot camp." We follow her mandate and limit ourselves to a couple of things on our to-do list each day.

Neither of us misses the nonstop, frenetic, must-get-out-of-bed-in-the-morning pace of full-time work. But after too many days of *grasses matinées*, sleeping till noon, we've put ourselves on a schedule. It's so easy to stay in bed and sleep—especially when there's little natural light in our studio to help wake us—so we've added some discipline to our days. The alarm goes off at seven; we get out of bed by seven thirty, tune in to France 24 for the news, have our breakfast while catching up on world events, do our e-mails and apartment chores, and head out the door by ten. Structure is a necessary partner when time is so abundant.

We've settled nicely into the roles with which we're

most comfortable: I do the bookkeeping, and Joe handles electronics; I'm the master of maps and navigation, and he gets us on the right bus and metro; I communicate with the locals, and he keeps us current via online newspapers; I prepare meals, and he does the dishes. Doing what we're good at helps keep us content.

I'm afflicted with gentle obsessive-compulsivity— I tend to think in spreadsheets—and I've come to realize OCD never goes on vacation. I create an Excel list of the places we want to visit and the restaurants we want to try. I add the number of the arrondissement to the to-do/see/eat/drink list in a separate column, sort by the neighborhood number, and voilà!—a well-organized road map for our jaunts in Paris. All our destinations in the 4th—the Marais quarter—are now listed together (the Musée Carnavelet on the history of Paris, Victor Hugo's home, the Mariage Frères Maison de Thé, and L'As du Falafel) so we can easily determine our route for the day. It helps that Paris has a numerical quartier system that lends itself to spreadsheets, but I'm sure we'll use the same approach for future cities. We'll just substitute the names of neighborhoods for numbers and let Excel map our itinerary. But this is definitely not gap year boot camp. Our arrondissement spreadsheets are friendly guides that help us wander more efficiently but don't dictate our pace.

PARISIAN ARRONDISSEMENTS 101

Having never been a resident of Paris before, I'm no expert on its neighborhood numbering system. Those who have resided here refer to the arrondissements with ease: "That museum's in the Fifth; I lived in the Ninth; my favorite café is in the Eleventh." One of my goals for our stay in Paris is to increase my fluency in arrondissement vernacular. I'm proud to say I'm now better than when we arrived and have picked up helpful hints along the way.

The twenty arrondissements are arranged in a clockwise spiral circle—think escargot shell—with the Louvre and the Palais Royale in the central 1st. Those in the know refer to the arrondissement by number only; you say simply, "I live in the Seventh," never "I live in the Seventh arrondissement." The first two numbers in a city's postal code indicate in which of the ninety-six French departments it is located. The last two numbers signal a location's arrondissement. Our address is 49 Avenue de Suffren, 75007 Paris. On the list of departments, Paris is number 75, and we're in arrondissement number 7. It's all so French—that is to say, logical. Each arrondissement has its own *hôtel de ville* (city hall) and mayor. Of course, Paris overall has its own *hôtel de ville* and mayor as well, but each local leader holds significant power over what takes place in his or her quartier. Finally, the signature deep blue and green—painted street signs affixed to corners of buildings wherever streets intersect list the arrondissement, so you always know where you are.

PARIS IS BURNING

Although the first several days after we arrived in Paris were cold, gloomy, and damp, the past three weeks have been glorious Indian summer: clear, blue skies, no humidity, and progressive warmth. Temperatures have broken the eighty-degree mark multiple times, and the last gasp of summer is winning the weather battle. We're close to experiencing *une canicule* (heat wave), because even evenings provide little relief from the heat.

It's a myth that Parisians don't wear shorts. When it's hot, they do indeed, and the shorter the better. No, they don't sport sneakers or Birkenstocks (those are the Americans and the Germans); women complement the shorts with strappy heeled sandals and stilettos and the men wear nice, leather flip-flops or white canvas slip-ons. And no matter the temperature, they sport scarves: striped and solid, bulky and dainty, muslin and wool (only men and women over seventy wear scarves of the silky Hermès variety). Most scarves are tied in a Parisian knot (folded in half across the middle, draped around the neck, loose ends inserted through the loop and pulled through), although the wrapped-multiple-times-around-the-neck-with-just-a-bit-of-a-loose-tail-hanging-in-front type is also evident. Over the past few sweltering days, Parisians have generally kept their scarves in their armoires, but there remain the die-hards who continue to wrap their necks despite the temperature. Are French necklines more susceptible to the cold than those in the rest of the world? Or is this all a corporate plot by Parisian scarf purveyors?

Since it's now October, I've started longing for fall color, but except for some luminous yellow poplars at Versailles, I see only brown. The French term for autumn foliage is *les feuilles mortes*, literally "dead leaves," and I can see that it's an apt expression for what we see in Paris. From green to gone is the life cycle of leaves here. The City of Light has many splendors, but autumn color is not among them. I do recall a semblance of New England glory the fall I spent in the Loire Valley, but in Paris the flowers are fading quickly, their early brown spots exacerbated by the heat, and the pink and purple dahlias have lost their crisp edges. I recently ran by the Tuileries flower beds, whose brilliance we sat next to only last week. They've already bleached several shades, the lines among the colors blurred.

This weekend, we take advantage of the warm weather and head to the Bois de Boulogne for a run. On previous trips, we've walked along the border of the huge park on the western limit of Paris, but we hear it's a great spot for runners, so we decide to explore. Completely contrary to what I expect, the park is covered with endless thickets of trees, except for two lovely lakes and two giant hippodromes. I would have been better prepared for what to expect had I paid attention to the first part of its name: *bois*, meaning "woods." I was expecting expansive green vistas and at least a few flowers, since some guidebooks describe the Bois de Boulogne as "one of the most spectacular parks in Europe." While large, it's far from my favorite park in Paris. I'll take Les Buttes Chaumont, Le Jardin de Luxembourg, or the Parc Monceau any day.

I must admit, however, that it is terrific for running. Hundreds of chalky limestone sand paths crisscross the woods, and the circuit of the lakes is wonderful, since people-watching distracts me from the pain in my thighs. We do eight miles through the park, each of us taking a different route, as my speed, compared with Joe's, is a crawl.

When the temperature sizzles at ninety-two degrees, we sit on a park bench, trading stories of our individual courses and downing multiple bottles of ice-cold water. Parisians are out in droves, and we watch walkers and runners pass by as we cool down. Families with babies in *poussettes*, lovers with arms entwined and hands in each other's back pockets, and groups of young people sweating in scarves amble by. Parisians have perfected the art of strolling, and try as we might, we have to work hard to slow to their pace.

Lower, more seasonal temperatures in the sixties are predicted for the end of the week, and we'll welcome the change in weather. Surely the investors in scarf futures want cooler days to prevail, and I'm looking forward to wearing the two new scarves Joe bought me yesterday at the open-air market on the Boulevard Raspail. Although he draws the line at wearing a scarf himself, we're doing our best to be Parisian.

PARIS AS PYGMALION

There's a Frenchwoman in our neighborhood who looks like a birthday cake. The first time I spy her, she's sitting outdoors at the corner brasserie with a double-decker platter of raw shellfish on ice in front of her. I'm running a routine errand at the Monoprix (musing, *Is any errand in Paris simply routine?*), and as I round the corner of the brasserie's terrace, a splash of color catches my eye. Am I seeing straight? There, amid the blacks, grays, and browns of the café crowd, is a woman bedecked in Lilly Pulitzer frosting colors of candy pink, lime green, and canary yellow. She's all alone, squeezing lemon on her *fruits de mer*, and appears to be having a wonderful time.

I immediately retrace my steps and slowly come back around the corner. I want to be sure to capture every detail so I can share them all with Joe. Is this confectionary vision really sitting at our corner café? Decades beyond "a certain age," she sits straight and dignified, and I can tell, even though she's seated, that she carries herself regally. On her head sits a layered hat with a pile of half a dozen floppy fabric brims, each in a different color and just a bit smaller than the one underneath, giving the effect of a multitiered cake.

On the Mad Hatter's arms are numerous flamboyant wooden bracelets of varying thicknesses, and from her ears dangle intertwining loops, all painted with flowers in colors that match her chapeau. On her shoulders is a satin cape of many colors, and around her neck a scarf (what else?), floral and dazzling. The table conceals what she wears below her waist. As if the candy colors weren't brilliant enough, her hat and cape are festooned with 3-D silk flowers and ribbons, adding to the birthday-cake effect. My gaze finally makes it to her face, much of it hidden by the brims of her hat, but her infinite deep wrinkles are in full maquillage, including rouge on her cheeks and intense pink on her lips, which she is careful not to smudge as she delicately slurps an oyster.

She remains in her seat, sampling her seafood, as I make my way home after fetching some groceries. I wonder whether Joe will believe my description, or will he think I'm just embellishing for the sake of a story?

Two days later, as we head home from the metro, voilà—there she is, slowly crossing the street in multicolored sartorial splendor. Her birthday-cake bonnet is again what first catches my eye. "There she is!" I exclaim. "You see, she really does exist!" This time I see her fully upright self, all the way down to her painfully thin legs in sheer pink tights and lace-up mauve shoes. She is maudlin, magnificent, and melancholy—all at the same time. Who is this woman, and what goes through her mind as she prepares herself to go into the world each morning? Does she see her confectionary costume the way others do and giggle just a bit?

I conclude that our colorful neighbor in pink and green loves what is reflected in the mirror. If not, how could she move with such measured grace and carry herself so proudly? Despite the stares and whispers as she passes by, she believes she's beautiful and struts her stuff with aplomb. Perhaps Paris has a Pygmalion effect on all of us fortunate enough to be here. She believes we're fine-looking and charming, and so we live up to her every expectation. Joe and I trade smiles, stand a little taller, and confidently stroll home arm in arm.

GOLDEN RINGS AND OTHER SCAMS

Guidebooks caution about scams abroad, yet I'm still surprised when I experience them firsthand. Today, we're walking along the river, admiring the sweep of the Seine and the dense tropical greenery carpeting the exterior walls of the Musée Branly. Out of the blue, a handsome, clean-cut young man swoops down in front of us and pops back up with a shiny gold ring between his thumb and forefinger.

"*C'est à vous, madame, monsieur?*" he asks.

We firmly reply, "*Non*," it's not ours and, without even looking at him, purposefully continue on. He tried his ruse, just as we've read to expect. Had we been unaware and hesitated for a moment about the 10-cent brass ring he presented, he would have told us the ring he found on the path was not his, and he couldn't possibly keep it for himself. When we finally relented and accepted the ring, he would have told us he'd just lost his job/was having trouble feeding his new baby/had sick parents who were in trouble—just fill in the blank—in the hope we'd pass along a few euros.

And then there are the teenage Romanian gypsy "deaf-mute" girls scurrying around the Champs de Mars and near the Place de la Concorde. I recently walked behind a bevy of them, dressed as typical teens but with cardboard clipboards and pens in hand, as they chatted effusively and made their way under the Tour Eiffel. At the wave of some invisible hand, they dispersed. Approaching unsuspecting victims, they shook their heads, repeatedly passing their fingers in front of their mouths and ears, indicating they could neither hear nor speak. Their communication faculties had been in working order as I'd followed them across the Pont d'Iéna to their *champs* of battle. They each carry a petition asking you to sign in support of their deaf-mute lot. But once you stop, take pity, and add your signature to their appeal (which cites the names of legitimate charities), they grab your sleeve and pester you until you relent, giving them their "minimum five-euro donation." Periodically, machine gun–wielding French soldiers in burgundy berets patrolling the major Parisian sights appear from around a corner, and the teens instantly fold their clipboards and scatter like mice. What amazes me is that people actually fall for this stunt and give these girls money. Why don't their ragged cardboard clipboards tip people off?

Not to the same degree, but cons nonetheless, are the waiters who attempt to get tourists to add tips on top of tips. By law, eating-establishment bills include a service charge for *les serveurs*, so it's not necessary to leave anything in addition. If you pay with cash, it's customary to leave any loose coins you may have received as change, but I have yet to see a French person paying with a credit card, in cafés and fine restaurants alike, leave an additional tip in cash. French credit card slips have no space to include service, so it's not even possible to add it. Thirty-five years ago, rude service and demands for unwarranted tips were to a certain extent expected in France, but nowadays attempts to garner an extra few euros are simply working folks being amiably resourceful. The French service industry has definitely evolved since it realized being nice is good for business. We had a waiter on the touristy Place du Tertre in Montmartre solicit an extra tip. The bill for dinner was 55 euros, and Joe handed over his American Express card. Our waiter arrived with his handy-dandy handheld credit card machine and asked, *"Soixante-cinq"*—65—*"d'accord?"*

"Non," Joe replied nicely, shaking his head and pointing to the "55" figure on the bill. Unsuspecting, non-French-understanding tourists we are not. Joe signed, the waiter shrugged with the hint of a smile, and we were on our way. We also had a waiter tell us that service was included on our bill, but not the tip. I'm just happy we understand what that actually means: service is included, but not an *extra* tip. Leaving loose change here and there is hardly a problem, but a year's worth of double tipping would do serious damage to our budget.

LES RESTAURANTS DE PARIS

"I drink champagne when I'm happy and when I'm sad. Sometimes I drink it when I'm alone. When I have company I consider it obligatory. I trifle with it if I'm not hungry and drink it when I am. Otherwise I never touch it—unless I'm thirsty."
—*LILLY BOLLINGER*

While I do love *une coupe de champagne* and have had a few since we arrived in Paris, Ms. Bollinger's words can also be said for *un verre de vin*. We've managed to occasionally say no to wine when we eat in, but every single time we go out, we're unable to resist at least a small *pichet* of it. Perhaps it's a social thing, but when we're in the company of others, a glass of wine is a must.

On Friday, October 7, we celebrate the end of our first month abroad with a dinner cruise on the Seine. It's somewhat touristy and expensive, but the food and wine are excellent, and what's more romantic than sipping a glass of champagne, gliding along the Seine, slipping through Paris as it sparkles?

Joe leans over and whispers, "As long as we're together, the next eleven months will be as special as our month in Paris."

I whisper back, "I can't wait to find out what comes next."

The lighting is low and romantic; the ginger lamp on our table offers an evening bathed in soft ocher. The food, the jazzy live music, the City of Light, and, of course, the company, make for an impeccable evening.

We've had multiple memorable meals in the *restos* of Paris, and early on they confirmed that we are indeed in France, land of *les Gauloises* and *les Gitanes*. Initially, when the evenings were warm, we opted for dining outside but quickly discovered we were the only two under the café awning not smoking. While cigarettes are no longer allowed inside restaurants, smoking remains legal at outdoor tables, and so sitting on the *terrasse* is the choice of most French, regardless of the weather. We resolved in our early days to eat inside more often.

One memorable meal was at Au Bon Saint Pourçain, a quaint, inexpensive, family-run restaurant on the rue Servandoni, tucked beside the *Église Saint-Sulpice*. We stop by one afternoon to make a reservation and are greeted by a scowling gentleman with a bushy black unibrow sitting on a wooden chair, holding court outside the front door.

"Je voudrais faire une réservation pour ce soir," I state.

He asks me at what time and for how many people and then simply affirms, *"Bon."* He writes nothing down and doesn't ask our name, but apparently we are set. We arrive that evening, and there he is again, greeting us with his ever-present frown and handing us over to the young waitress. As we delight in our traditional French cuisine (hearty *boeuf aux olives*), along with a bottle of the private-label wine (all you're asked to choose is white or red), we admire the pen-and-ink portraits of the gentleman, which include his distinctive eyebrow, hung on the wall and gracing the restaurant's postcards.

In the totally quirky category is Chez Louisette, a strange place from another time. Our visit to this bizarre saloon is also our last, but we're happy for the experience. Desperate to escape the maze of the Paris flea market, le Marché aux Puces, and its aggressive hawkers selling surplus junk, we follow the music and duck into a red-checkered-tablecloth joint down a dark alley. An amalgam of sideshow and frat party, Chez Louisette features an accordionist and a woman in her seventies belting Edith Piaf standards. Green, red, and gold tinsel hang from the ceiling over long tables set for communal meals. The carnival effect is amusing (we appreciate the chanteuse's rendition of *"Non, Je Ne Regrette Rien"*), but the food is mediocre and the subsequent singers pale in comparison to "Edith." Neither Joe nor I have ever been a fan of the circus—it always seems so sad—and so, as we leave, Joe mutters, "This place is a bit too 'sideshow' for me."

The evening after our lunch at the flea market, we discover a boîte of a totally different kind. At Café Laurent, for the price of an expensive French coffee (a tasty blend with Grand Marnier and whipped cream), we have a relaxing evening of sophisticated music under tawny lighting in a lively quartier. *Pas très cher*, all things considered. Paired with the almonds on the table, our coffee becomes dinner. The café is in the classy boutique Hôtel d'Aubusson in Saint-Germain. Christian Bernard is hunched over the piano, coaxing expressive, jazzy notes from the keys, à la Schroeder of *Peanuts* fame. Each night he plays with "invited musician friends," but he is what makes the music special. "This is what Paris is all about," Joe comments, as we nestle closer together on the upholstered banquette.

We relish eating out in Paris, but the food and wine of the southwest beckon. We'll soon leave the city behind, but the *verres de vin* and *coupes de champagne* will surely continue.

AU REVOIR, PARIS, FOR NOW

Paris inspires all who visit to make the city their own, convincing couples she exists just for them. Is it the art, the flowers, the food, the fashion? Or perhaps it's the bridges, the boulevards, the parks, and the wine. Or maybe it's *les lumières*, the Tour Eiffel, and the Seine. Lovers who have come to Paris since time immemorial imagine her enchanted for them and them alone. And so it is with us, in our conceit. She makes us believe in the monogamous bond between a city and two lovers, just as she does all other couples who stroll her boulevards, cross her bridges, and sip her wine. Paris is ours and will always be ours, even as we leave her. Before our reappearance next spring, thousands of others will walk hand in hand, making the city their own, but "our Paris" will always be there, awaiting our return.

However, I must admit that, as much as I love Paris, a piece of my heart also belongs to the French countryside.

Thus, looking at the City of Light in the rearview mirror isn't as difficult as I imagined. Knowing we'll be back in April for the marathon and again for a final week at the end of our year softens the blow of our departure. It's time to hit the road, head south, and reflect on our month in Paris. We'll have plenty of driving time to reminisce about our favorite Parisian delights as we make our way to the vineyards of Sancerre, the castles of the Dordogne, and the desolate beauty of the Lot.

III. *La France Profonde*
October 2011

HEAVEN IN A WINEGLASS: SANCERRE

I WAKE UP AT FIRST LIGHT wondering where we are. My foggy morning brain eventually clears when I feel the slippery bedspread on top of me and the sagging bed below and with one eye glimpse the dingy orange curtains covering the windows. We're in Sancerre in the Loire Valley, hilltop home of my favorite Appellation d'Origine Controlée (AOC) in the world. Two hours south of Paris, we've landed in a depressingly shabby hotel room in the heart of white-wine heaven. As we check in, Joe observes, "It's terrific for the budget but terrible for our mood" and suggests we spend as little time here as possible.

Paris became our comfortable home away from home, and we've gotten used to awakening to the sounds of fellow apartment dwellers. But now that we're on the road, I expect there will be many mornings when I have to concentrate hard to remember where we laid our heads the night before.

Needless to say, despite any initial doubts I had about this trip, now that we've been in France for five weeks, the reality of our gap year is finally sinking in. Unlike my tenuous affirmation to the British gent in the Paris hotel elevator on our arrival, who quipped as he squeezed into the closet-size space beside our luggage, "What—are you staying for a year?" I can now assert with confidence, "Yes, we're in Europe until next August; we're staying for a year." Joe and I have agreed to tuck away any anxiety about finding jobs when we return by refusing to think about employment searches until late next spring.

I do my best to get inexorable Father Time to heed my daily mantra: *Stop, s'il vous plaît! Or at least slow down a little!* And to every moment that passes, I plead, *Stay! Please don't go.* The French expression *je vais en profiter* continues to follow my every thought. Yes, I'm going to appreciate and savor every moment of the time we have here. While a consummate anticipator of the itinerary ahead (especially the day Chris and Caroline join us in December), I'm doing my best to be a good Buddhist, living in the moment of every single day. And today, while we explore the pleasant town and rolling vineyards of Sancerre, I want to adopt a gentle pace that allows us to savor every sip.

Of all the wines in the entire world, Sancerre *vin blanc* (made from the sauvignon blanc grape) is my favorite. This rich terroir also produces rosé and red wines from pinot noir grapes, but while we're here in my personal AOC paradise, I'll stick to white. I experienced my first glass as a student in Tours. I carefully wrote its name in the little notebook I carried with me: Sancerre. The je ne sais quoi of this crisp, minerally, faintly citrusy white wine got my attention and wouldn't let go. Caroline wrote in a recent e-mail, "Have fun touring the vineyards, but I hope Mom isn't swimming in a vat of Sancerre." (Be honest, Caroline, you love Sancerre as much as I and would be doing the backstroke beside me.) While not quite a swim, we do go to a generous wine tasting at the Henri Bourgeois Estate in Chavignol (home of the famous Crottin de Chavignol, a savory little goat cheese). The Sancerre sampling is free, unlike most such offers in the United States, which can set you back as much as $40 for two. After eight varieties of white—each with a generous pour greater than a simple tasting—we purchase six bottles, knowing there will be ample opportunity to drink them in the ensuing weeks.

"I still prefer a big, buttery California chardonnay," Joe admits when I ask for his review of the tasting, "but we've agreed to eat and drink local, so light and crisp it is."

Bleary-eyed, we head back to our joyless room at the sparse Hôtel du Rempart. To allow ample funds for the purchase of good wine, we opted for the low-rent, concrete auberge. Our third-floor walk-up is depressing, and the gloomy gray sky outside doesn't help matters. But our palates still taste of Sancerre, so we contentedly lie down for post-*dégustation* naps.

Joe falls asleep immediately, as is his wont, and I take the time to lean back on my rock-solid pillow (is it filled with sawdust?) and analyze our sorry little space. The French pride themselves on their logic and symmetry of thought, but I have always been amazed by the inability of budget hoteliers to center a picture over a headboard. The pastel drawing of the Sancerre hilltop in a cheap plastic frame that hangs over the drooping bed is at least six inches to the left of center. The wall screams for horizontal artwork, but there the vertical print hangs, askew. Cheap French hotels also have an aversion to colors that match. The walls are upholstered in pallid blue thin-wale corduroy, the floor is covered with a threadbare maroon carpet long ago punctuated with divots from cigarette burns, and the curtains are the color of carrots. I look over at Joe and wonder if he's read my thoughts and is dreaming of being back in Paris. *Is this what we're in for?* I ask myself, as I drift off after surveying our surroundings. *A dream year of afternoon naps in dreary, disappointing lodgings?*

Summary of our two nights in Sancerre: heaven in a wineglass and hotel hell.

TWO FOR THE ROAD: THE DORDOGNE

While we may not be Audrey Hepburn and Albert Finney in a white Mercedes convertible in *Two for the Road*, we do love exploring the back roads of Europe. The rolling hills of the Loire are behind us as we head for the Dordogne, land of white limestone canyons, feudal castles, foie gras, and truffles. Joe and I have loved solo traveling since we were in our twenties. Being together in the middle of nowhere, never knowing what's around the next corner— it's us against the world and our kind of adventure. It doesn't appeal to all—in fact, friends have told me they would find it downright dull, lonesome, or terrifying and that they can't imagine spending even a week alone with their spouse—but we've always relished discovering the byways of France all by ourselves.

Joe and I are both eldest children (he of three and I of eleven), and I've found that firstborns, like many only children, often have a fierce need for quiet time alone. In my case, eighteen years in tight quarters with a family of thirteen left me with a ravenous hunger for solitude. I savor my alone time and always have. As an adolescent, I retreated to the treasured tranquility of the bedroom I shared with my sister, where I developed the ability to lose myself in a Nancy Drew mystery or a Rosamond du Jardin romance to tune out the beehive of noise and activity that was home. Joe has similar memories. We're natural introverts whom silence restores and inactivity refreshes, much the way others muster vitality by being in the midst of the fray. We go inside to recharge our batteries, gird our loins, and gather the energy we need to be social. I can recall disappearing from business functions down a deserted hallway and from family reunions to an empty bedroom for some short-term restorative calm. While there was nothing lonelier than being young and single and living in New York City, surrounded by millions and not knowing a soul, being swallowed by the great cities of Europe with just Joe is bliss. The two of us are like heroes in a picaresque novel, with little need to be social other than with each other.

After spirited en route discussions of US and French politics, our children, and the approaching World Series, Joe muses, "Do you ever think we'll run out of things to talk about?" as he reaches for my hand and we descend to the meandering Dordogne River. Over the past twenty years, the Dordogne has become a popular spot for international tourists and country home—buying Brits alike. The pound's favorable position vis-à-vis the franc in the 1990s spurred the buying spree, not to mention the area's beauty and wealth of Hundred Years' War English history. The tourist trade has kept pace with the appetite of the crowds, and flower-bedecked hotels, cafés, and restaurants now sprout from every formerly abandoned nook and cranny imaginable. About a seven-hour drive south of Paris, the Dordogne has jammed narrow roads, castles and hill towns crawling with tourists, and countless canoes and kayaks creating noisy gridlock all summer.

It's early October, however, and the crowds have disappeared now that many hotels and restaurants are closed for the season. Although British accents are audible in even the tiniest of towns, the region has reclaimed its quiet, authentic charm. We rent a canoe one sparkling fall day (we've finally found some brilliant autumn color) and paddle our way twelve miles downriver from Vitrac to Beynac, past feudal villages clinging precipitously to cliffs, medieval fortresses, and lonely châteaux high on distant hills. The garrulous owner of Canoë-Loisirs, from whom we rent the boat, reports he has only ten canoes on the water today; in July and August he rents his entire fleet of eight hundred daily.

The Dordogne boasts dozens of quaint villages that rise impossibly over rocky bluffs. We decide to forgo the windshield tour (many of the "must-see" towns are as far apart as forty miles of treacherous, twisting roads) to stop and fully explore just one or two. It's all in keeping with our anti–boot camp pacing, and as much as I have to rein in my natural inclination to see everything the guidebook recommends, I'm really starting to realize the benefits of a slower speed. We have lunch in Beynac on a terrace by the river and then hike the steep footpaths, peeking into tight alleys and ivy-covered passages, all the way up to its daunting château that towers over the valley.

Our Dordogne-discovering tempo has been just right, leaving us plenty of time to relax in our accommodations at the Vieux Logis. Our three-night stay at this intimate Relais & Châteaux property is the first hotel splurge of our trip, our Sancerre hellhole a distant memory. In the picture-perfect village of Trémolat, the inn is nestled in a sharp bend of the Dordogne River. Claude Chabrol filmed his movie *The Butcher* here, taking advantage of towering plane trees and the hamlet's charm. In keeping with our intention of watching movies that add local flavor, we search for the film online, to no avail.

It's a challenge to adequately convey the subtle beauty of the gardens and the romantic solitude of this wisteria-covered former farm and priory. We book the "simplest" room at the inn but are pleasantly surprised when we are upgraded to a first-floor *déluxe* room that opens on the garden. Joe and I wear ear-to-ear smiles as we're escorted to our accommodations. The walls and ceiling have dark, exposed beams that date from the time our arm of the hotel was a tobacco barn, the floors are terra-cotta, and patterned curtains and bed linens in Provençal blue and yellow brighten the room. The ultraprofessional service, always softened with warmth, of Relais & Châteaux properties is consistent and without equal.

We have two alarms at Le Vieux Logis. Joe's watch buzzes at 7:30 a.m., and then the bells of the solid twelfth-century Romanesque church on the town square chime at eight. The promise of exploring the extensive garden outside the tall French doors finally gets us up and out.

Chris coined a family expression when he was nine years old and we were staying at the Wilderness Lodge in Disney World. This magnificent hotel, designed and outfitted as an authentic Pacific Northwest hunting lodge, had a stunning, ten-story atrium entrance with a giant timbered chandelier, dozens of overstuffed easy chairs, comfy sofas, and an engaging working train set. Aaron Copland's *Billy the Kid* suite played in a continuous loop to help set the stage. We were in our room settling in, and Chris was itching to explore the hotel with six-year-old Caroline. Desperate to speed up the unpacking process, Chris came up with this unique appeal: "Come on, guys, let's go—we need to take advantage of the lobby!" From that day forward, if we stay somewhere that merits it, Bohr family trips always include plenty of time for "taking advantage" of our lodging's public spaces. Thus we appreciate the lobby, the gardens, and the various cozy salons of Le Vieux Logis by absorbing every detail and relaxing for as long as possible. Even the prospect of seeing more castles of the Dordogne can't lure us away.

We stay well past noon at Le Vieux Logis on our final morning, but it's time to get back on the road. We drive along winding back roads for an hour, until we reach the lovely Dordogne town of Sarlat-la-Canéda for the tail end of its bustling Saturday-morning market. Sarlat is a gorgeous, golden-sandstone fourteenth-century town, and its old town center remains car-free. We wander the cobblestone streets and admire its architecture, agreeing that the town is improbably beautiful.

While we would love to stay in Sarlat to further explore its stone buildings and winding streets, we get back in the car for an additional two hours, leaving the Dordogne behind to motor deeper into *la France profonde*. We have an appointment with Sophie, the owner of our next weekly rental, in Saint-Cirq Lapopie. We reluctantly take our leave but look forward to what we'll discover at our next stop: the Lot.

MY LAZY AMERICAN JAW

Six weeks into our journey, and I no longer have to think so hard about speaking French. I recall that at this point in my year here as a student, my lazy American jaw finally started forming the words more easily and the effort became less substantial. Previous trips have been frustrating: just as the phrases start flowing, our vacation is over and it's time to go home. When we arrived in France this time, I tripped over even the simplest phrases and imagined myself as the Tin Man, needing Dorothy to provide emergency oil to loosen my jaw—on both sides, *s'il vous plaît.* Speaking French requires much more in-and-out movement of the lips and cheeks—exaggerated at times—to pronounce words correctly and achieve the appropriate intonation.

Much to the consternation of L'Académie Française, the elite group of forty *immortels* in charge of ensuring the "purity" of the French language, there is increasingly more Franglais used in everyday speech, especially in Paris. A wireless connection is pronounced "wee-fee," a runner goes *jogging*, those who want a calorie-free soda order *Coca-Light*, and everyone says *bon week-end* on Friday afternoon. Next to the signs for the *boulangerie*, pâtisserie, *boucherie*, and *crèmerie*, you now find signs for the *sandwicherie*. I'm keenly aware of my Americanness when I'm in France and do my best to avoid the more blatant Franglais whenever I can.

Now that we're in the sticks, it's been so much easier to understand what people say. Parisians tend to run everything together, dropping endings and forming words deep in the backs of their mouths. And of course, the terribly chic and cool young people in Paris speak an undecipherable argot. Except for a wooden plank nailed to a tree whose painted letters announced SNACK BAR as we canoed down the Dordogne, French is so much more pure outside the capital.

As I converse with a waiter who asks about our camera, I recall a Franglais episode from soon after we arrived in Paris. We decided we needed a lens cap attachment for our new Sony. Before heading into the camera shop, I Google-Translated the appropriate photography-related vocabulary and figured out how to describe what we needed. And, as I've so often found, the phrase *le petit truc* (the little whatchamacallit) came in very handy.

"Mais oui, madame, zee cap kee-per," the guy behind the counter replied to my query. I'd agonized all morning over exactly how to communicate what I needed, and he made all my worry for naught with his instant Franglais response.

"I could have handled that one," Joe observed, and agreed to be the communicator the next time we had an issue with technology.

I'll need to continue to work my jaw when we cross the border into Spain in a couple of weeks. Despite having taken seven years of Spanish before and then concurrently with French, I haven't had the opportunity to practice it for years. I suspect that most of what I'll be doing *en español* is translating road signs and menus but hope that at least some of what I learned in class will return. Communicating in other languages is one of my elemental joys. Joe, on the other hand, recently admitted that he "gave up" on French, even though he took it for four years in high school, when he learned nouns could be masculine or feminine. As a rational fourteen-year-old, he concluded that such a convention was stupid. I've done my best to explain the whole gender thing and how it goes back at least as far as Latin, but to him, it remains nonsense. No matter how compelling my explanation, he still comes back to the basic question of why make a language even harder than it has to be? I'll be sure to ask L'Académie Française the next time I correspond, but I'm afraid some questions simply have no answers.

In the meantime, I'll focus on keeping my jaw loose and my oil can ready.

SAINT-CIRQ LAPOPIE

The French department of the Lot is about one hundred kilometers to the south and east of and thirty years behind its more developed and savvy neighbor, the Dordogne, at least in terms of exploiting tourism. Whereas the Dordogne is relaxed and slow in the off-season, the Lot comes to a virtual halt after mid-September. Its eponymous river flows through a deep valley but is narrower than the Dordogne waterway, and we see not a soul taking in its pleasures. I insisted on adding the Lot to our itinerary because I'd heard and read for years about Saint-Cirq Lapopie, an astoundingly dramatic clifftop village that instantly transports visitors back to the Middle Ages. I look forward to inhabiting the soul of a French peasant woman and staying in an authentic stone dwelling. My travel companion is notably less enthusiastic.

We squeeze past a gargantuan coach bus packed with elderly tourists (Joe accurately observes that "Europe makes their cars small and their buses colossal"), improbably hugging tight roads carved into rock walls along the river. As we venture deeper and deeper into the province, Joe voices trepidation. "Is the Lot just one shuttered village after another?" It's baseball playoff time back home—his beloved Yankees are in the running—and he fears being cut off from the action. "I wonder if the Lot has even heard of the Internet," he muses. Everything is abandoned and will remain so until next June, when the sun again warms the limestone cliffs and tourists scurry to umbrellaed cafés. In the meantime, all is silent along the River Lot, including Joe as his anxiety level rises.

We arrive in Saint-Cirq Lapopie in the late afternoon. We meet our spunky landlord, Sophie, in the riverside campground at the base of town, just as the sun dips behind the castle and the long fall afternoon shadows disappear. Visitors must park in lots just before the town's gate, where cobblestone streets rise sharply and wind uphill at vertical angles to the top. But we're residents for the week, so we have parking privileges. Sophie ably guides us up and around the town's perimeter and then down its impossibly steep main street into a tight passage that will serve as our driveway for our stay.

Guidebooks uniformly describe Saint-Cirq as one of the most beautiful villages in France—indeed, it's a member of the association Les Plus Beaux Villages de France, whose green-and-red shield is proudly displayed as we enter town. In the Middle Ages, a variety of crafts, such as wood turning, blacksmithing, and tanning, dominated village activity, and in recent years, international writers and artists have taken up residence in the summer months. Joe has once again started to speak as Saint-Cirq shows the promise of life: a few shops and restaurants are open, and scattered tourists are making the steep climb up the tight main street. Some of the action can be attributed to the fact that it's Saturday, but we hold out hope that a modicum of activity will continue for the next seven days.

Sophie advances to open our rental's squat wooden door, flecked with lichen, and six-foot Joe quips, "I trust the ceilings will be higher than that door." Indeed they are, and he has ample room to stand up straight. As Sophie shows us around our cozy three-story home (one small room on each floor connected by vertiginous open stairways), she advises us on what to do and where to eat in the village. Our cottage is just as I pictured—it's a beguiling stone and half-timbered house with a sharply pitched tile roof and two little outdoor spaces: a pebble-covered courtyard through which we entered and a grassy, terraced garden out back.

Sophie informs us that the house is over four hundred years old and that when it was first built, the ground floor, now the kitchen, housed the animals. Their body warmth rose to the second floor, now a sitting room with a wood-burning stove, which was where the family lived and slept. The third floor, an attic bedroom with a steeply sloped ceiling, was added years later. I am enchanted. *Why go anywhere else in the region,* I think, *when Saint-Cirq is pretty and atmospheric and filled with flowers?* The town and our home are dripping with medieval charm, so there's no need to travel to find more. Always-practical Joe quickly brings me back to reality, of course, reminding me that we need to make a shopping run to Cahors, capital of the Lot, at least a half hour away, to stock up on toiletries, starter logs, and food before the remaining daylight fades and temperatures plummet.

Saint-Cirq is indeed picturesque, but it is also the definition of lonely. After seemingly interminable days of isolation, even natural introverts like Joe and I need the company of others, if only to observe them eating, drinking, and laughing. After twenty-four hours, it becomes clear that Saint-Cirq is like everywhere else in the Lot: in the off-season, there is absolutely nothing going on. Our hope that Saturday would not be the only day of the week blessed with activity is dashed as we discover that we are two of the handful of people actually living in the town. We take multimile hikes along ridges above the river, including one that has us cross a gorge over a long-abandoned railroad bridge, where we pass no one, and wander through hamlet after desolate hamlet, their every window barred.

"I guess the visitors we saw were day-trippers," I lament.

And while our house is enchanting, it has no heat— it retains the cold in its brick and stone walls—and we spend hours stoking the fire in the cast-iron stove. It's no wonder they eat belly-warming crocks of piping-hot cassoulet with sausage and beans and gulp goblets of dark purple *vin noir de Cahors* in the region. Downing the stuff helps us ward off the nighttime chill; we also wear fleeces to bed and throw additional blankets on top of the duvet. Still, we see our breath in the mornings. The only thing that gives us the courage to abandon the shelter of our pile of blankets is the prospect of a kitchen warmed by an open oven that toasts our morning baguettes and the gas flame that boils water for coffee.

In addition to lacking heat, our enchanting icebox has no Internet, confirming Joe's worst fear. We chose the property because of its old-world charm, but we should have paid more attention to current conveniences. We recall the weeks on end when we sprinted through the business rat race at home and yearned for just one day of disconnected peace. But now that we're completely away from it all—and have been for weeks—we realize that being unplugged is not as heavenly as we'd hoped. We're uncomfortable being off the grid, and solidifying additional plans for our trip is impossible.

"I suppose we've allowed the romance of the road to blind us to our very real need for the modern world," I sigh.

"We?'" questions Joe with a halfhearted smile. "This is *your* bucolic vision, babe. You know I'm a city boy at my core."

In our hungry search for connectivity, we become like compulsive smokers who furtively huddle in the shadows outside shuttered *bistrots* and in McDo (McDonald's) parking lots in Cahors, anxious for a signal and a fix from home. *Has it really come to this?* we think, then agree that yes, it has. One drizzly afternoon in Saint-Cirq, Joe cowers from the elements on a stoop in front of a closed café with free Wi-Fi to get a dose of the wider world. The grumpy old Frenchman putting out his trash across the street doesn't much like the look of Joe's iPad (or maybe just Joe) and glares at him, hoping this will send him scurrying. But Joe is connected, and he isn't leaving his post so easily. The geezer then comes over, gesticulating and grumbling, *"Qu'est-ce que vous faites?"* over and over. Joe tries to show him he's just checking the baseball scores, but the monsieur is having none of this and continues on, creating a scene. Joe finally surrenders his hallowed spot and comes back to the cottage, annoyed and defeated.

Our descent into disconnected gloom teaches us a valuable lesson: our ability to appreciate the wonders of the Old World requires being connected to the New. From now on, access to the Internet will be critical. We resolve to book no more wireless-free abodes, be they country inns or home rentals, and to carefully consider the isolation factor of where we decide to stay. We may opt for a desolate, bucolic location once again, but it will be a deliberate decision and it will simply have to have Internet, elusive in *la France profonde*.

LE CAFARD

Seven weeks in, homesickness hits and hits hard. We're in Languedoc-Roussillon in southwestern France, the Lot is behind us, the Yankees are out of the playoffs, and the fall weather has turned decidedly colder under steely gray skies and thick cloud cover—never a good thing for lifting one's spirits. Though we never imagined our adventure abroad would be daily champagne and constant merriment, we didn't expect the blues to make their appearance so soon.

Endless desolate, medieval stone hamlets have darkened our mood. Everything we see has been touched not only by the savagery of the Hundred Years' War between the French and English in the fourteenth and fifteenth centuries but also by the thirteenth-century Cathar Crusade. Prior to our trip, I read extensively about the Cathars and decided that we must visit the departments of the Tarn and the Aude, in which this shameful yet fascinating period of French history took place. The bloodthirsty military campaign of the pope, ironically named Innocent III, to eliminate the dualist offshoot of Catholicism in the Languedoc region of France was conducted with abandon against the heretics and spared no one—men, women, children, and the elderly were all slaughtered. And when Catholics refused to give up their Cathar neighbors, one religious leader (a monk, no less) famously declared, "Kill them all. God will know his own."

In a sunnier clime, all this history might be remote and intriguing. But against a backdrop of unrelenting gray, it leaves us feeling fogged in and low. After visiting so many places that witnessed sieges, starvation, plagues, pestilence, and butchery, even the cheeriest of souls would succumb to its grip. The French have a fitting expression for this dark visitor: *le cafard*, which means "the cockroach."

Yes, we're now suffering an inconvenient melancholia, tinged with some serious *mal du pays* (homesickness) that's reared its ugly head without warning. Perhaps we've had our fill of cold, antiquated spaces and lonely, abandoned stone villages. Or perhaps the total absence of others to provide even a bit of people-watching diversion has brought us down. Is it simply the loneliness of being disconnected from the rest of the world, day after day after day? Maybe we're just in a temporary trough of the normal vicissitudes of travel. To put it simply, we miss our children and we miss our country—we've come down with a serious case of *le cafard*.

We left Saint-Cirq after a week of steaming dinners and shivering nights and headed farther south, driving deep into Cathar country. Despite knowing that immersing ourselves in the brutal extinction of the Cathars might not be what we needed to improve our dispositions, we plowed ahead toward our next destination: Caunes-Minervois, just north of Carcassonne. We stop and hike the steep Cathar hill town of Cordes-sur-Ciel, where the region's heretics took refuge, and take a long midday break for a sunny, outdoor lunch in Albi (home of Toulouse-Lautrec), with its austere, imposing redbrick cathedral of Sainte-Cécile, unlike any other church in the world. Joe notes that the cylindrical exterior of its nave looks like a space shuttle ready for launch. Sainte-Cécile was built after the Cathars were wiped out to remind others thinking of defying Rome, lest they forget who was in charge.

We get back on the road and drive farther south into the Montagne Noire (the Black Mountains) and then down to the constricted streets of the village of Caunes-Minervois, where our Internet-enabled hotel awaits. It's been over a week since we communicated with our children, and both of us are lost in reverie about what we'll learn when we fire up our laptops. Chris had just had an interview the last time we spoke. Did he get the job? I wonder. Caroline was coming down with a cold. Is she now feeling better? Did my latest Amex payment go through, and is the house we hope to rent in Spain still available? Joe speculates about the problems Chris was having with his car and whether the colleague who was giving Caroline trouble has backed off, as well as how the New York Giants fared last weekend.

Our home for the next three nights is the difficult-to-find Hôtel d'Alibert. As soon as we see that the age-old townhome, highly recommended by several guidebooks, is in the heart of the medieval quarter, we know we're in for logistical difficulty. Joe deftly squeezes our car into the tight, deserted streets and waits while I check in. The affable but quirky owner (you cannot arrive at the hotel between 2:00 and 5:00 p.m., because he is napping—it says so right on the door) lets me in through the French doors of the hotel's restaurant at just after five. The front portal remains inexplicably locked all day.

He shows me to our large, airy room with plenty of heat (things are looking up), and then we wind down dark spiral stairs, through a series of stone arches, to the barn-like garage at the back of the building. After demonstrating the necessary gyrations of twisting and turning the locking mechanism and then tugging and pushing the huge double wooden doors open, he tells me to walk out the alley and make the first right, then another right and yet another right, and there I will find my husband sitting patiently in the car. *Sacré bleu,* I think, *just wait till Joe sees where he has to drive to maneuver the car into this garage.*

I present Joe with the good news first—there's a warm, cheerful room awaiting us, but he has to drive through a tight maze in order to park the car. As always, he masterfully negotiates the alleyways of Caunes-Minervois and guides our little rental into the stable at the back of the inn.

The coda to our arrival in Languedoc-Roussillon is this: "Yes, the hotel has free Wi-Fi," the proprietor confirms when we inquire, "but it is not currently working; there have been some problems, I'm afraid." We are both enraged and on the verge of tears. Here we are in yet another deserted town with no means to connect. We drag our devastated spirits up the spiral stone stairway to our room and drop our luggage, and *le cafard* attacks with a vengeance. For the rest of the evening, in a fit of pique, we seriously contemplate the possibility of returning home but finally agree that all will seem better in the morning. After our night of frustration and reflection, the morning light bolsters our resolve to rally.

CARCASSONNE: FORTIFIED CITY EXTRAORDINAIRE

My first starry-eyed imaginings of Europe were of a turreted, walled, fairy-tale city like Carcassonne. When I was growing up, my family had a multivolume set of orange-clad Childcraft books, each with a name like *The World Around Us*, *Folk and Fairy Tales*, and *Poems of Early Childhood*. I loved every volume and read them again and again, but my absolute favorite was *Life in Many Lands*. It included stories of children in Mexico, Holland, and China, and of course the one I remember most is of a young French girl, Nanette, in an embroidered dress and lacy headdress, who lived in a crenulated château with her grandmother.

As we approach Carcassonne and its fifty-two turrets and double-walled fortifications, the romance of Nanette's story floods over me and I'm reminded of when I first fell in love with France. We pull off the highway onto a back road's crest, a gauzy vista of the city before us. Perhaps it's the afternoon light streaming across golden autumn vineyards, or maybe it's my childlike love for my subject, but my photos capture the uniquely dreamlike quality of Carcassonne. We could sit here all day, absorbing the beauty of this bewitching city.

A healthy lunch of green salads and ham-and-cheese crêpes—comfort food à la *française*—on the central square of Carcassonne lifts us up even more. Our café's free Wi-Fi and the fact that we've spent the warm, sunny morning exploring also help. People-watching in the largest fortified city in Europe is excellent—the best we've had in weeks—and we're so happy to no longer be alone. We expected to see many tourists at this haunting monument to the past but didn't anticipate such an international crowd. People and languages from around the world surround us; in fact, it's the first time we've heard anything other than French and English since we left Paris.

Carcassonne boasts its share of griffins and other medieval beasts whose ghastly faces dampened our dispositions over the past weeks, but there's a difference between having them glare at us when we're all by our lonesome in cold, deserted villages and experiencing them surrounded by happy people, the sun shining down.

Friends and family have often heard the story of my arrival in Carcassonne as a student during a blustery January snowstorm in flimsy canvas sneakers, the city's inns and hostels all full. After I banged the huge brass knocker on the timbered gate of a youth hostel housed in a convent—but closed for the month—an elderly nun in full black-and-white habit, wrinkled as a walnut, opened the padlocked doors. She took pity on shivering me and offered me a bunk in an unheated stone chamber.

Some of my anticipation for visiting this *bastide* stems from wanting to revisit with Joe the site of my snowy stopover so many years ago. We pass through the city gate and make our way up the curving cobblestone path, winding past hawkers of plastic swords and knight costumes, followed by artisan workshops and cafés housed in stone arcades. Years ago, en route to the top of town before I stumbled upon the convent that rescued me, I briefly stopped in the one open bar for a *chocolat chaud* to thaw my frozen fingers and warm my belly. And there it is. The little place remains, tucked on the left of the twisting street, still in business and bustling. We stop for a quick look and move on. We have less luck finding the convent as we wander back and forth and around the church on the summit's square. Just where I think the dorm of my memory should stand is a gilded, four-star establishment: l'Hôtel de la Cité. While it would make a good story to claim the frigid convent hostel of my youth has been transformed into a luxury hotel, I'm afraid l'Hôtel de la Cité has been in that spot for one hundred years. We eventually give up searching for what appears to exist no longer, and I decide to preserve my memory of that snowy night in Carcassonne exactly as I remember it. I will not let the reality of today interfere.

Having rallied with a tasty lunch, some time with Wi-Fi, and an afternoon in Carcassonne, we conclude our constitutions can handle a true Cathar experience—barbaric stories, bloody ghosts of brutality, and all. We plan a hike for the following day to the hilltop bastion of les Châteaux de Lastours and cross our fingers that sunny moods will prevail.

LES CHÂTEAUX DE LASTOURS:
A CATHAR HIKE

My emotions get the better of me, and I am indeed haunted by the annihilation of the Cathars as we ascend the steep, rocky spur above the village of Lastours. The bloodthirsty religious fervor of the Crusaders who slaughtered these believers in a Christianity different from that of Rome is unthinkable, yet such fanaticism still exists today. How uncomplicated it must be to live life with a set-in-stone worldview, believing in a forever war between good and evil. Those who live in a moral world of black and white, with no ambiguities, must find it easy to navigate life, not questioning what is right and what is wrong but simply following established dogma. Such thinking terrifies me. But was it really what the Cathars believed that incited Rome to launch a crusade? More likely, it was the loss of power, taxes, and valuable Cathar-owned land.

The Châteaux de Lastours are four castles perched high in the foothills of the Montagne Noire, isolated by deep surrounding valleys. Cabaret, Surdespine, and the Tour Régine march in line along a crest, while Quertinheux is on a slightly lower neighboring pinnacle. The castles and proximate villages welcomed fleeing Cathars during the Albigensian crusade and thus were a target of the brutal Crusader leader Simon de Montfort. I find it hard to say or even think his name without adding the epithet "sadistic bastard."

It takes us thirty minutes to negotiate the switchbacks and stoop through a dark, eerie cave to the châteaux. We spend an hour scrambling from one castle rampart to the next, exploring the crumbling windows and towers of each. It's windy, with a hint of drizzle, and the gloomy weather helps us summon life long ago: difficult, cold, and under constant threat. The precipitous hike down on slippery scree is more difficult than the ascent, and we're happy we've brought our trekking poles with us. Back in the car, we drive to a promontory opposite the châteaux to the *vue panoramique*, where we take in the castles from across the valley. Just as with Carcassonne and impressionist paintings, the view from afar is the best and brings all into focus.

We have bread, cheese, and a bottle of chilled Sancerre back at our room at the Hôtel d'Alibert and are happy not to eat some form of duck for our evening meal, for once in many weeks. It's amazing how duck dominates menus in southwestern France: duck breast, duck rillettes, duck confit, duck gizzards, foie gras in its many forms, stuffed duck's neck, duck cassoulet . . . We even saw duck heart on a menu. About a week after arriving in the Dordogne, I recalled what a Canadian we met at the Paris flea market told us when we shared that we were headed southwest. He and his fiancée had just left the Dordogne, and he predicted, "Yes, I see duck in your future. . . . I see significant duck in your future."

LOST HORIZON: ANDORRA

We leave Languedoc-Roussillon and make our way farther south, deep into the bowels of the French Pyrenees, toward the Spanish border. Our five-day trip into the mountains is a pleasant but strange one, filled with little surprises.

Our scenic four-hour car ride is slowed in a mountain village as we zip into an alley to avoid a face-off with three eighteen-wheelers negotiating their way through. Just where we've backed up, the road takes a turn that makes the passage of each long truck between the stone buildings a tricky proposition. The geometry just won't work because, as Joe, ever the engineer, puts it, "the ten-pound trucks won't fit through the five-pound road." The drivers get out of their cabs, scratching their heads, gesticulating wildly, and surveying the situation from a variety of angles. We have ringside seats for all the backing, filling, and eventual liberation of the three vehicles.

Our next obstacle appears on what is barely a lane twisting farther into the mountains toward our next destination, Molitg-les-Bains. Around a sharp bend, we're blocked by a most astonishing sight: a herd of sheep, a pack of dogs, and a shepherd making their way ahead of us. Keeping our distance, we're spellbound by the way the shepherd orchestrates the procession from behind, whistling, clucking, and waving his staff. The dogs respond immediately, following his every order to move the sheep along and rescue those that stray. We need to pick up our pace, but I'm sad when the road forks and the herd veers up a mountain path. With a quick wave, we continue on our way.

Our two days in the spa town of Molitg, where we stay in the Château de Riell, a baroque folly of a hotel, are a bit surreal. Not sleeping in yet another cold medieval building is a welcome change. At first glance, the crenelated-tower château in the middle of the woods appears to be from perhaps the sixteenth century, but we learn it was actually built in the nineteenth, in the baroque style, by its eccentric original owner. Our room is warm and inviting, and its many windows look out onto the thick surrounding woods.

We eat our meals at the Grand Hôtel, an eerie health resort down the road. The antiseptic dining room is far from full when we arrive, but additional patrons soon file in as if in a trance, one by one, and each diner is led to his or her assigned table with an already opened bottle of wine waiting. No orders are taken and no one speaks as food starts arriving. We appear to be the only guests sitting as a pair and ordering off the menu. It's difficult to put our finger on what makes the mood and these people dining alone so strange, but there's a Stepford quality to it all. "I'm surprised they're not all wearing light blue hospital gowns," Joe remarks. The gentleman sitting next to us by his lonesome appears frail, as do many of the others. He quietly finishes his meal, drinks exactly one glass from his bottle of red wine, and slips away for additional time in the eerily lit healing-water chamber on the lower level. The Grand Hôtel seems more sanatorium than spa, with its ethereal inhabitants in search of cures for who knows what ails them.

The following morning, we hit the road for the tiny principality nestled in a remote valley of the Pyrenees. If ever there were a spot that calls to mind James Hilton's slightly spooky novel *Lost Horizon*, it is Andorra.

No, Andorra is not Tibet—not even close—but there is something otherworldly and about the place. Even its architecture reminds us of the red-and-white Potala Palace high in the Himalayas, with its symmetrical square windows climbing the hill. We've decided to detour into this tiny country before a final stay in France and then our entry into Spain. How many people can say they've been to Andorra, after all? On our approach, we wind through colossal, primary-colored, futuristic ski compounds sprawled across the valleys with architecture unlike anything we've ever seen. Tucked between the French and Spanish borders, Andorra is a cross between a lit-up duty-free shopping mall and outfitter extraordinaire, much like a Pyrenean Moab or Boulder. Its main industry is tourism, and visitors come in droves for inexpensive, tax-free electronics, watches, perfume, and liquor, as well as to ski, hike, and rock-climb.

What adds to the anachronistic, neither-here-nor-there-ness of the principality is the official language of Catalan. A romance language related to French, Spanish, and Italian but altogether different, it's impossible for me to decipher; it might as well be Russian. But most people we meet at our rustic guesthouse and in shops and restaurants speak at least some French, albeit thickly accented. The gentleman who cuts Joe's hair (yes, he decides to get a haircut in Andorra, just to be able to say he did) speaks Spanish, so I am able to communicate, "Just a trim."

We learn there are three types of schools in Andorra—Catalan, French, and Spanish—and you go where you are most comfortable culturally. Almost no one speaks English, which is fine with us, but the language mash-up is a unique experience. We say *merci* to someone, and they respond with *de nada*, in Spanish, but if we say *gracias*, they often come back with *merci à vous*, in French. As our waiter in a tapas restaurant explains, in a mixture of Spanish and French, "We are very international here."

After three days, we head back into France for six days in the small town of Puylaurens, an hour east of Toulouse, lured by the prospect of a highly rated inn, for our last taste of France before we return next spring.

PUYLAURENS: HOME OF MARIANNE

When we arrive in Puylaurens after the long drive from Andorra, things look grim at first glance. The entire town except our hotel, the marvelous Cap de Castel, is concealed behind closed shutters and gray roll-down steel security doors. "Great," we sigh, "yet another abandoned place." It finally dawns us, however, that this is the important French holiday la Toussaint (All Saints' Day), and almost all businesses are closed for the entire weekend. November 1, All Saints' Day, falls on a Tuesday this year—an excellent excuse for a four-day weekend. It's difficult to find anything open on a Sunday or on any day of a holiday weekend in all but the largest cities in France. We've had more than one disappointment and change of plans because we've forgotten that Sunday means closed. It's a reminder of the differences between France and the United States and of the so-true adage that while Americans live to work, the French work to live.

We've witnessed several anecdotal incidents in France that confirm the profit motive does not reign supreme. On multiple occasions in Paris when we lunched near the Eiffel Tower or walked through a park, we saw men in business suits reclined on benches, taking long midday naps. I can't imagine businesspeople in Manhattan daring to take a full hour of a workday to snooze in the sun. We've also seen restaurateurs turn away business at 2:05 p.m. because they stopped serving lunch at two o'clock. Most likely, the cook had already gone home, and working overtime was out of the question.

After a long day of hiking the farmland hills in the surrounding countryside, we polish off our last bottle of Sancerre and relax with our usual in-room dinner menu of bread, cheese, and ham. We change things up a bit with an *epi*, a French loaf composed of a series of rolls strung together, thereby providing much more crusty crunch than a regular baguette.

Once la Toussaint is behind us, the shutters open, the steel walls lift, and Puylaurens is back in business.

Although not particularly picturesque, it's a vibrant town with plenty of citizens on the streets, especially at the busy market on Wednesday morning. Wholly unexpected is the discovery that Puylaurens is the birthplace of the French Republic's moniker and my namesake, Marianne. Just as Uncle Sam is a symbol for the United States, so Marianne is the symbol of France, representing *liberté, égalité, fraternité* and appearing on its stamps and official seal and on euro coins. We learn that the first use of Marianne as a symbol of France was in a song of the revolution (*"La Guérison de Marianne"*), composed in 1792 by the cobbler-poet Guillaume Lavabre—a native son of Puylaurens. Who knew?

On the eve of our departure for Spain, we have one final candlelit dinner at our warm, rustic hotel, prepared by the adorable twentysomething chef, who comes out of the kitchen to bid us adieu. Housed in buildings from the 1600s and expertly renovated with exposed beams, earthen-tiled floors, ocher-painted walls, and abundant gardens, the inn has been a find. It's a member of the Hôtels de Charme et de Caractère association, which is how we discovered the little gem, and it definitely lives up to this label. The owners are warm and attentive and help us map leisurely but satisfying hikes through the surrounding gently rolling farmland. The *jardinier* answers my every question about the gardens and is as in love with the lavender as I am. Adding to our delight is the fact that the nightly tariff is well below our budget, as are the epicurean pleasures we've tasted here. There are definitely advantages to traveling off-season.

A SIGNIFICANT MILESTONE

November 7 is an important date for us. First, it's Chris's twenty-seventh birthday, and just as it was so difficult to be away from Caroline on September 21, the day she turned twenty-four, we hate being so far from our son today.

The second reason is equally important and makes the distance somewhat easier. One month from today, the kids fly into Milan to travel with us for two weeks in Italy. And while we don't want our upcoming four weeks in Spain, Portugal, and Morocco to fly by, we eagerly anticipate the arrival of our children from across the pond.

Reason number three to note the date is that two months ago today, we arrived in Paris to start our sabbatical. We've had our ups and downs, including the almost fatal bout with *le cafard*, but we've learned that we need connectivity and people to watch and must be wary of isolation. So, with two months of travel wisdom under our belts, we prepare to immerse ourselves in Spain with the glimmer of a visit with our children on the horizon.

IV. The Iberian Peninsula
November 2011

BELLA BARCELONA

W E KNOW FRANCE is definitively behind us when our train pulls into the Barcelona Sants station an hour late. Our 6:54 a.m. TGV (*train à grande vitesse*) left Toulouse right on time, and the train to which we transferred in Narbonne departed not a second late as well. But all bets for an on-time arrival are off now that we've crossed into Spain.

The train slows to a screeching stop at the border, and I woefully harken back to my overnight trip to Madrid in the '70s. In the dead of night, my fellow backpackers and I were awakened at the Spanish border town of Irun, gathered our belongings, got off the French train, and stumbled forward two hundred yards to board the Spanish train because the French wheels wouldn't run on Spain's wider track gauge. This is still true for many of the trains in Spain, and the unlucky passengers crossing the borders into and out of France must do the border-train shuffle. Luckily, this is not the case for our variable-gauge train, which runs from the Mediterranean coastal towns in France to Barcelona. Rather, they widen the distance between the wheels of each car to accommodate the wider tracks of the Iberian system.

"What a way to run a railroad," Joe quips loudly so I can hear him over the incessant wheel-expanding clanging in the background.

Now that we've arrived in Barcelona, the familiar doorbell-chime greeting of "*bonjour messieurs, dames*" each time we walk into a shop or hotel has been replaced with a simple, straightforward "*hola.*" And the abundant red-and-yellow-striped flags, street signs, and billboards (only a few words of which I can decipher) remind us that we're not yet fully in Spain—we're in Catalonia, as we were in Andorra. Here and there I spot a familiar word: *bella*, for "beautiful"; *carrer*, for "street"; or *gambeta*, for "shrimp."

Barcelona genuinely surprises us. We arrive with no preconceived notions and thereby will allow the city to unfold for us on its own. We've read only enough of our guidebook to help us reserve a room and then stopped, concentrating our time and energy on the logistics of moving from one country to the next. All unpacked and settled into our hotel (wanting to keep *le cafard* at bay, we decided against accommodations in the shadowy old quarter and opted for a bright place with all the modern conveniences in the center of town), we turn to each other and ask, "Now what?"

Just after our very first wake-up in Spain, we have an unexpected, laugh-out-loud moment. In the well-lit hotel breakfast room, painted pale green and decorated with plentiful plastic oranges and daisies, we are the only two Americans filling our plates from the buffet. Imagine our surprise when the English-language rock music playing in the background launches into Cee-Lo Green's original version of "Forget You." We practically drop our *huevos* in our laps.

"Are they really playing the uncensored version?"

I ask as Cee-Lo drops one f-bomb after another.

No one else in the cantina even flinches. Ah, the beauty and innocence of listening to another country's music while you have no idea what the lyrics mean.

The fact that we arrived in the rain and that showers continue for two days dampens neither our spirits nor our introduction to Barcelona. There's an upbeat vibe to this city—it's a happy place with happy people, and the energy is contagious. Joe and I fall into step, our temporary travel depression a distant memory. Compared with their neighbors in France, Barcelonans' bodies are broader, their hair is darker, and people move with an unmistakable lightness of step. The bread doesn't come close to the French variety, but the fact that all forms and colors of tapas are available all day is a pleasant plus. While no other system surpasses the Paris metro in my book, Barcelona's subway is clean, easy, and efficient. The colossal, central public market, the Mercat de la Boqueria, just off the main pedestrian way, La Rambla, makes the open-air markets we visited in France look like roadside farm stands. Filled with hundreds of stalls selling every type of fresh seafood, meat, cheese, and produce imaginable and fringed with strings of hanging hams, the lofty-ceilinged indoor market buzzes with activity and chatter.

Joe declares, "This is a vegetarian's nightmare," and I observe, "We don't have to worry about being by ourselves anymore. The people-watching opportunities are priceless."

Tourists elbow to elbow with locals jostle to buy groceries and snap photos of exotic sea creatures on beds of ice, every variety of fruit and vegetable piled high, and the brown-and-red awnings of Spain's beloved *jamón* merchants.

Barcelona is much like Los Angeles geographically, nestled between high hills and the sea. There are even Barcelonan surfer dudes, boards perched on their shoulders, heading off to catch the waves along the beach. To help us discover more surprises, get our bearings, and orient ourselves to the far-flung highlights of the city, we join other tourists and take one of the ubiquitous hop-on/hop-off, open-topped buses that snake through town, stopping at the major sights.

The number-one stop for any Barcelona visitor is Antoni Gaudí's Sagrada Família church, the architect's unfinished masterpiece, still under construction and not to be completed for another twenty-five years. This sand castle sculpture in the middle of a residential neighborhood is unlike any structure we've ever seen, with its intricate details and lacy spires. We're equally fascinated and charmed by Gaudí's colorfully tiled Park Güell, carved into a hill, its paths delineated with irregular, organic fences and jagged overhangs. And the fanciful buildings that undulate in the chic Eixample district make us stop to marvel at the magic of their mosaics and vibrant serendipity. I'm embarrassed to admit I had no idea how much Gaudí and the Catalan *artistas modernistas* influenced this lovely city.

"I wish I were a designer," I sigh, "so I could be inspired by the work of Gaudí and his contemporaries."

"How about you just be inspired?" Joe chuckles. "If we're ever able to buy another house, you can do it à la Gaudí."

Beyond these visionaries' whimsical work, so many other buildings in Barcelona are simply striking structures whose windows are graced with attractive shutters in yellows and greens and are always open, unlike those perpetually closed in France. Every window has a balcony of wrought iron or stone, beckoning its residents outside. We visit the Picasso Museum, hidden in the dark recesses of the ancient Barri Gòtic quarter. It houses much of Barcelona's other famous resident's early work. Despite Joe's teasing, I once again yearn to be an artist. My creative juices would be spilling over, and I might never want to leave this color-filled city. But then I recall that in reality I'm already embarking on a new career and am grateful that it aligns perfectly with my plan for personal fulfillment.

ROAD RAGE, RELAXATION, AND DOGS

The second week of November, it's a balmy seventy-eight degrees, and we lounge by the pool in the Valencian sun. We now understand why hordes of Northern Europeans flock to the Spanish coast to escape long, dark winters. We're six hours from Barcelona en route to southern Spain. Home for two days is a low-slung hacienda set amid sprawling citrus groves just inland from the Mediterranean. Everywhere we look, flat brown bowls overflow with tiny, sweet tangerines, and a pile of dried peels between us is evidence of how much we're enjoying them.

I noted on our arrival, as we made our way up the winding, mile-long driveway to the relaxed Mas de Canicatti, lined with spiky hedgerows of lavender, heather, and agave, that it would be the ideal start for an afternoon run. Always a reluctant runner, I would prefer to continue sunning myself by the pool, but we're training for a marathon, after all. Joe and I both head out, our bellies filled with citrus. The highlight of my five miles is a pomegranate bush on the approach road. I've never before considered how or where this exotic fruit grows, but I stop in my tracks as I spy a golden-leafed bush with apple-size orange-red fruit weighing down its branches among the lavender. What a surprise! I now know the provenance of the delicious seeds in our morning fresh-fruit salad.

The hacienda's tranquility is a welcome relief after our frustrating drive from Barcelona. The city center behind us, we quickly realized that serious struggles with directions were on the horizon. Language wasn't the problem; the lack of clear markings was. Even when we allowed for time to get used to the nomenclature and unfamiliar coding, the sparse, very small, and often contradictory signage didn't come close to the clarity of abundant road signs in France. Nonetheless, we managed to find our way to the Mas de Canicatti after a detour or two along the way.

After a relaxing two days surrounded by orange, lemon, and lime trees, we're ready for another day of tackling Spanish roads. The landscape south of Valencia quickly resembles that of sunburned Tucson, with rough, rocky peaks rising to the west and scrub pine and cactus dotting the arid flats.

I study Granada's location on the map and am struck by how far south the city is: a quick sixty minutes from the Mediterranean. The three main cities in southern Spain, or Andalusia (Granada, Córdoba, and Sevilla), will be completely new territory for us, and we're anxious to explore.

We make the drive to Granada with minimal road-sign rage and are amazed at how the snowcapped Sierra Nevada rise so quickly in the southeast from the desert landscape of the city below. We head south thirty kilometers to the tiny hilltop village of Chite ("Chee-tay"), where we've rented a traditional three-story house, Casa Conejillo (Rabbit House), halfway between Granada and the coast. It will serve as home base as we explore Andalusia for the next two weeks.

When we drive into Chite, the first thing we notice is how many of man's best friends roam the streets; all have collars and all are friendly, but their owners are absent.

Joe remarks, "I thought we'd left the *merde* behind in Paris, but here we are in the land of a thousand dogs and all they leave behind."

Given the name of the village, we imagine the fun we'll have coming up with new, more appropriately descriptive pronunciations.

The tiny town is anything but touristy. It's a genuine Andalusian village with very real inhabitants, most of them over seventy. There is one smoky corner bar (where I pick up our house key) and one neighborhood restaurant. Over the course of our stay, each time we pass the two establishments, the locals hanging outside give us the once-over. In fact, none of the Spanish villagers hesitates to stare at us for minutes on end, as we do our best to respond with smiles and sunny *holas* as we walk by. When we're being watched, it's difficult to relax and observe our surroundings, which would be our intent if we patronized the Bar Nuevo or the Cafe Garvi. But as the focal point of intense local scrutiny, we feel the indignity of being treated like intruders. When we're the object of attention, our tendency as introverts is to focus inward, retreat into our skin, and not return the stares, knowing our every move is being evaluated. We're uneasy with the scowls, so we fix many of our meals in Casa Conejillo and never venture inside the local establishments.

"I'm actually feeling kind of angry," I share with Joe midway through our stay. "I know they mean no harm, but do you think they realize how they're making us feel?"

"I'm right there with you," Joe replies. "I wish we could explore more of Chite, but those glares are pretty inhibiting."

We talk a lot about how we would treat obvious visitors at home and agree that our response would be just the opposite. "Is it a small-town thing?" we ask each other, and acknowledge that we might trigger the same behavior in a tiny midwestern town.

Chite has its own quirky "charms," of course. Whereas in other small towns we've been awakened by church bells, in Chite we have several recurrent alarms. At six thirty it's the chorus of roosters from the yard next door; at seven it's the neighborhood dogs inevitably involved in a sunrise skirmish; at eight and every fifteen minutes thereafter, it's the familiar peal of bells from the church down the hill; and, most unusual of all, from eight thirty onward, the intermittent honking of horns from small white trucks circling through town interrupts the morning calm as the drivers alert villagers to their daily wares of fresh bread, meat, and produce.

"We're up, already," Joe groans as he rolls over.

I cover my head with a pillow. "We get the message!"

We experience another village oddity as well. On one random morning, we awaken to the acrid stench of burning. The village houses are stacked one upon the other like interlocking stair-step Legos as they climb up a sharp hill, and our neighbor's terrace is directly below our bedroom window. We open the shutters and, sure enough, discover the gentleman next door burning a toxic mixture of grasses and palm fronds that must include something rubber, because the smell is simply awful. We were planning to do our wash this morning and hang it on our terrace to dry, but our neighbor's conflagration forces us to turn our living room into the laundry room. It would have been nicer to dry our clothes in the sun, rather than draped over the furniture, but the noxious, billowing smoke makes that impossible.

Over the course of our stay, we learn that burning your refuse in Chite is standard practice. There are individual fires all over town as the residents get rid of rubbish by burning it in their backyards. It's illegal to start an open fire almost anywhere in the United States, but I guess we all have our ways of dealing with waste.

During our stay in Chite, Spain is holding national elections. As a result, we endure a mixture of strangely Soviet-style political propaganda from both the Right and the Left, all accompanied by rousing patriotic anthems blasted from huge speakers mounted on vans roaming the streets. We're happy when the elections are decided (the conservatives oust the socialists after eight years) and have to deal with one less bizarre interruption. The evening after the election, however, the campaigning continues when two Jehovah's Witnesses knock on our door. Whereas at home we would send them packing after a few curt words, we're in another country and don't want to offend.

"*Buenos días,*" I say, and Joe follows with, "*Hola.*"

"We speaks *inglés,*" the woman says, and I respond, "*Hablo un poco de español.*"

The two of us lapse into a polite, lopsided chat, the woman speaking Spanish and I responding in English, our male companions helplessly observing the exchange in silence. They're from Madrid, I learn, and I say that we're Americans. After I share some details of our yearlong trip, she reveals that they're on a ministry trip around Spain. I finally make an excuse about having dinner in the oven, and, with a friendly wave and an *adiós,* they leave us with a bilingual pamphlet and move on to the house around the corner.

"Will I ever understand the conversations you have with the locals without you having to translate?" Joe asks. I assure him there will be plenty of non–romance language countries ahead in which neither of us knows what's being said.

"Terrific," he responds. "I'm tired of being on this side of the language barrier by myself."

We find our house in Chite cold, both literally and figuratively, and it never manages to grow on us. While the indoor chill may be pleasant to return to as an escape from the heat of a scorching summer, in November at the end of the quiet, dog dropping–filled streets, it is downright depressing. We agree it was probably a mistake not to have paid the extra few hundred bucks to turn on the heat, but we had decided to economize. Long, hot showers and steaming cups of tea keep us warm, and we leave the house to hit the road daily to discover all there is in Andalusia.

SWEET HOME ALHAMBRA

I could live in the Alhambra, but on this first visit, I have to content myself with wandering its palaces and gardens for as long as I can in the rain.

While Carcassonne has a dreamy, storybook aura from afar, it can be a cold, depressing place on close examination. In contrast, the Alhambra appears stark and plain on the outside, but up close and from inside, its elegance delights and invites you to pull up embroidered Moorish pillows and stay. Carcassonne is a fortress in which to cower and be protected; the Alhambra is a garden sanctuary for relaxing and settling in. Although the skies on the day we choose to visit are a foreboding gray, the beauty and warmth of the place shine through.

"If it's this impressive under a veil of drizzle," I comment, "it must be stunning in the sun."

The Alhambra (from the Arabic for "red fort") is a sprawling complex of very different structures perched on a plateau on the crest of a hill, all within the protection of massive fortress walls. Its construction over centuries followed no master plan; individual buildings were added piecemeal over the course of alternating rules of Muslims and Christians, resulting in a hodgepodge ensemble. The oldest and most westerly section is the imposing Alcazaba fortress, built on Roman ruins and providing wonderful views over Granada straight below.

Beyond the Alcazaba stronghold and hanging over the deep ravine of the Darro River are the crown jewels of the Alhambra: the fourteenth-century Nasrid palaces of the Moorish rulers, designed to be "paradise on Earth." We wander through the various rooms of the beautiful intertwined building, awed by the delicate tile and plaster decoration of the ceilings and walls, and gaze out the arched windows that rewarded residents with vistas across the surrounding countryside. Unlike so many other enormous European castles, the Nasrid palaces were built on a human scale—they are elegant, rather than grand— with smaller rooms, gardens, and hallways that offer intimate spaces into which I wish I could crawl with a good book and a cup of tea for the afternoon.

Joe suggests, "Let's hide in a garden until dark and stay the night under the stars. It might be warmer than going back to Chite."

Washington Irving stayed at the Alhambra for three months in 1829, and the palace tour includes the room in which he lived. I've done my best on our trip to "read local," and the entertaining travelogue Irving wrote as a result of his sojourn in the palace, *Tales of the Alhambra*, is a brilliant literary companion for our visit. (If they'd made it into a movie, we'd have watched it.) The book helps me conjure up the Alhambra's days of former glory and the captivating characters who lived there. No standard guidebook could appeal to my emotions and evoke the sensual pleasures of the Alhambra as Irving's romantic collection does. It's difficult to leave the palaces, but there is more to see.

Plopped next to and sharing a wall with the Nasrid palaces is the circle-in-a-square, sixteenth-century residence of Charles V. Boys will be boys, and so, after the Moors were defeated, the Christian monarch in charge built his own imposing palace to dwarf that of the conquered. Were his Renaissance masterpiece on a piazza in Florence, I would be amazed. But built as it is, crowding the delicate Moorish palaces, it just doesn't belong in this context. We do a cursory circuit and then explore the baths, the Santa María church and the *Granada parador*, once a mosque, then a monastery, and now a four-star hotel at whose restaurant we make reservations for Thanksgiving dinner. Finally, we head for the sultan's Generalife summer palace on the upper part of the grounds as the rain picks up in earnest.

I've always appreciated the symmetry and serenity of a quadrangular Catholic cloister, and the Generalife palace has several similar spaces where rooms open onto central courts filled with the soothing sounds of running water: cascades, reflecting-pool fountains, and gurgling rivulets. It's easy to imagine the refreshing cool they provide under Granada's grueling summer sun. Slicker hoods and umbrellas up, we use our imaginations to picture them in brilliant summer glory. Joe and I promise to come back and see them for ourselves someday.

MORE MOORISH MUSINGS

The following day, we return to Granada to explore the rest of the city, including the massive cathedral (the second largest in Spain, after Sevilla's), the checkered Plaza Nueva, the dark alleys of the Alcaicería (formerly the silk market), and the Albayzín labyrinth (the hillside quarter of the Moors). Perhaps it's because everything pales in comparison with the Alhambra rising on the summit above, but for some reason the city below fails to move us. We climb the hill facing the Alhambra on the rise across the river, through the winding streets of the Albayzín, to reach the Mirador de San Nicolás, an incredible viewpoint on a church plaza. While the neighborhood maze is interesting, the whole point of the climb is to see the Alhambra once again, from a new vantage point. When we finally reach the top of the stairway and make a hard turn to our right to face the masterpiece across the ravine, we have a mouth-dropping-open moment. "Oh, wow!" is all we can say as we take in the ensemble from afar.

As we halfheartedly say goodbye to the view and make our way down the winding cobblestone streets, a sight that never fails to unnerve me appears. A woman in a head-to-toe burka with frightening grilles across her eyes is walking in front of us with her husband, pushing a stroller. I've heard and read the arguments from both women and men about the merits of the burka—how it allows women to praise God; how it's specified in the Quran; how women honor and respect their husbands by wearing it. But no matter how I try, I don't buy it.

Many Roman Catholic religious orders are based in Granada, and we pass several priests and nuns on the streets as we head back across town from the Mirador to the parking garage. We cross paths with a tall, regal cardinal in black-and-crimson ecclesiastical regalia: short, gilded cape over his shoulders and red miter on his head. The young novitiate in tow scurries just behind, carrying the dignitary's briefcase and other paraphernalia.

We round the corner onto the Gran Vía de Colón, and I stop dead in my tracks. Is it possible we're following two more burka-clad women? That's three in one day in Christian Granada. What are the odds? As we approach, it suddenly hits me. These women aren't Muslims in burkas at all. They're Catholic nuns in long gray-and-white habits, their brows pushed down and their cheeks pinched tight by wimples. The woman in her burka and the nuns in their habits: Are these femininity-erasing garments that different? Cardinals ascend to power adorned in royal colors and ornamentation, but nuns, unable to become priests, are stuck in black, brown, and gray. Muslim men wear Western clothing, while their women hide under identity-robbing burkas. Two of the world's largest religions share obvious points in common—a patriarchal culture and the oppression of women. I'm astounded that I never before made the connection.

SCENES FROM ANDALUSIA
Alpujarras: Close to Chite is the Alpujarras, a mountainous area south of the Sierra Nevada into which the Moors fled after the Christians retook Granada. Deep canyons are dotted with villages of characteristic flat-roofed Moorish

houses and are rich in challenging hiking trails. We grab our trekking poles, jump in the car, head for Pampaneira, one of the Moorish villages, and start a multihour hike into the Poqueira Valley.

We have one of our most pleasant lunches in Spain when we return to the village, because the woman who owns the quiet *taberna* and serves our food—along with her husband, who cooks in the kitchen—loves practicing her English. We have a spirited discussion about Spanish politics (she believes the new party elected will make everything even harder for the Spanish people), the European economy (it's very bad and getting worse), and her children (they're grown, on their own, and she wishes her son hadn't married a Frenchwoman). I fill her in on Chris and Caroline (what they do for a living, how much we miss them, and that they'll visit in Italy next month), and Joe fills her in on politics (we both voted for Obama and are dismayed about the polarization of America's two parties).

Córdoba: The focus of our visit to Córdoba is the architectural gem completed in 987 AD and the most important building and symbol of the city: the Mezquita, in the heart of the historic center. Formerly the Great Mosque of Córdoba and then a cathedral after the Christian Reconquista, it's known to locals as the Mezquita-Catedral. As is the wont of conquerors, the Catholic hierarchy needed visual assertion of its superiority over the vanquished Moors and thus built a grandiose Renaissance cathedral nave and plopped it jarringly in the middle of the spacious, graceful Muslim place of worship. While the bulk of the mosque was kept intact, the new center drove a willful dagger through the heart of the original building. Learning that Spain's King

Charles V approved the clumsy addition, Joe quips, "Big mistake, Chuck. Very bad move." Even the king himself is said to have lamented his decision by telling local religious leaders, "You have destroyed something unique to build something commonplace."

Perhaps the only positive thing that can be said about the redesign is that much of the original beauty of this sublime mosque was preserved. In most cases, victors level the structures of the conquered and build their own replacements from the ground up. But in this case, the Mezquita's iconic arcaded hall of 856 red-and-white-striped double arches, crafted from the marble remains of the Roman temple upon which it was built, remains. However, the once–bright and airy Mezquita now has little natural light, since the vaulted openings facing the courtyard of orange trees were cemented over during the Christian conversion. What a sight the mosque must have been in its heyday, filled with thousands of worshippers praying on their mats in streaming sunlight.

From the Mezquita, we wander through the whitewashed old quarter and stumble on the historic synagogue, a cozy space filled with refined carved woodwork, exquisite stucco decoration, and an upper-level, out-of-the-way women's gallery. It's become routine for us to acknowledge the inferior position of women in all of the world's great religions as we visit each place of worship. I bristle as we walk through the historic streets of Córdoba and see two-foot-high dark-wood latticework covering the bottom of every window. The screens that hid women from public view are constant reminders of how much things have evolved on this front, at least with respect to nonreligious matters, in most of the Western world.

We head back toward the Mezquita after reading

about the subjugation of Jews during the Inquisition, one of Spain's bleaker moments. The stark choices offered were convert, leave, or die, and all but three of the synagogues in the country, including the one in Córdoba, were destroyed. The mosque, cathedral, and synagogue all live together harmoniously within one hundred yards of one another in 2011. But in the 1400s, the hierarchies of the three religions just couldn't play nice, and in varying measures, the rules of the day declared that whatever faith was in charge must assert itself by destroying, or at least suppressing, the others. Behaving badly in the name of religion is all about power with no consideration for spirituality.

All over Spain, and certainly in Córdoba, the juxtaposition of the world's three great monotheistic faiths—Christianity, Islam, and Judaism—is everywhere. These entrenched institutions have me reflecting, as I do so often, on my own Catholic upbringing—twelve years of parochial school and four years at a Jesuit college—and I can't help but think that somewhere through the ages, they've all lost their way. As I did in Cathar country, I imagine that the founding fathers of each religion would not be pleased with what unfettered adherence to man-made dogma has done to their original teachings. These male-dominated religions have taken their core convictions—belief in a higher power, do unto others as you would have them do unto you, and peace among neighbors—and turned them into rules and regulations and a worldview that rejects all whose daily practices differ from theirs. I left my adherence to such bastardizations in a wooden pew long ago.

Gibraltar: The *autovía* north of Marbella passes over a crest heading west, and suddenly two lone mountains appear miraculously in the distance: the great Rock of Gibraltar and Jebel Musa, its shadowy twin across the straits in Morocco. It is a jaw-dropping, incredible sight: the rock and our first glimpse of Africa in one frame.

From this vantage point, Gibraltar appears physically detached from the continent as it looms in the morning mist. While two-and-a-half-mile-square "Gib" may be attached to Spain at the tip of a peninsula, the two are as distant as two contiguous places can be. Still angry over having lost Gibraltar to England in 1713, Spain makes few concessions to its neighbor. Until you are almost on top of the colony, there are no signs directing you there. Billboards aplenty announce La Línea, the Spanish town through which you have to drive to reach Gibraltar, but it's as if this little piece of Britain doesn't exist as far as signage is concerned. Shortly after breezing through passport control, we find ourselves driving across an airport tarmac. Gibraltar is so narrow that the airport runway spans its width and traffic must stop several times a day for incoming and outgoing flights. Gridlock reigns.

The view from the top of the rock is sweeping; we can see the Costa del Sol to the east, the ships and container cranes of the busy commercial port of Algeciras to the west, and across the sea to the shores of Africa outlined in the distance to the south. We play with the precocious macaque monkeys that live on Gibraltar, explore its caves, and then head down to town for a lunch of fish and chips.

"Let me order for you," Joe insists, as he proceeds to chat up the waiter about the soccer game on TV. "It feels so good to finally be able to speak the lingua franca."

We watch British bobbies in dark blue helmets direct throngs of schoolchildren outfitted in gray-and-maroon uniforms with pressed white collars, knee socks, and polished leather shoes across the street. Experiencing a slice of the UK jutting into the Med and surrounded by Spain is fascinating, but our visit is too short.

"I know we didn't plan it," Joe mentions, "but if we can find cheap flights, how about if we go to London for Christmas? I could use a dose of English for an entire week."

"Done," I agree. "That sounds like just what we need."

Ronda: Dramatically straddling a gorge that divides the town in two is Ronda, one of Andalusia's iconic white hill towns. It was here that modern Spanish bullfighting traditions developed, and the highlight of a visit is its appealing Plaza de Toros. Ernest Hemingway and Orson Welles, both fascinated with *la corrida de toros*, were summer residents of Ronda, and their writings helped popularize the town. Completed in 1785, the bullring is a delicate sandstone structure, white on the outside and painted a soothing yellow and rust inside. Its 136 Tuscan pillars and covered benches lend the structure the air of a cloister, rather than a violent arena, although it's impossible to ignore the angry red streaks of blood ground into the sandy ring. If the central circle housed a garden sanctuary and a bubbling fountain, I would enjoy our visit much more. It's too bad the brutal ritual of bullfighting takes place in it and spoils such a noble piece of architecture.

Salobreña: On two occasions, we head to the coast for runs by the sea. Twenty minutes south of Chite, the *autovía* dumps us directly into Salobreña, a beach town overrun by Brits and Scandinavians and with a broad, kilometer-long seaside boulevard, perfect for stretching our legs. The weather on both days is superb: midsixties, brilliant blue skies, and pure sunshine. The first time, I run back and forth along the water, but my second run takes me away from the beach, down a sandy trail that cuts through flat acres dense with eight-foot-tall sugarcane. *How lucky am I not only to be running along the Mediterranean on such a gorgeous day,* I think, *but to have found this uniquely sheltered, deserted trail as well?* Doing something ordinary in an extraordinary place makes me feel like my normally sluggish, nonrunner body could jog forever. After putting two miles behind me, I see, off in the distance, dozens of brown goats, clanging bells and all, with an elderly gentleman prodding them along. The herd is headed straight for me, and the distance between us closes quickly. I slow to a walk and then sink into the sugarcane thicket to allow the pack to pass by. What a sight and what a run.

On my way back to the beach, I recall that the previous night we added *The Sun Also Rises* to the list of movies we've watched so far in Spain (along with *Vicky Cristina Barcelona, The Way,* and *Women on the Verge of a Nervous Breakdown*). I say to Joe when we meet at the car, "We won't be in Pamplona for the running of the bulls, but I just managed a jog with the goats in Salobreña."

Thanksgiving at the Alhambra: Thanksgiving has always been my favorite holiday. It's such a simple notion: spending time with loved ones to give thanks for our blessings. The retail mania of Christmas and crass commercial trappings of most US holidays have bypassed Thanksgiving, except for Black Friday, of course. We don our best outfits, have a fine dinner, and feel privileged to be eating at the *Granada parador*, part of the Alhambra complex, although we badly miss our children and traditional holiday favorites (duck with rice is the closest thing to turkey and stuffing on the menu). We do our best to focus on feeling special as the only diners in the restaurant celebrating the American holiday.

Torremolinos: We're most anxious to see Torremolinos, one of the unforgettable settings in *The Drifters*, James Michener's classic account of disaffected '60s American youth and their overseas adventures. I recently reread the book we both devoured in college, and driving into the actual town that reached mythic partying proportions in the novel was a decidedly gratifying experience.

"I'm sure Michener wouldn't recognize the place," Joe observes, looking up at the pastel high-rises.

"I'm gonna hold on to the image of what it looked like in the book," I say, as we pass a laid-back seafood shack along the infamous Torremolinos beach. "This place looks like it might have been a hippie hangout," I add, as we duck in for lunch. We dine on fried shrimp on paper plates, while rain pounds on the plastic roof of the *chiringuito* (an informal food joint), and chat about how the built-up seaside venue no longer looks the way it did when Michener's mixed bag of characters crashed here in cheap hotels almost fifty years ago.

SEVILLA FOREVER

We love Sevilla even more than we did Barcelona. Cities have distinct personalities, and Sevilla's is festive. We arrive in town on a Saturday, the biggest evening for a twilight stroll. The entire city appears to be outdoors and partying—young parents push strollers, elderly couples walk arm in arm, teenagers speak a mile a minute, lovers of all variety and ages are entwined on corners, and international tourists are laughing and drinking. The Spanish paseo, the ritual end-of-the-day promenade, is in full swing, and we need no convincing to link arms and join the crowds. For no reason other than celebrating life, hundreds of people spill out of bars and restaurants into the streets and fill the city with chatter, laughter, and clinking glasses as revelers across generations take advantage of the night air.

With only two days to see the capital of Andalusia, we're efficient with our time and draft an itinerary that includes touring the cathedral (the largest church in Spain and the third largest in the world, behind Rome's Saint Peter's and London's Saint Paul's); climbing the Giralda (a former minaret converted to the cathedral's bell tower), which one ascends via a corkscrew ramp, rather than stairs, as did the Moorish muezzin on horseback five times a day to call the faithful to prayer; wandering the residential Triana district across the Guadalquivir River; crossing the Parque de María Luisa to see the grand Plaza de España from the 1929 exposition; and exploring the narrow streets of the Barrio de Santa Cruz (the former Jewish neighborhood).

Finally, but actually number one of our musts for Sevilla, is flamenco—not just a touristy show with food served and drinks poured, but the genuine, traditional version. Joe does the research, and we settle on the show at la Casa de la Memoria, deep in the barrio. It turns out we've chosen well; the performance is mesmerizing and emotionally intense in a way I wasn't expecting. Young artists, including a guitarist, a singer, and two gorgeous dancers, hold us transfixed for an hour in our front-row seats. They're clad in black trimmed in intense colors and wear thick-soled shoes with tiny nails embedded in the toes and heels to enrich the sounds of their footwork. The intimate venue is a candlelit courtyard in a seventeenth-century palace, with just two rows of chairs surrounding the performers on three sides. Inspired by those who lived in southern Spain across centuries—the Moors from North Africa, the gypsies, and the Spanish—flamenco emanates from deep inside and movingly combines the romantic, passionate, and celebratory influences that wove the tapestry of modern Andalusia. We're spellbound by the dancers, who move so boldly with emphatic claps, sensual hip undulations, and muscular stomping. Their centered confidence and erect carriage are infused with sexual tension and longing. *He's totally in love with her,* I think, as they circle each other slowly, deliberately, and then burst into rapid-fire movement. The drama and urgency of their art touch my soul, and I know I've never experienced a more ardently charged live performance. I know Joe agrees, as I see that his eyes, like mine, are welling with emotion.

We quietly leave the courtyard as if in a spell. Joe finally breaks the silence and, pulling me close, suggests, "How about some flamenco lessons back home?"

"Where do I sign?" I reply, hugging him back. For many days we can still hear—and feel—the percussive clapping and rhythmic, ear-splitting feet stamping of this proud art form that grabbed our hearts and won't let go.

Sevilla's architecture, clad in characteristic mustard and burgundy, is fetching, and though the combination may not sound attractive, it works on the stately Sevillan buildings. The Moorish influences of pretty arches, flowered patios, and enameled tiles add colorful touches. Carriages pulled by sleek horses enhance the city's romance, as do the many cobblestone pedestrian ways.

The official motto of Sevilla, "No8Do," is omnipresent: on sewer caps, buses, and even Christopher Columbus's tomb in the cathedral. Loosely translated, it means "Sevilla forever," but the more formal meaning, tied to a legend involving a skein of yarn (the "8" in the emblem) and the loyal subjects of King Alfonso X, is "Sevilla has not abandoned me." Unfortunately, we have to abandon Sevilla days before we want to. Now we know better—we should have cut our stay near Granada in half and then spent a full week in and around this splendid metropolis.

CULINARY SCORECARD—FRANCE: 10; SPAIN: 3

I've waxed poetic about the yummy food we sampled all over France at fine-dining restaurants and roadside bistros alike, but it's difficult to come up with even a few meals in Spain that I would label memorable. Thus, France scores 10 and Spain just 3 on our Gap Year Culinary Scorecard.

The first of Spain's points is for sangria. It's one of my perennial favorites (and Joe is now an aficionado), and we've downed multiple fruit-filled pitchers of the thirst-quenching nectar over the past weeks. Spain scores a second point for paella, although one—in a beachside *chiringuito* on Playa Burriana, along the Costa del Sol—is significantly better than the others. Owned and run by an aging, ponytailed hippie named Ayo, the eponymous open-air restaurant specializes in paella, made in view of diners in a four-foot-wide pan in an outdoor kitchen. The beachy surroundings do add some local flavor, but our plates of saffron-infused rice would be delicious wherever we had them. Accompanied by a pitcher of sangria and our bare feet in the warm sand, the dish makes for a delicious afternoon.

The final point for Spain goes to tapas in general. We do our best to try as many tapas and *especialidads de la casa* as we can (including Spain's beloved and very pricey *jabugo jamón*). In Barcelona, we have flash-fried artichoke shavings that are out of this world, and in Sevilla, an *escalivada* (grilled eggplant, tomatoes, onions, red peppers, and garlic, mixed and molded into a squat cylinder) topped with warm cod is finely prepared and bursting with flavor. Also in Sevilla, we are served a bowl of salty, vinegary, very ripe olives the size of small plums that are the best we've ever had. Andalusian gazpacho, although more finely pureed and much creamier than the soup in the States, is often offered on tapas menus and is filling and tasty. Most of what we sample, however, simply fills our stomachs and leaves us with no yearning for more.

So, as we move along, we continue our quest for memorable local food and drink and maintain our highly subjective, country-specific scorecards. France is in the lead by well more than a head. We'll be in Portugal for just a couple days—too hasty a visit to make an informed judgment. We have little idea what we'll find in Morocco, but we project that Italy will give France a run for her money. Since we'll be heading to London for Christmas, we expect that British cuisine will score even lower than Spain's. *¡Qué lástima!*

THE SUN MAKES ALL THE DIFFERENCE

Our quest to follow the sun and sixty-five-degree temperatures prompts a quick visit to Portugal at the end of our Andalusian adventure. We'll leave the Iberian Peninsula for a week in Morocco, and there our southern trajectory will end. We then fly northeast to Milan, where we'll meet Chris and Caroline at long last. My heart physically aches just imagining our reunion. They're no longer little, but they'll always be our "babies," and I need to hug them close. Video calling has definitely lessened the distance between us, but I long to have the four of us together, sharing the details of what's gone on in all our lives in the three months we've been away. If it weren't for being with our children and the prospect of skiing in the Dolomites, I might suggest we keep heading south to continue stalking the sun. At every opportunity, I bask in the warmth of Mediterranean sunshine, drink in the vitamin D, warm my inner essence, and bronze my outer self.

To brighten my mood and lighten my spirit, the sun makes all the difference. Joe however, sticks to the shade, so we've developed our very own half-and-half routine whenever we dine alfresco: our table must be half in the shade and half in the sun so I can get my rays and Joe can keep his cool.

With Mother Nature smiling, we spend two glorious days in Moncarapacho, a village just inland from Faro on the southern coast of Portugal. The Vila Monte Resort, a Relais & Châteaux property we book for the paltry, off-season sum of 70 euros a night, welcomes us with majestic palms, a sunny suite, and a lofty-ceilinged dining room looking toward the ocean. It's quiet and has solid Wi-Fi—just what we need to regroup, repack, and gird our loins for our African escapade. We have lots of research to do before we board the ferry to Morocco.

When we check in, Joe is happy (and I am thrilled) to discover that, unlike Spanish restaurants, which rarely open before 8:30 p.m., the dining room begins service at the reasonable hour of seven thirty. Always ravenous by six and unhappy to fall into bed with full bellies, we prefer eating much earlier than the Spanish.

"It looks like the Portuguese follow our eating

schedule," Joe says, smiling.

Our stomachs growl steadily by early evening, and we count down the hours to dinner, anticipating the culinary creations of the hotel's Orangerie restaurant. Sitting in the waning sun and turning to my computer and some long-overdue writing, I look at the time on the screen and suddenly realize that Portugal is in a different time zone—it's an hour behind Spain. *Oh não, quão terrível!* my stomach shouts. *Not two but three more hours before we eat!* In Iberia, we can't seem to avoid protracted, famished waits for late dinners.

As with Sevilla, we wish we could prolong our stay in Portugal. To a person, everyone we meet is beyond pleasant. When we venture into tiny Moncarapacho, three local women practically fall over themselves to show me how to get to the post office and accompany me the entire way, making sure I reach my destination. In addition to Portuguese kindness, the biggest revelation is the language itself. Portuguese, as a romance language, looks similar to Spanish when written, but I'm astounded by how different it sounds when spoken. Its many *sh* sounds and its cadence sound central European to me. Previously, I was exposed only minimally to the written language, and I'm sure I've often guessed a speaker's tongue as Slavic when he or she was actually speaking Portuguese.

Our sun-worshiping pilgrimage now takes us across the Strait of Gibraltar to northern Africa. While a trip to Morocco has long been on my travel list (another Francophone country!), I'm not sure I believed I would have the opportunity to actually visit. But my hope is now a reality.

V. Moroccan Adventure
December 2011

THE *MARRAKESH EXPRESS*

THE THOUSANDS OF SONGS Joe loaded on his iPod and that we play through the car radio have made for good company on the road. With such a wide selection, he always comes up with the fitting mix for every leg of our trip. Feeling adventurous, enthusiastic, and, I'll admit, a little anxious, we head southeast from Portugal toward the Spanish coast belting "Marrakesh Express" along with Crosby, Stills, and Nash.

Our destination is actually Fès, not Marrakech, but the song captures our mood just the same. The holiest city in Morocco, formerly a scholarly and commercial locus of North Africa and Muslim life and a five-hour train ride from the port city of Tangier, Fès is many fewer hours south than the distant Marrakech, an eleven-hour trip usually accomplished overnight, so we choose to visit the closer city and stay in its medina, the walled ancient city.

Our early-morning ferry trip across the Strait of Gibraltar from Tarifa, Spain, to Tangier, Morocco, is a speedy, hour-long ride with a fiery sunrise as backdrop. We spend most of the trip waiting in line to have our passports checked and stamped. Looking at and listening to our fellow passengers, we appear to be the only

Americans aboard. Some travelers are Spanish, but most hold Moroccan passports and speak Arabic.

"My heart is beating just a little faster," I mention to Joe as I lean into him.

"I think my heart has stopped," he admits.

We take deep, cleansing breaths as we load up our backpacks, pull our duffels from the rack, and make our way onto African soil. Incessant haggling, and our firm "*non, merci*" in response, begin the moment we disembark the ferry. A half dozen men in multicolored djellabas, the traditional floor-length Moroccan robes with pointy hoods, insistently offer to help with our bags as we make our way up a steep, switchbacked steel incline, over an elevated platform, and then down a final ramp to the chaotic taxi zone.

A gaggle of taxi drivers offering their services approaches, but one who speaks clear English stands out. Once he agrees to take euros as payment (we haven't yet withdrawn Moroccan dirhams), we accept. He loads our bags in the trunk of his cab, and before we know it, we are whisked away through the streets of Tangier, the sights of the port town whizzing by. After a couple-mile ride, we arrive at the brand-new train station on the eastern side of town, the red Moroccan flag with its green pentagram flying overhead.

Offers to help with our bags resume at the station, but we continue to decline assistance in both of Morocco's languages, having learned how to say *la, shukran* in Arabic from our helpful cab driver. Once inside the station lobby, however, we're left alone, watched over by the Police Touristique, part of whose mission is to protect travelers from being hassled.

Our two first-class fares for the three-hundred-kilometer trip to Fès are a mere $30 total. First class, for just a few dollars extra, buys us reserved seats in a cabin with six passengers, rather than the eight in second class. Handwritten signs indicate that credit cards are accepted, but when we present our Amex we are told we must pay cash: the system is down.

"I wonder," says Joe, "if the system is ever up," as he pays for our fares with the dirhams we've just withdrawn at the ATM outside the station. "All aboard the train, handsome," I reply as Joe passes me my ticket. I grab his hand, the '70s classic rock song echoing in my head. "It's time to ride the *Fès Express.*"

Moroccan trains are labeled "express" but are far from fast—there are no TGV bullet trains in this country. Twenty minutes after leaving the station, we're plodding through the dusty outskirts of Tangier, and Joe and I have instinctively cuddled closer. Joe whispers, "Not only are we no longer in Kansas, but we've officially left the Western world." At every train crossing on unpaved roads, a wide-ranging parade of jalopies, horse-drawn carts carrying multiple passengers and a jumble of wares, donkeys burdened with baskets overflowing with cargo, and pedestrians in djellabas wait patiently for the train to pass by. Dogs and cats freely roam, and goats graze on phantom grass along the railway bed with nothing to prevent them from wandering into the path of a train. A never-ending trail of debris and rusted appliance skeletons lines the shallow gully that parallels the track. How do the few people who live in these desolate towns possibly generate so much garbage?

Our compartment companions are three young Moroccan women. One is dressed conservatively and talks incessantly, using her headscarf as a hands-free device for holding her cell phone tight to her ear. The other two are Morocco's answer to *Jersey Shore*, their chunky bodies sausaged into tight, dark outfits. They have long black hair, high leather boots, and thick layers of makeup. The tableau of the three young women across from us is completely incongruous with what we witness through the train window.

I attempt to write the postcards we purchased at the station, but my thoughts keep wandering back to *The Sheltering Sky*, the haunting movie adaptation of Paul Bowles's powerful novel, which we watched together in bed last night. Although Bernardo Bertolucci's film transforms the sinister tone of the latter part of the story into a desert romance, I can't help ruminating on how hopeless and empty I felt when I read the book's ending so many years ago. *How will we feel after our encounter with Morocco? I wonder. Alienated? Forlorn? Or will a stay in Fès be à la Bertolucci—an unforgettable chapter in our very own love story?*

An hour outside our destination, a lumpy man in masking-taped glasses and two-day stubble enters the compartment and takes the one empty seat. He chats in Arabic with the young women and then turns to me. I'm sitting next to him, so, in accented English, he strikes up a conversation, alternating between English and French once he discovers I also speak the latter. When I tell him we're going to Fès, he lights up.

"I was there last week with my brother and sister-in-law from Toronto," he bubbles. "We had a wonderful time, and I can recommend our excellent guide."

We've been advised by everyone we've spoken to and every guidebook we've read that the only sensible way to see the Fès medina (the warren of lanes inside the looming city walls) and guarantee safe passage back to your hotel is with a local guide. Our new friend is an affable, gentle soul who shares with me all the medina sights he and his family saw.

"My sister-in-law, Beatrice, who looks a lot like you," he shares, "was amazed at all the guide showed us and for such a low price—only two hundred fifty dirhams" (about $30).

Before I can protest, he calls the guide (Mohammed is his name, naturally) and hands me the phone. After promising to call when we arrive at our hotel, I pass the phone back to our friend. He gives me Mohammed's phone number and continues to wax poetic about him until we arrive at Meknès, his stop.

"Thank you," we say. *"Shukran."* We shake hands, and as the train pulls away, there he is on the platform, searching for us and waving goodbye.

"What a nice encounter," I say to Joe.

"I only caught about half of it," Joe grouses. "Now fill me in on what you committed us to."

We arrive in Fès in late afternoon, golden shadows lengthening, descend from the train, and drag our bags over the makeshift dirt path that bumps across the tracks and into the station. Over the course of the five-hour train journey, as scenes of Morocco progressed outside our window, we realized the extent of our unfolding adventure. We inhale deeply and head for the throng of taxis and drivers hovering and ready to pounce, eager but tentative about what we will find deep in the heart of Morocco.

IMAGINATION VERSUS REALITY

I have a limit for adventure, and I find it in Morocco.

In Fès my efforts not to be an ethnocentric American

fail me. I'm uncomfortable in its foreignness, and I can't hide how I feel. Despite my resolve not to write about the country's sights and smells and what I feel as a spoiled, judgmental American voyeur with little knowledge of Moroccan culture, this is who I am and the lens through which I experience this distant city.

If ever there were a destination whose reality does not match my imagination, it is Fès. All the exotic details I anticipated are there: beautiful tiled archways, delicately carved buildings, caftaned pedestrians on sandy streets, donkeys bearing burdens down alleyways, deliciously spiced food, buzzing calls to prayer, men in bright leather slippers, women in vivid headscarves.

But I am not prepared for the pervasive deal making and inescapable subterfuge. My inability to discern who is being honest and who is playing us goes against my basic nature of taking people and situations at face value. If, as Churchill said, "Russia is a riddle wrapped in a mystery inside an enigma," then Morocco is a high-pressure deal hiding behind a humble presentation disguised as a simple greeting. Everyone in Morocco wants to sell us something; every urchin in the street has an angle; every Ali, Said, and Hassan has advice; and everyone wants a cut. After just hours in Fès, we have no idea who is duping us and who is telling the truth.

Maya Angelou once wrote, "People will forget what you said, people will forget what you did, but people will never forget how you made them feel." So it is with Morocco: I may eventually forget the details of our days here, but I will never, ever forget how it made me feel. I like communications to be clear, I need to have the facts, and I want to be in control. But nothing is clear in this North African country, and Fès definitely doesn't allow me to be in control. I feel the sands shift beneath me every time someone approaches us and we encounter cultural differences I'm simply not ready for.

My fascination with Morocco began when I read *The Drifters*. And while reading *The Sheltering Sky* years later gave me pause, I knew I had to follow Michener's characters one day. But Morocco on the page and Morocco in reality are two different things, and I'm not prepared for my visceral reactions to our experience.

Our week in Morocco leaves me believing that perhaps some places are best left as postcards in our imaginations. Is the chasm between my world and what we find in Morocco simply too great for me to bridge? Are the accretion of an overt state religion, practices that underline the inferiority of women, incessant scams and duplicity, rampant poverty, and inescapable garbage just too much all at once? While I may never be able to fully answer these questions, I do know that I will leave a country I expected to love certain I will never return.

FORT APACHE, RIAD FÈS

By the time we close the door of the taxi—a rusty, beat-up, beige Mercedes sedan, ubiquitous in Morocco—outside the walls of the old town, we're completely drained. As each kilometer passes, our faces glued to the windows as we make our way along the broad, traffic-jammed boulevards of the Ville Nouvelle (built *à la Haussmann* during the French occupation) toward the medina gate, we expend every ounce of our remaining energy absorbing the scenes of Fès. I comment that the heaps of detritus and vibrant parade of djellabas reinforce that Fès is not a Western city.

"But it's just like Paris," Joe observes, pausing for a

moment, "had the Germans decided to bomb it."

Our cab slowly circles Batha Square near our drop-off point outside the medina, and a teenager approaches, grabs the cab's door, and runs beside us until we stop. He asks the driver where we're going and, as we pay our fare and unload our bags, presses us to use him as a guide. We firmly say *non* and *la, shukran* as we pass through the gate, but he is adamant and continues his in-our-faces pitch on the multiblock bag drag all the way to our hotel.

"You would be lost without me," he insists, but, no thanks to him, we've managed to follow the royal-blue tiles on the walls that direct us to our destination. Our duffels trailing behind us through the twisting medina maze, we're keenly aware of the scene: the two of us looking, without a doubt, about as American as apple pie, a young Moroccan remora attached without our consent until we cut left into a dark alley and stop at the locked door of our hotel. The teen insists we reward him for his services, which at that point amount to his simply being a pest. We ring the hotel bell announcing our arrival and he becomes indignant, continuing to demand money as the door closes behind us. We let out audible sighs of relief, our backs resting against the main portal, in the peace and quiet of Riad Fès.

When we were planning our trip to Morocco, security was paramount, since we'd been warned of pickpockets and hustlers, swindlers and scoundrels. Yes, we are concerned about personal safety, but we also wanted to be close to "the real Morocco." Thus, we booked a proper *riad* hotel (formerly a traditional home or palace with interior gardens and fountains) inside the medina's imposing walls. Riad Fès, a splurge hotel extraordinaire, fits the bill perfectly. Compared with prices on the Continent, even luxury accommodations are affordable in Morocco.

What we didn't anticipate, however, was becoming virtual prisoners of this lovely oasis. Squaring the serene beauty of our hotel with the disarray outside its protective walls is an ever-present challenge. The Alhambra-like atmosphere of the *riad*, with murmuring fountains, open-air courtyards, handmade mosaics, carved wooden archways, low plush sofas, embroidered cushions, and bottomless pots of sugary mint tea, is warm and welcoming. In sharp contrast is the medina, a never-ending cacophonous hustle housing a colorful menagerie pecking and sniffing its way around the grimy pathways underfoot. The real Morocco is indeed knocking at our doors, but are we brave enough to leave the sanctuary of our *riad* to explore it?

The first time we venture out alone, we wind through the maze to the gate through which we entered and up the street to the ATM on Batha Square. The mundane act of withdrawing money becomes a singularly stressful pursuit, as we're keenly aware of being observed. Unlike the scrutiny in Chite, however, which felt more curious than hostile, these stares appear ominous, as if someone might actually grab our cash or assault us. Stress sweat running down our backs, we decide to be brave and sit for a time to people-watch on a concrete bench in the middle of the square. I feign calm, taking in the peeling billboards in Arabic and French and the crowds passing by, but within minutes an inebriated Moroccan starts cursing at Joe, waving his arms and threatening bodily harm. So much for heroics.

We hastily retreat through the gate and back to Riad Fès, nursing our wounds with some restorative tea.

As the largest car-free (though not always motorbike-free) urban district in the world, old-town Fès is an almost-intact medieval city—a congested labyrinth of twisting dirt lanes (some barely two feet wide, allowing only one-way foot traffic), and even map-loving explorers with a good sense of direction like me find themselves hopelessly lost after a few tortuous blocks. Towering stone walls penetrated by just a few city gates encircle the entire medina, so once you're inside, it's tough to escape.

We mention to the hotel manager, a gentle man named Radouan (pronounced "red one"), that we met a man on the train who put us in contact with a guide to help us explore the city's scrambled geography. We stop our story once we see the look on Radouan's face.

"Well," he says, shaking his head as he presents us with hot scented towels to wipe away the grime of our venture outside the walls and serves us tea and biscuits, "it was all a scam. That man probably gets on the train at the same stop several times a day, finds first-time visitors, chats them up, and calls his accomplice, an 'unofficial' guide who would not have given you the tour or the service you want. And your contact would have gotten a healthy cut of the faux guide's fee."

I'm deflated to discover that the friend we made on the train was actually a con man. He was so nice and seemed so genuine that I wanted to believe him. And while I generally consider myself trusting but not naive, perhaps I actually am. That man was one of our first encounters with the unique economy of Morocco, where nothing is ever quite what it seems.

So, heeding Radouan's counsel, we arrange for official guides—trained, badged, and sanctioned by the tourist office—one for each of three days. At 300 dirhams apiece ($35), our personal tour guides are a bargain. First we'll explore the medina, then circle the ramparts to visit spots of interest and panoramic viewpoints outside the city walls, and, finally, take a drive into the countryside. We're ready for more Moroccan adventure outside Fort Apache, Riad Fès, but this time we'll have seasoned escorts beside us.

MOROCCO: THE FIVE SENSES

Two hours after we arrive in Fès, a motorbike gently revs outside our hotel window. The droning builds to a persistent hum, and Joe declares, "That's no motor—it's a call to prayer."

We're experiencing our first *adhan*, one of the five broadcast daily by the neighborhood muezzins. The ritual summoning of the faithful reaches us from mosques throughout the city for a full fifteen minutes. While the first couple times are exotic, after relentless iterations the overt reverberation of the state religion is unsettling. It wakes us before the sun is up, interrupts our dinners, and is a frequent reminder throughout the day of just how pervasive Islam is in Morocco.

The main attraction in Fès is the bustling medina itself: people living as they have for centuries, crowding the alleys, buying and selling goods in the local souks, greeting neighbors, and delivering bread to public ovens for baking. Our first stop with our inside-the-walls guide, another Mohammed, is the Bab Boujloud, commonly known as the Blue Gate, a monumental horseshoe entry for all variety of human and animal traffic into and out of the medina. Amid the morning hubbub, we stand with Mohammed, looking foreign and out of place as we gaze into the depths of the forbidding lanes ahead. There are nearly eleven thousand retailers in the nest of pathways, many of them family-owned and most conducting business in cramped stalls that line the main streets. The tiniest shops are no more than cubbies a few yards wide and a yard or two deep. Larger retailers have tight corridor entrances, the bulk of the premises tucked behind multiple storefronts and packed to the rafters with merchandise. Within the medina, no freight can be delivered by truck; it's carried by beasts of burden or handcarts or on human shoulders. We're often pushed aside by donkeys carrying seven weighty LPG (liquefied petroleum gas) cylinders, the maximum load for a single animal, which make their haunches as wide as the passageways themselves.

In the course of our medina meanderings, we pass open-air butcher stands with a variety of animal parts hanging on hooks and bleeding into the street. These meat purveyors differ from those in Paris and Barcelona in that there are no display lights and antiseptic white counters, nor do labels identify the offerings. Rather, the butchers operate out of small, dark stalls with wooden cutting boards, and the provenance of the meat is no mystery: still-attached heads, hides, and hooves help identify the bloody stumps. Joe points out a six-pack of forelegs held together with twine. "For soup stock, perhaps?" he asks.

Across the alley from the hoof display is a vision that will haunt me forever. Bloated, grimy hands are butchering a goat, its head on the chopping block, blood pooling in the dirt below. "I prefer not to think about where the flesh that reaches my plate came from," I tell Joe, but in this Fès quarter, there is no disguising the process. The medina represents dizzying, often disgusting sensory overload, and we haven't even gotten to the Chouwara tannery, the highlight of any trip to old-town Fès. We've heard about this anachronistic sweatshop, seen pictures in guidebooks, and believe ourselves prepared for the experience. How wrong we are.

The tannery, the largest commercial enterprise inside the city walls, makes its presence known long before we arrive. "What is that stench?" Joe asks. Mohammed simply smiles. As we start up the multiple crooked staircases that lead to a broad wooden terrace that overlooks the open-air operation from two stories above, the stink is overpowering. We breathe through our mouths and press the requisite sprigs of mint to our noses to mask the reek, but the smells are so strong that we gag. Gawking over the tannery tableau, we're transported back to the Middle Ages. The method for transforming animal hides into soft, supple leather has not changed in hundreds of years. What lies below is positively primitive—a curing and dyeing process as manual today as it was in the 1200s, when the tannery first opened. Dozens of four-foot-square earthen wells, like so many finger-painting pots, are filled with foul liquids and skins being stomped on by barefoot laborers in shorts. The camel, cow, goat, and sheep hides have pungent smells of their own, and in combination with the tannery's special curing cocktail of cow urine and pigeon guano, the odor that results is overwhelming. The skins are then stretched, scraped, and dyed by hand in the next series of honeycombed pigment pots before they are baked in the sun on the tannery roofs.

The accumulation of what we see and smell is almost too much to bear. But I temper my misgivings with the thought that the primitive operation remains a critical source of income for the people of Fès. I glance over at Joe and imagine him thinking, *Babe, I can't believe I let you talk me into coming to Morocco*, because, of course, this detour to Africa was all my idea. I finally muster the courage to ask him a question as I attempt to take his hand. When he gives me a clipped response and moves away, I decide to delay conversation until we're back in the shelter of our hotel. This certainly isn't the first time Joe has been upset with me on the trip, but I can tell this one will take some doing to work through.

The tannery exit is beyond the large retail space, and we receive a full-court press to buy a leather jacket as we pass through. After ten minutes of being nice, I just want to scream, *What about 'la, shukran' don't you understand?* I do my best to recognize that by Moroccan standards, we're incredibly rich—moneybags with four legs, in fact, since we're able to travel so far from home. And while intellectually I know they're just trying to make a living, I somehow feel the gentleman who presses us so hard feels entitled to our funds. *I really do feel bad about having to say no—I can't buy something from everyone,* I rationalize, but I'm self-conscious at the thought nonetheless.

Mohammed has the nerve to question my lack of a purchase: "Was there something wrong with the jackets they showed you?" he asks. We reiterate what we thought we made clear at the outset of our tour: we aren't in the market to buy anything, especially $300 worth of light blue suede. *He must now understand,* we think as we leave the tannery, its rancid smells clinging to our clothes and our hair.

But we are wrong.

Mohammed drags us to the shops of his friends, where they attack with abandon and the selling fury of a timeshare hawker. It becomes clear that even "official" guides receive commission on the sales they bring to retailers. Joe says, "I'm thinking a good map or a medina GPS [a boy who takes you where you want to go for a few dirhams] would have been a better idea."

We've now arrived at a carpet cooperative where, we understand, we'll be shown how the merchandise is designed and fabricated. No such luck. We're plunked down for sweet tea in a tiled showroom awash in carpets. They are indeed works of art, but we're not going to buy one. Joe sits, ill at ease and angry, and my mistake is being polite, commenting with a smile, "The carpets really are gorgeous."

That does it—they have me in their sights and direct all attention to me, the soft one. Joe is promptly marginalized as our private show begins. We're presented with dozens of rugs of various sizes, weaves, and colors, each rolled out by four workers in front of us. We're soon knee deep in carpets, the entire production narrated by the head honcho—a fast-talking schmoozer in a striped djellaba who reveals he is a lawyer. "I wouldn't want him arguing a case against me," I whisper to Joe. Each time we protest, stating we don't want a carpet and have no home in which to put one, his response is to show us more. "You'll buy one," he insists; "we just have to find the right one."

As Joe becomes even more annoyed, it's all I can do to fight the urge to flee. The master marketer's tactic is to embarrass us into a purchase. His workers are sweating after rolling out enough carpets to upholster all lanes in the medina, and he stresses that his wares are the handmade creations of widows and orphans. We're angry with ourselves for being so nice and not firmer about no purchases, and we're exasperated with Mohammed for ignoring us. But at the same time, we're keenly aware of not disrespecting our guide and these industrious merchants by simply walking out. I feel trapped and claustrophobic because my drive for diplomacy overrides my need to disappear, and, frankly, we're now so deep in the medina,

God only knows how we'd find our way back to the hotel on our own. I just want out and ignore what's being said as I plot our escape.

When the guy finally takes a breath, we tell him outright, with no room for misinterpretation, that we aren't buying this morning, this afternoon, or tomorrow, with cash, on credit, on layaway, or with delayed shipping. No carpet. No rug. No nada. *La, shukran.*

Mohammed is no help; he's getting a cut, after all. He just sits there extolling the virtues of every carpet they present. We finally break free, perspiring and agitated, into the alley. Does Mohammed understand the extent of our annoyance? Apparently not. Our next stop, after more lane meandering, is a workshop where we see Berber carpets made on traditional looms. Having learned from my mistake of being complimentary in the previous establishment, we remain silent during the tour and promptly leave before the sales pitch can begin.

To help Mohammed save face, or perhaps because I imagine the tour will end only when we make a purchase, I buy a $20 bottle of argan oil in a tiny cosmetics stall. I've read about this peculiar oil with its skin-healing properties, and I'm curious to try it. Goats climb argan trees, endemic to Morocco, to reach the fruit on the upper branches. Berber women collect the undigested pits from the goats' feces and then grind the kernels to release the precious, nutty oil. Mohammed pushes additional emollients on us, but I grab my oil in a definitive statement of *it's time to go.* My fight-or-flight response has become overwhelming, and, feigning exhaustion, we beg off further sights and ask to return to the *riad.*

Our medina tour/selling session on steroids ends after four very long hours. We've learned the hard way that saying no in Morocco is excruciating work, but talking about it may be even harder. We say not a word to each other all afternoon and get through dinner only with the aid of copious amounts of wine, until Joe finally breaks the ice. "Listen, I'm sure one day we'll look back on today's tour and laugh, but for now I'm dead tired and all I want is a really good night's sleep."

I nod, fold my napkin, and drop it on the table.

The following day, we meet with guide number two, Ahmed, for a brief car tour of the medina ramparts. Along the city's outer walls, we approach a disturbing sight, and, as with the tannery, the smell heralds what's to come. It isn't clear initially what we're seeing, but as we circle closer, our guide confirms our suspicions: it's pile upon pile of hides for sale. The two-acre muddy lot is stacked twelve feet high with recently harvested sheep and goat skins awaiting donkey and human transport inside the walls. The skins are abundant because of the recent Eid al-Adha celebration (the Festival of Sacrifice), which commemorates Abraham's willingness to kill his son at God's request. Allah eventually intervened and provided Abraham a sheep to sacrifice instead, and Muslims re-create this narrative by slaughtering an animal. The pelt pile is shocking, the odor overpowering, and luckily our driver has no plans to stop. We pass as quickly as traffic allows, but the scene lingers long after we've returned to the refuge of our hotel.

The panoramic view of the medina from the *riad*'s rooftop terrace includes the expected green (the revered Muslim color of life) minarets, flapping laundry, and gardens on the flat tops of the stone buildings. While the residents of Fès are hardly rich by Western standards, the people we see appear hale and hearty. And if the vista from the terrace is any indication, every residence in the medina, even those unstable and crumbling, can afford multiple rooftop satellites. The white devices, their faces like blossoms turned toward the sun, are affectionately known as "flowers of the medina." When ancient and modern worlds collide, this is the result. The jarring juxtaposition is appealing, in a science fiction sort of way.

An hour south of Fès are the Middle Atlas Mountains. Our sweet guide, Idriss, takes us in his van on a private tour of the Atlas countryside, including the hardscrabble Berber village Imouzzer, where we'll meet an elderly woman who lives with her family in a cave, the traditional tribal dwelling. Idriss leads us through muddy market stalls and down a dirt lane to a walkway carved in the stone. Joe and I give each other quizzical looks that ask, *Are we really up for this?* but then head down rocky steps into the cave.

A spacious home built into a cliff face, this is not. We find ourselves in a humble, one-room, all-purpose abode dug out of the ground. It's oval, with a low ceiling just taller than Joe, and its walls are whitewashed. At one end of the space is a rustic wood-burning stove on which a large pot of water boils. At the other end are blanket-draped banquettes that double as beds in the evening. It's a pleasant enough spot, except for the absence of electricity and running water. The warm, bright-eyed matriarch invites us to sit as her middle-aged daughter and adolescent granddaughter pour us sweet *louiza* tea (the two of them bickering, as mothers and daughters do, about the tea's proper preparation), a lovely lemon-verbena infusion scented with freshly picked leaves. After a few minutes of questions and answers with Idriss translating, the grandmother decides it's time to dress me up in traditional regalia and enthusiastically drapes me in a woven white cloak, black babushka, and chunky red necklace. We take pictures to prove my transformation into a Berber princess, but if she attempts to adorn Joe, I know he'll allow no photographic evidence. We stay with our generous hosts about twenty minutes, then say goodbye with an effusive *shukran* and, in accordance with Berber tradition, pass some dirhams to the matriarch for her hospitality. We leave our visit with these three generations of women, appreciating that they are proud of the hole in the ground they call home, have no embarrassment about their way of life, and are happy to have shared it with us. For this family, the village of Imouzzer is all they know of the world; there is no reality outside it. We leave with just one question unanswered, one we haven't dared pose: Where are the men in the family, and where do they reside?

Our sensory experience of Morocco ends on a delicious note. While we've hardly had a representative sampling, since we ate all meals in our *riad* restaurant (the sleek and dimly lit L'Ambre), Moroccan cuisine has pushed Spanish fare even farther down the Gap Year Culinary Scorecard. France is on top, with Morocco in second and Spain a distant third. The Moroccans got it right early on—centuries ago—with the sweet-and-savory craze and have long understood the appeal of mixing the two.

We sample all manner of traditional Moroccan appetizers, including candied carrots, diced quince, chopped eggplant and red peppers, mashed curried cauliflower, minced zucchini and green peppers, lima beans with lemon and olives, and pumpkin puree with cinnamon. All are delicious and uniquely spiced. Our main dishes include *pastilla*, a sweet-and-salty phyllo dough pie with shredded chicken, nuts, and powdered sugar; and several delectable *tagines* (Moroccan stews with attitude): *kefta* (lamb meatballs in a piquant tomato gravy), beef with olives, carrots, and preserved lemons; and shrimp in a slightly sweet pepper-and-tomato sauce, all served with a side of fluffy couscous. We drink several local wines, both white and red, and for dessert there is *briouot* with honey (Morrocan baklava) and *pastilla* with cream (a Moroccan mille-feuille). All these dishes are listed on blackboard café menus in the medina, but we're brave enough to try them only at Riad Fès. I'm disappointed at our cowardice, but we can't bear to eat outside our oasis.

The sounds, smells, images, feelings, and tastes of Fès assault my senses and evoke profound, explosive responses. I feel them viscerally, and they leave me unsettled and anxious. Yet I push them down, deep down; Morocco will be behind us soon.

DEPARTURE DIFFICULTIES

Leaving this country is one of those hellish experiences you read about in a travel magazine's letter to the editor.

Joe receives an e-mail from Royal Air Maroc late Sunday afternoon: "Your Tuesday flight to Casablanca has been canceled." We're still booked on Tuesday's connecting flight to Milan, but they've rebooked us on the Wednesday-morning flight from Fès to Casablanca. It makes no sense at all. We panic briefly, imagining ourselves unable to escape Morocco to meet Chris and Caroline in

Italy on Thursday. We enlist the help of Radouan, who informs us, "Oh, Air Maroc does this all the time. If the flight isn't full, they just cancel it." He makes several phone calls and then lists our options for getting to Milan. We decide the most reasonable alternative is to leave Morocco a day early. Given our squeamishness about the country and how anxious we are to see our children, the early-departure decision is an easy one. Radouan calls Royal Air Maroc and rebooks our flights for Monday. We receive a confirmation e-mail, are hugely relieved, and agree that spending an additional night at the Milan airport won't be so bad.

The Fès-Saïss airport is a quick twenty-five-minute cab ride away at five in the morning, with no daytime donkey- and horse-cart parades jamming the streets. Before we know it, we're at the head of the line for our 6:30 a.m. flight. "In just three days we'll be with the kids," I say. I lean into Joe, and he squeezes me tight.

The young woman agent looks at our names, studies the computer screen, looks at our passports and then up at our faces. This back-and-forth goes on for several minutes, until finally she shakes her scarved head and says, "No. You're not on this flight." When we protest, she consults a colleague, who studies the screen and confirms her assertion. "No, you have no reservation," she says. Meanwhile, the check-in line builds as Joe's anger and my panic rise. *We have to get out of here*, I think. *I just want to leave, and I want to leave now. I will not go back into that city for another night.*

The agent aloofly insists there is nothing she can do and pushes us aside. Joe holds it together enough to ask with whom he can speak about the "mix-up," and the agent hands us the customer service number. I pull out our "just for emergencies" cell phone, but the battery is dead. "God only knows where I packed the charger," I say to Joe, my heart sinking. We ask the agent if she has a phone we can use, and without looking up she points to a pay phone near security. I scrounge for the dirham coins I have left, pump them into the phone, and get through.

"I'm sorry, but the system canceled your reservation," the airline representative who answers reports. "There's nothing I can do." The clock is ticking, and as Joe is about to let loose a few choice expressions, we're out of coins and the phone goes dead. It's important to us that we be there when the kids arrive, but I feel powerless in this oh-so-foreign country and am on the brink of surrender, slumping under the phone, when Joe remembers the last e-mail I looked at the night before was the airline confirmation. There's no airport Wi-Fi, but maybe, just maybe, the e-mail is still on my screen. I furiously pull my laptop from my backpack, and bingo! There she is in black and white—the Royal Air Maroc message, our confirmation code in bold.

We're running out of time. I rush back to the counter and show the agent my open laptop. She knows better than to ask me to wait, so she types in the confirmation code, and, miraculously, her indifference evaporates. "I'll get my manager," she states.

A dude in a baseball hat—the least official-looking airline manager I've ever seen—materializes from the back. He steps to a terminal and, after we watch him execute a "system override," tells us, "All is okay." We let out audible sighs of relief, my panic subsides, and Joe is once again able to speak. We grab our luggage, pass through the worthless security system (the fellow on duty has no uniform, looks like he was pulled in off the street, and never once looks at the X-ray screen), and are summarily ushered onto the tarmac. I have never, ever been happier to be strapped into an airline seat, ready for takeoff. When we're finally in the air, I'm still trembling.

We disembark in Casablanca and wait an interminable four hours for our flight to Milan. At long last on our way to Italy, I reflect on what I'll say about our visit to Morocco. Perhaps something like, "Bertolucci's exotic love story, it was not" and, "Should you crave adventure and have a desire to visit northern Africa, by all means see Morocco, but see it only once."

The country has exhausted us.

VI. Back on Terra Familiar
December 2011

REWIND

THE MIRACLE OF JET TRAVEL whisks us from the disquiet of Morocco and, in a matter of hours, returns us to a civilization that is comfortable. Setting foot in Italy feels like coming home.

Back from the wilds of Africa, we check into an ordinary, well-lit budget hotel, a quick shuttle ride from Milan's Malpensa airport. Normally, a nondescript, antiseptic hotel would not be our fancy, but its simplicity is a most effective succor after the complications of Morocco. We're so happy to be back in Europe and need some downtime to sleep in, regroup, and finalize travel plans before the kids arrive. How many ways are there to say, "We're excited"? Joe and I compete to see who can come up with the most as we anticipate our children's entry into our gap year.

Before Morocco settles permanently into my memory bank of journeys, however, I have a compelling need to chew over our adventure and my intense reaction to it. I soon find myself in tears over a carafe of chianti and a plate of prosciutto. It appears I buried my fears, reservations, and sadness while in Fès, repressing my feelings in the thick of the experience, unable to share them with Joe. It isn't until now, when we've returned to the relative safety and familiarity of the Continent, that I can come from behind my detached facade and allow my feelings to surface. Talking about how we feel has always been Joe's and my best form of therapy, but for some reason I avoided this path in Fès. My only explanation for why I held my thoughts so close is that I was traumatized. Just as physical symptoms of stress often appear after the stressor has passed, so my deepest emotional response to Morocco spills over under fluorescent lights in the dining room of an Italian airport hotel.

"Why did that country leave me so shaken?" I ask Joe, always my obliging sounding board. "Why did I take it so personally, and why do I still feel so emotional about it all?"

"I'm sure it's because it was all so foreign," he replies gently, leaning in across the table, "and it boils down to what you said when we were there—it all has to do with how it made you feel: uncomfortable, ill at ease, suspicious. Polar opposites of what you usually are. And let's be honest, Marianne; that's exactly how I felt as well."

"Here's to putting Fès behind us," I toast, our glasses of red wine clinking, "and to enjoying where we are now: Italy."

ITALY—A FUNNY COUNTRY

Now that we've succeeded at putting Fès in perspective, Italy has us belly-laughing in a way we desperately need. We return to our room after dinner and are hit with blistering heat. "What is this, Dante's *Inferno*?" Joe protests. He futilely searches for the climate controls and then heads to the front desk to have them reduce the temperature. He returns, laughing, with brilliant advice: "'If it's too hot, just open the window. We cannot control the temperature.'" So much for Italian energy conservation. I join him in laughter, open the window wide, and let in the refreshingly cool December air.

Next in Italy's humor progression is the book I find among the pulp fiction paperbacks stacked on the lobby's bookshelves. There are dozens of titles in the Segretissimo spy series, all with sensational titles and covers illustrated with busty, weapon-wielding women in various stages of undress. But my favorite of all is *L'Abito Non Fa la Monaca*. It features a pretty young woman fully clothed in black-and-white religious garb holding a smoking gun, a fierce look in her eye as she shouts at her adversary. I'm quite sure I got the translation right but double-check the Internet to be sure. Yup, translation on target: *The Habit Does Not Make the Nun.* "I wonder if there are more nuns-with-guns titles in the series," Joe says, and we chuckle every time we think about it.

The fun continues over our second dinner in Italy. Spy-nun novel in hand, we head back to the hotel restaurant to toast our first full day in Italy. Our frog-eyed waiter, fiftyish, with shoulder-length gray hair slicked back, down, and into a flip, is ceremoniously clad in a crisp black tux. He greets us ever so graciously and shows us to our table. The formality seems excessive for the simple surroundings and modest menu, but he's reveling in his role and we get a kick out of watching him. It's quickly apparent, however, that his sartorial splendor is all for show. While he acts as if he were one of the waitstaff at le Grand Véfour, he has the abilities of an absentminded professor. When we ask if he speaks English, he stands tall and proudly declares, "But yes, of course." He translates some menu items for us, but most of what he says makes absolutely no sense. We stifle giggles.

In the end, we opt for dishes we know, like gnocchi and penne. I think I'm safe when I take his advice on the antipasti dish he confidently declares is a salad, but I end up with a protein platter overflowing with salami. We order a carafe of the house chianti. Pencil poised on his order pad, he closes his bulging eyes, shakes his head, and announces with regret, "No more. It is finished." We then point to a valpolicella on the menu and receive the same response. We try twice more, with no success. When I ask what they do have, he walks to the wine table behind us, and we can tell he's having a hard time figuring out which bottles match the menu listings.

After several agonizing minutes watching him fumble, I get up to see if I can help. Thank goodness, a twentysomething waiter arrives just in time and puts us all out of our misery. He quickly finds a bottle of red that works for us and opens it, and Joe finally toasts, "Here's to Italy—a very funny country. May she always make us laugh."

A MILANESE SURPRISE

Milan was to be a convenient location for meeting our children—nothing more, nothing less. But when we find ourselves with an extra day, we take the train and wander the city on a cursory half-day tour. We board the *Milano Express* blind, having done absolutely no research on what to see. All we know is that the city is a center for haute couture, has a magnificent duomo, and is home to La Scala, the famed opera house.

On the ride into town, I study the map we picked up

at the hotel to sketch a route. I fortuitously stumble on the notation that Leonardo da Vinci's *The Last Supper* is in Milan. Shame on us for having had no idea it was under our noses, but what a lucky surprise. Surely a day that starts with such an auspicious discovery will turn out well. We arrive at the terminus and head a few short blocks away to Santa Maria delle Grazie, a fifteenth-century convent in whose refectory the masterpiece is housed. We promptly buy two tickets for the 3:00 p.m. visit and head toward the center of Milan for lunch, the Duomo di Milano, and La Scala.

We first come upon the Duomo, which we find quite appealing. It's a confectionary vision from Oz, flamboyant yet graceful and topped by a forest of soaring spires. Adjoining the Piazza del Duomo is the elegant, black-and-gold Galleria Vittorio Emanuele II, the upscale shopping arcade built in the late 1800s to provide direct, sheltered access from the Duomo to La Scala. The structure is composed of two perpendicular glass-vaulted ceilings intersecting under an octagonal dome and covering the streets below. The construction is much larger in scale than any of its predecessors and was an important step in the evolution of modern, enclosed shopping malls, many of which use the Milano-inspired term *galleria*.

After pizza under the soaring skylights, we head to the Piazza della Scala, hoping for a brief tour of the opera house. But when we arrive, we're met by a dense crowd held back by metal barriers and bump into carabinieri with every step. It makes sense when we learn that the evening performance of Mozart's *Don Giovanni* will launch the new opera season and that Italy's glitterati, including Mario Monti, the new prime minister, will attend. The inside of the theater is off-limits for the day, so we content ourselves with the view from the street. The missed opportunity to see the building's interior actually suits us—we're tight on time and don't want to be late for our appointment with Leonardo.

We arrive at Santa Maria with plenty of time to study the information about *The Last Supper* posted in the foyer. I'm astounded to discover that US bombs damaged the convent during World War II, blowing its roof off and exposing da Vinci's treasure to the elements.

At three o'clock on the dot, a guide leads our group down a hallway and into the refectory. Keenly aware that we have a brief fifteen minutes to take in da Vinci's mural masterpiece, we do our best to absorb the setting and details of the painting, since no photos are allowed. We struggle to push aside our pop-culture baggage (references in Dan Brown's *The Da Vinci Code*) so we can simply marvel at the magnificent work in front of us. It's difficult, however, to completely disregard the notion that the figure to the left of Jesus is not actually John but Mary Magdalene, given the individual's evidently feminine characteristics. Covering much of the refectory's far wall, *The Last Supper* measures fifteen feet high by twenty-nine feet wide, and its composition is haunting. Although we've seen the image that depicts Jesus announcing to his apostles that one of them will betray him reproduced countless times, to actually see it where da Vinci painted it and knowing it was once within inches of complete destruction is remarkable. Fifteen minutes is hardly enough time to satisfy us, but, just as we were ushered in, we're briskly escorted out.

We take the train back from the genius of da Vinci to the brilliance of our hotel, buoyed by the knowledge that after a pleasant pasta dinner we'll have only twelve hours until we reunite with our children.

LAUGHING ALL THE WAY

Expectation sometimes exceeds the event you await, but not so with Chris and Caroline's arrival. Their familiar American faces leap from the airport crowd in full color as all others blur to gray. From the moment they bustle through the international arrivals door, all is right with our world and I can barely control my excitement. I'm jelly-kneed but on my toes and ready to pounce. There's nothing more beautiful than Caroline's smile and hearing Chris call me his pet name: "Maman!" The four of us converge in a "family hug," as we call them, no one wanting to be the first to let go. Joe finally announces, "Guys, our Fiat awaits," to get us moving toward the exit. The children's broad smiles are the fulfillment of any parent's dream.

Caroline asks, "How much Italian have you learned?" and I remind her, "We've been here only three days, *mia bella!*"

Chris pipes in, as he always does, "When do we eat?"

"The minute we arrive in La Spezia," Joe assures him.

We cram ourselves and our eleven bags into our rented minivan, make our way to the autostrada, and head south to the sea, packed to the gills. Our itinerary for the kids' visit includes the Ligurian coastal town La Spezia, from which we'll explore the Cinque Terre and Pisa; skiing in the Alps; and Verona, city of romance and Romeo and Juliet.

We never laugh as hard as we do with our children. Joe and I are not perfect parents, but we love our kids dearly and must have done something right to be able to have so much fun when the four of us are together. It's early December, and so, always the sentimental one,

Caroline has brought a CD of our family's favorite holiday carols to foster the Christmas spirit. We sing along with Nat King Cole and Bing Crosby as we head south to La Spezia, anticipating being together for two full weeks in Italy, laughing all the way.

THE CINQUE TERRE: DELIGHT AND DISAPPOINTMENT

For years we've dreamed of visiting the Cinque Terre (Five Lands), terraced along the Ligurian Sea, and hiking from one medieval seaside village to the next. Reachable only by water until the arrival of the railway, it's one of the destinations we most looked forward to visiting with our children. But Mother Nature had other plans at the end of October 2011, when she unleashed a torrential rainstorm along Italy's northwestern coast. The fury of the downpour triggered landslides of unprecedented proportion that left rivers of sludge, trees, and debris in their wake. Three local residents were swept to sea, their bodies recovered weeks later off the coast of France.

The disappointment of four thwarted hikers doesn't compare to the devastation experienced by the people of the Cinque Terre, but we're let down nonetheless. "I feel selfish even thinking about it," I admit to Chris.

"I know, Mom," he replies. "I was just feeling the same thing."

The five towns, from south to north (from closest to La Spezia to farthest away), are Riomaggiore, Manarola, Corniglia, Vernazza, and Monterosso al Mare. Vernazza, lauded by many as the most striking visually, bore the brunt of the mudslides, along with its northern neighbor, Monterosso. The former is off-limits to visitors; only aid workers and residents may get off the train at the stop. When we envisioned our visit to the area long before the storm hit, our plan was to take the train from La Spezia to Riomaggiore and then do the five-hour trek along the trails linking the picturesque towns, a total of eight rocky, roller-coaster miles. Unfortunately, all but the flat, paved trail between Riomaggiore and Manarola, the Via dell'Amore ("Lover's Walk"), are closed, too damaged for hikers to pass. So, a very loose Plan B in place, we take the twelve-minute train from La Spezia to the southernmost town of the Cinque Terre to see what we will find.

There's little evidence of storm damage in Riomaggiore. The fact that few other visitors walk the main street that slopes to the slim harbor, the multihued town spilling down to choppy water, is most likely the result of the cool off-season and not the fall floods. The Cinque Terre towns are overrun with tourists in the summer, but in December we almost have Riomaggiore to ourselves. We make the easy walk along the deserted Via dell'Amore—just short of a mile—into Manarola and continue through and past the town to where the trail is unsafe and barricaded. Corniglia, the next and only hilltop town of the five, clings to the cliff in the distance, tempting, beckoning us to hike. But the dramatic walk must wait for another day, when the path has been restored. Today, we head back into Manarola to catch the train.

As we wait on the seaside platform, we marvel at (and take dozens of pictures of) the gradations of light that result from the sun peeking in and out of angry cloud cover. A blue, cloudless sky would have been pleasant, if only for the sun's warmth, but wouldn't have produced the variation of ghostly shadow and luminous radiance of this morning. We watch waterspouts—tornadoes on the sea—rise in the near distance from turbulent gray waters, but close to the shore the sea calms to a tranquil, intense turquoise.

The train drops us below Corniglia, perched on a promontory overlooking the sea. We ascend infinite stairs to the deserted town center, which, like its two neighbors to the south, is a jumble of sherbet-hued buildings of peach, raspberry, tangerine, and lemon. We scramble down the north edge of town along a steep, winding stairway to the cramped harbor and pebbly beach below. The primary colors of the fishing dinghies—navy, red, yellow, and royal blue—contrast with the pastels of the town above. How much fun it must be in the scorching summer to make the long, rocky descent and then dive into the cerulean sea. We amuse ourselves taking funny family pictures along the angled cement pier, water lapping at our sides.

Back up in town, Chris, ever looking forward to his next meal, asks the question I've already anticipated: "So, anyone else hungry?" Caroline spied an inviting trattoria, the only one with its lights on, when we initially walked through town, so we head there directly and are the only patrons in the cozy place. As so often happens in Europe, we're presented with a platter of the slippery daily catch and promptly order a variety of fresh seafood. We chat with the elderly, married owners about the storm, and they express their gratitude that their home-cum-restaurant didn't sustain much damage. "Thanks to you, you visit Cinque Terre, never mind the storm," the husband says.

Joe responds, "And *mille grazie* to you for your hospitality," as the wife takes the platter and they head to the kitchen to prepare our lunch.

The train's next stop is Vernazza, and although we're not permitted to disembark (the town was under thirteen feet of mud, which reached first-floor balconies, immediately after the storm), we can see the damage from our window. Six weeks into the recovery, a film of dried gray mud still coats the pastel facades that line the main street, leaving the town an ashen imitation of its prior self. Construction equipment blocks the way to the harbor as workers continue to clear residue from the storm. We're able to get off in Monterosso, however, where they've made significant progress toward getting the town back to functioning. Whereas Vernazza runs uphill, perpendicular to the coast, Monterosso hugs the waterline in classic beach-town fashion. There's an eerie, grimy debris field at the southern end of the coastline, piled high with refrigerators and other appliances, furniture, boat fragments, sinks, boxes, trees, and clothing, waiting for a refuse barge to haul it away—the remnants of people's lives heaped haphazardly along the shore. Sandbag stacks remain in place, lining the base of most storefronts in what were likely futile attempts to keep floodwaters out. Town leaders vow that what was once a string of animated restaurants and shops will once again house a brisk tourist trade this spring. Their promise appears on track as Monterosso reverberates with the constant motorized sounds of heavy machinery and moving equipment.

We return to La Spezia on the late-afternoon train with a mixed bag of emotions. The Cinque Terre towns are worthy of their reputation as top Italian destinations, and we're grateful to have been able to visit them. But we're also saddened not to have experienced them, their residents, and their challenging hiking trails fully. The best we can do is spread the word that the Cinque Terre will soon be back, as scenic and lively as ever, ready to welcome and reward visitors. I add it to my list of places to which we must return someday. The next time it will be summer, the devastation will have disappeared, the communities of the five lands will be thriving, and we'll complete the entire coastline hike of our imagination.

SILLY PISA

Pisa turns adults into adolescents who do silly, childish things, the four of us included, and all because its tower is pitched at a bit of an angle. The tilted column elicits giddy joy as people marvel that it remains upright after so many years.

We arrive in Pisa on a sunny morning with almost balmy temperatures. On a backpacking trip over thirty years ago, Joe and I made the requisite trip-to-Italy pilgrimage to Pisa to see the famous tower. I remember being astonished then, as the kids are now, at the beauty of its setting, lovingly called il Campo dei Miracoli (the Field of Miracles). The most famous bell tower in the world, the cathedral of Pisa it stands behind, and the baptistery farther on form a harmonious ensemble of brilliant white marble set against the deep, contrasting green of the surrounding lawn. Today, the cobalt blue of the sky completes the tricolor palette. The grassy rectangle sits below intact massive walls on the edge of the feudal city and is set apart from all around it, in no way suffocated by the congestion of buildings along its perimeter. The Leaning Tower itself is actually rather delicate, at 185 feet tall (much shorter than many imagine), and its massive cathedral neighbor provides perspective, reinforcing their differences.

Once we take serious shots of the lush square and its world-famous structure, we move on to the silly stuff.

Would a trip to Pisa be complete without a bunch of funny forced-perspective photos with the tower? Not a chance. We stage a picture of Caroline pushing with hands upright, bracing with her back, and aligning the appropriate body parts so the camera shot is just right, creating the illusion that she's preventing the tower from falling. We then have Chris hug the pillar, his arms wrapped around it flawlessly and then appearing to lift it off the ground. Since our visit is a family affair, Joe and I also pose in juvenile fashion. The "phunny photo" merriment continues as we watch other tourists in their silliness, adjusting themselves to hold the famous tower on their hands or catch it in their arms. Families struggle to position each other, couples bicker about how best to pose, and multiple strangers ask us to take pictures of them in wacky, twisted stances. Even the most solemn visitors put their poise aside as they jockey for the ideal zany shot.

ONE PART ITALY, TWO PARTS AUSTRIA, THREE PARTS HEAVEN

Deep in the Dolomites, the craggy, limestone Italian Alps, is the mountain paradise of Val Gardena. From our earliest imaginings, the broad-brush plan for our gap year always included several days of skiing with the children in this enchanting part of the world at Christmastime—our family gift to each other. How incredibly fortunate I am to have the joys of my life—Joe, Chris, and Caroline—along with skiing, a passion of my youth, come together in a snowy Alpine wonderland.

We head north from La Spezia on the autostrada, and as we scoot around Verona, the white peaks of the Dolomites rise in the distance. The temperature steadily drops as we speed toward Bolzano, and it's below freezing when we exit the highway, heading east. The architecture changes the minute we leave the highway, and Caroline, so like me with her GPS brain that always needs feeding, asks, "Are we really still in Italy?" Residences in warm shades of stucco with orange tile roofs become brown and white A-frame chalets adorned with flower boxes and rustic wooden lodges with inviting balconies. Have we entered a frosty slice of Austria even though the map maintains we're in Italy?

Val Gardena is in the South Tyrol province, part Austro-Hungarian Empire until 1918, when Italy annexed it after World War I. Although residents speak Italian, German is the mother tongue and dominant culture and the area is officially bilingual. It's a slow thirty-five kilometers to our destination, on winding, snowy roads that wind deeper into the mountains and eventually down into Ortisei in Val Gardena.

The young staffers at our hotel, the grand Gardena Grödnerhof, are genuinely and uniformly warm and kind. The incredibly pleasant and helpful Mathias (should I mention he has beautiful blue eyes?) checks us in, and the four of us settle into our comfy suite, the perfect space for our winter getaway: a main bedroom for Joe and me, an adjoining sitting room with a pullout couch for the kids, and a bathroom to share. The beds are under thick, fluffy duvets; the walls are a fragrant natural wood; there are huge closets for all our ski clothes, which the kids hauled over with them; and an outside terrace looks over town a hundred yards away, the snowy mountains towering behind. Some think us crazy to stay in such close quarters with our adult children when we travel, but we wouldn't have it any other way. Doing so with Chris and Caroline and overhearing their private chitchat and whispers—they speak a language all their own—only adds to our enjoyment of being together.

As we're settling in, there's a knock at the door, and a hotel staffer appears with a tray of champagne flutes for a welcome toast. "Happy?" Joe asks as he joins me on the balcony, bubbly in hand, and puts his arm around my shoulder.

"Do you really need to ask? " I reply, our children's laughter in the background. "It's all just as I imagined."

The children join us outside, and after a few minutes in the cold, Chris suggests, "Shall we go down and take advantage of the lobby?"

After another round of drinks, we take a chilly walk at dusk through the quintessential ski town, and although darkness falls quickly, we can see the shadowy outline of the mountains framing the village. The combination of the rocky peaks and the energy of the town, now glittering with shop lights and peppered with skiers returning from the slopes, brings a flood of memories of trips gone by. My dormant ski juices have thawed, and my excitement about the days ahead, schussing downhill, begins to rise.

"How long's it been since we went on a family ski trip?" Caroline wonders out loud.

"Has to be at least eight years," Joe guesses. Work, everyday life, and college tuitions can sometimes eclipse our passions, and I remind myself that this is exactly what our gap year is about—putting those passions front and center as we temporarily set aside the daily grind. We've hit the jackpot for doing just that in Val Gardena: a dramatic Alpine valley technically in Italy but with the appearance of the Tyrol, and which is certainly skiing heaven.

A PASSION FOR POWDER

Tempering my excitement is a healthy dose of anxiety. Looking from our hotel window to the mountains beyond, I feel a quickening—a tingling mix of anticipation and nerves. I'm certainly not getting younger, haven't been on the slopes in years, and don't know what to expect in the Dolomites terrain. Will everything come back easily? Will muscle memory guide me down the mountain?

I needn't have worried. Strapping on my boards feels as natural as walking down the street, and once I've snapped my boots in place, I'm ready to go. Finding my rhythm on the slopes is indeed like riding the proverbial bike. I'm reunited with an old friend as if no time has passed, Chris, Caroline, and Joe all crisscrossing the trail ahead of me. It appears that all of our bodies have seamless recall.

Why is it that pastimes of our youth have such unique staying powers? Like Proust's madeleines, do they imprint us forever with their joys? Why do we so often put them aside as adults, never finding the time to delight in them as we once did? Self-help books extol the virtues of revisiting activities pursued in youth to help chase away the blues. And so it is with skiing. Introduced at fourteen, I immediately fell in love and saved my babysitting money to head to the mountains whenever I could. All my friends loved to ski, which made it especially attractive, and the fact that Joe is gifted at the sport guaranteed we would go often.

The snow gods cooperate by releasing a layer of fresh powder the night before our first day out. The Alpine scenery sparkles in the early winter light as we make the ascent by gondola and then cable car, the jagged limestone peaks rising toward fluffy clouds. As we stand poised on the Seceda summit and survey the terrain, anticipating the glorious seven-mile descent, I marvel at the fact that two short weeks earlier, Joe and I were grappling with the rigors of Morocco. We couldn't be in a more different place now: a mountainous wonderland with Chris and Caroline, the wind in our faces—the heady stuff of my dreams.

As we settle in for our final Val Gardena dinner, we review our stay. Joe and I bask in the soft glow of the dining room, observe Chris and Caroline eating their meals, and exchange conspiratorial glances. "March?" I whisper to Joe, and he knows exactly what I mean.

He nods yes, his eyes lighting up, and orders a second bottle of wine. I conjure up our gap year calendar and mentally make adjustments to our itinerary. It would be such a shame to have found this place and not return. Soon. I mark my mental datebook for March 2012, when we'll be on our way to Eastern Europe and just the two of us can come back to Val Gardena as the capstone to the three months we'll spend in Italy.

AU REVOIR, LES ENFANTS

We conclude our family trip in Verona. We stay in a hotel appropriately named Giulietta e Romeo, dine at a trattoria with the same name, shop at the open-air Christmas market, and take pictures at the mythical home of Juliet under its romantic balcony in a cobblestone courtyard. I do my best to enjoy the time, but as our sad parting looms, I find myself sobbing in the shower on our last night in Italy, though I pull myself together and manage to dress for dinner tear-free, not wanting to ruin our final family evening.

The French have it right when they kiss and say *au revoir*—"until we see each other again," not "goodbye." And that's what we say to our children when they leave us to go home. "We'll see you in less than four months, Dad," Caroline consoles Joe, but she's working as hard as he is not to cry. "Maman," Chris says, rubbing my back, "the next time we visit, you'll be in Paris and ready to run the marathon."

Joe and I both nod and try to smile, but for now it's time to say, "Until we see you again." And so off they go, through security and to their gate, just four days before Christmas. While Chris's film-editing work is on hiatus for the rest of December, Caroline, a NICU nurse, must work through the holidays; otherwise, the kids would be staying through the twenty-fifth. We yearn to board the plane with them, to remain in their company and head back to our familiar United States. But we busy ourselves with our own departure details and the mechanics of getting to another terminal to catch our EasyJet flight to London. The decision to leave for England on the heels of the kids' departure is a perfect foil for our melancholy; distraction is a very helpful antidote.

We settle in at our gate, and I do my best to lose myself in a book. But the chattering holiday travelers passing by make me feel the physical absence of the grown-up Chris and Caroline I just hugged goodbye so keenly that my face twitches and then crumbles, the tears I've held back all day spilling over. Not only do I miss my adult children, I realize in that moment, but I miss them as children as well. As happy as we are to see our sons and daughters grow, share the joy of their successes, help them deal with disappointment, and beam with pride as they become young adults, it's painful to say goodbye to their youth. Sitting on a molded plastic chair at a sterile airport gate, I love who my kids are now but I miss their little selves—like friends I no longer see—and I feel fleeting but unmistakable loss. I share my thoughts with Joe and lean my head on his shoulder. His voice thickening with sentiment, all he manages is, "I know, babe, I know."

The announcement of our flight to Gatwick interrupts my wistful reverie. I shake off my funk and strap on my backpack, and we're on our way to London— stiff upper lip and all that. It's time for new adventures sans children; we're back to being on our own, back to being just two for the road.

HAPPY CHRISTMAS IN MERRY ENGLAND

Much to our delight, we find London experiencing springlike temperatures and are able to leave hats, scarves, and mittens unpacked. For the entire week of our stay, although the skies are overcast, we have only one afternoon of gentle drizzle. Having been to London many times for both business and pleasure, we forgo rigorous sightseeing and simply stroll the streets. It's terrific weather for wandering, peppered with breaks in whatever pubs we find welcoming. In years past, pubs were murky chimneys of omnipresent cigarette smoke, but now that indoor smoking is outlawed, I've become a huge fan of the neighborhood hangouts. I like the camaraderie and everyday conversation that pervade them, as well as the fascinating people-watching.

In Chequers Tavern, the dependable pub behind our hotel, we meet a witty duo, an American expat banker and his German colleague, who work in London. "So, why are you both in the UK?" we ask, and they tell us they both have English women in their lives who keep them here. They're fascinated by our gap year undertaking; they ask questions about logistics and our itinerary and seem genuinely in awe of what we're doing. "You're telling us you quit your jobs and sold everything just to bum around Europe?" the American asks.

"That pretty much sums it up," Joe replies. Our festive evening with the financiers ends abruptly as they're pulled away to an office Christmas party, but we're gratified that the escapades of two fifty-five-year-olds have impressed two thirtysomethings. It's just the emotional boost we need, since the memory of the kids' departure lingers and the prospect of Christmas by ourselves is still rather sad. Every once in a while when we're feeling melancholy, it's nice to hear that others deem what we're doing cool. Outside affirmation so far from home, especially by international bankers, is always welcome.

Joe is especially pleased with the relaxing change of not struggling with a language barrier, and I appreciate the opportunity to temporarily relinquish my role as translator in chief. As usual, the moment we arrive on British soil, we find it difficult not to affect an English accent and sprinkle our speech with "brilliant," "ring my mobile," "dodgy," and "takeaway." We quickly learn to say "Happy Christmas" instead of "Merry," search for where to make reservations for "Christmas lunch," not "dinner," and anticipate the arrival of "Father Christmas."

Few restaurants advertise the Christmas meal other than brightly lit cafeterias or stuffy, overpriced dining rooms in the fanciest of hotels. We find Greig's on a list provided by our own hotel, a warm neighborhood inn that will serve a reasonable prix-fixe meal and promptly make a reservation for Christmas Day. But the following evening, while having a drink at Chequers, we see that its specials blackboard is decorated with green- and red-chalked holly and berries and advertises Christmas lunch: pigs in a blanket, turkey with the fixin's, cranberry sauce, and mince pie—all for just 10 pounds. Joe is certain I'm kidding when I first remark, "That menu sounds really good." But once he realizes I'm seriously suggesting we eat at a pub on Christmas, he quickly warms to the idea. "Why not?" he says. "I haven't had mince pie since your mom used to make it."

Chequers serves a variety of draft beers and a nice French sauvignon blanc, so, in the spirit of eating local, we decide to celebrate Christmas at the neighborhood tavern. The bartender says they'll be serving all day, from 11:00 a.m. until 7:00 p.m., no reservation needed. Trying to be respectful patrons, we ring Greig's multiple times on Christmas Eve to cancel our reservation but are unable to get through.

Christmas dawns like an April morning. After a quiet breakfast, we head through deserted London streets to the Jesuit Church of the Immaculate Conception on a quiet lane a fifteen-minute walk from our hotel. The ninth-century building is warm and modern inside, a welcome change from so many cold, aloof churches on the Continent. We've decided for reasons of nostalgia to attend the 11:00 a.m. high mass, a joyous liturgy sung in Latin that harks back to the Catholic church of our 1960s youth. We sing *Adeste Fideles* and *Gloria in Excelsis Deo* along with the congregation, a bit melancholy with no family beside us but feeling very British indeed as we greet our neighbors with *"Happy* Christmas."

We take the short walk to Grosvenor Square to salute our flag and pay our respects by waving *"Merry*

Christmas" to the American embassy and the statues of presidents FDR, Eisenhower, and Reagan. We then head to Chequers, our mouths watering as we anticipate our holiday meal. But when we arrive, the pub is shuttered—no lights, no patrons, doors locked. Our plans for Christmas lunch at our neighborhood tavern promptly evaporate. Was it a communication issue of two countries divided by a common language? How could we have misunderstood so completely? Standing in front of Chequers, Joe and I are crestfallen at the prospect of spending Christmas in a charmless cafeteria. But then we remember Greig's. Lady luck prevented us from canceling our reservation, and if we hurry, we'll arrive right on time.

More upscale than the corner pub, Greig's serves us a tasty Christmas meal of prawn cocktail, turkey, stuffing, gravy, parsnips, and brandied Christmas pudding. The atmosphere is festive, and we fit right in with the international mix of diners, all of us popping open our foil-covered Christmas crackers and wearing red and green tissue-paper crowns.

For the balance of our week, we enjoy our favorite London activities: high tea, eating fabulous Indian food, the changing of the Queen's Horse Guards, a play in the West End (live theater may be the only bargain in town), and several long runs in the incomparable parks. Why Chequers was closed for Christmas and the subsequent several days remains a mystery; we leave London before it reopens.

Although we shared Christmas dinner with neither the royals at Sandringham nor the locals at Chequers, we did have a nice, quiet celebration, Christmas pudding and all. At the end of the day, there's nothing as comforting and heartwarming as being with family at this time of year, and we agree that this will be the last one on our own. Any future gap years must start *after* and end *before* the holidays.

VII. An Italian Winter
January 2012

BUON ANNO

ENTHUSIASTIC SMILES ON OUR FACES, we fly back to Italy from London and take the train south from Milan to Rome. New Year's is one of the few holidays we actually *prefer* celebrating by ourselves. Other than our studio in Paris, the only reservation we made prior to leaving the States was for New Year's Eve and New Year's Day at the Cavalieri, a five-star Hilton–Waldorf Astoria property. "Being business road warriors and getting all those hotel points is finally paying off," Joe crows as we check in, gratis, at Rome's premier address.

The sumptuous Cavalieri sits on acres of parkland high on Monte Mario, just north of the Vatican. "Look, there's Saint Peter's dome!" I exclaim to Joe as we walk the grounds. Built in 1963 for the sophisticated la dolce vita cocktail crowd, the hotel is up to par with the exception of its ugly modern exterior brickwork, chipped and missing in places. A favorite among diplomats and high-end business travelers, it's filled with such types and their families for the holiday. In contrast with the arrogance that often characterizes such establishments, the staff is uniformly friendly and everyone greets us with *"Buon Anno."*

Our palatial, mahogany-filled room is richly draped in palettes of blue and gold, and I immediately fall back on the bed piled high with pillows. The marble bathroom includes a travertine sink, a bronze wastebasket on claw-foot legs, and a shiny towel warmer. "Joe," I say as I go through our welcome paperwork, "it says our New Year's Eve package includes breakfast, Wi-Fi, the spa, and access to the Colosseo Lounge. We get free drinks and an appetizer buffet every night." Having settled into such a splendid spot, we agree to stay put in the Cavalieri to revel in luxury for every one of our forty-eight hours.

Just for fun, we check out the Capodanno ("New Year") menu at La Pergola, the hotel's Michelin-starred rooftop restaurant (the only three-star in Rome). "Let's come here tonight," Joe suggests. "We can have dinner, champagne, wine pairings, and music—it's a bargain at just twelve hundred euros per person."

While not everything at the Cavalieri is as dear as La Pergola, the prices are still vertiginous, and we head straight for the simple spread at the Colosseo Lounge for our New Year's Eve repast. Bubbly flows freely, and we make a meal of pistachios, focaccia, grilled vegetables, and cheese. On so many New Year's Eves past, we counted down years and then months to our mythical gap year departure. But this year, with no more days to cross off the calendar, we toast to being in Rome and envision adventures for the next eight months. Fuzzy with champagne, I murmur, "Let's please not even *think* about having to look for jobs next year." But my declaration belies my anxiety about rebuilding our lives stateside as Joe pours me a refill.

The new year arrives quietly as we take in the twinkling lights of the Eternal City from the terrace and watch fireworks bursting from every corner. We head to the Cavalieri bar for sambuca, and Joe takes out his wallet for the only time during our two-day stay.

WANDERING ROME

Rome is a museum with no ceiling or walls and something to see at every turn. Modern buildings push against ancient, crumbling structures, evidence of civilization long gone. But you must depend on your mind's eye to guess the provenance of the remains and conjure up past glories, since explanatory plaques are sparse. The relics we pass on our walkabouts—a derelict wall here, a lichen-covered, headless statue there—are unmarked, and even insistent Internet searches yield nothing.

Coexisting with the past glories of the Roman Empire and the precision of Renaissance sculpture are a gentle shabbiness and ever-present grime. Swaths of graffiti cover bridges, buildings, and street signs. Efforts to tackle the visual scourge are futile because Rome's prolific street artists quickly paint over any progress that's been made. Litter is an ongoing problem in any urban landscape, but in Rome it seems worse—though nothing could be as bad as Morocco. Joe comments, "It seems like people can't be bothered to take care of their city. Don't they appreciate what's here?" as we step over gaps in the sidewalk, now convenient garbage disposals packed with crushed cans, candy wrappers, cigarette butts, and other junk.

Romans have never wanted for water. Known for its plentiful supply, thanks to aqueducts that tap frosty mountain streams, the city boasts fountains on almost every corner, both ornate sculptured basins and simple *fontanelle* for drinking. Often referred to as *nasoni*, given their proboscis shape, the public faucets offer a supply of clear, cold water that's not only safe but delicious. The genius of quirky creativity—you plug the end of the spigot with your finger, and the water spurts out a hole on top in a nifty drinkable jet.

THE BRIDGE OF SAN LUIS REY

On Friday, January 13, we stroll around perpetually crowded Saint Peter's Square, dodging packs of tourists dutifully trailing behind guides holding distinguishing flags. Joe points to the group of middle- and upper-aged travelers whose leader hoists a numbered paddle. The lettering below specifies COSTA, with a distinctive blue-and-yellow logo. "They're from an Italian cruise line," Joe says, resident expert marine engineer, ever interested in all things maritime. Walking back toward the Tiber and our apartment across the river, we pass four charter buses parked along the Via della Conciliazione, the approach road to Saint Peter's. The front windshield of each is labeled *Costa Concordia*, and Joe guesses the ship is docked in the port of Rome at Civitavecchia. Later that evening, Joe reads online that the *Concordia* left port at 1900 hours, heading north along the coast off Tuscany.

Over cappuccinos the next morning, Joe scans the headlines and groans, "Oh my God, no." The *Costa Concordia* hit a reef, ran aground overnight, and is now lying on its side near Isola del Giglio, in the Tyrrhenian Sea. Short of breath and shaking, we turn on the TV and see that many are confirmed dead and scores are missing. Are some of those we passed in Saint Peter's Square the previous afternoon now dead? Might we have exchanged smiles with passengers now injured or unaccounted for?

I have a *Bridge of San Luis Rey* moment and wonder, *Why*

them? Why the specific people who died in this tragedy? In Thornton Wilder's novel, Brother Juniper is steps away from an Incan rope bridge when it snaps, plunging five people to their deaths in the chasm below. The friar tries to discover whether it was simply happenstance—being at the wrong place at the wrong time—or part of God's omniscient plan. Questions unanswered, I find myself tearing up as we watch the unfolding story and the images of the grounded ship. *Be mindful and live in the moment,* I think. *We have no guarantees about next year, next week, or even tomorrow night.* We leave our breakfasts untouched and turn off the news, and I grab Joe for a protracted hug before we tentatively head out for another day in Rome.

OUR STORY DOES NOT COMPUTE

Renting a car should be routine and always has been—until we try the transaction in Rome. We reach the tangerine rental-car kiosk deep down a side corridor of the Roma Termini, the sprawling central train station, to pick up the sedan we reserved for a week. Passports presented, credit card relinquished, we sign the stack of forms that accompany the rental of a car. We're ready for our keys, but the diligent agent, with spiky hair a uniquely European shade of metallic orange that matches the kiosk, begins a battery of questions we've never been asked before. I take the lead after just two questions, knowing Joe's short fuse is about to ignite.

"Where you live?"

"No permanent address; we're traveling around Europe for the year."

"But where you live?"

"Well, not really anywhere for now."

"You have no address?"

"No."

"Where you staying in Rome?"

"We're leaving Rome, in one of your cars, we hope."

"When you leaving Italy?"

"In about two months, we think."

"You not know?"

"No."

"When you leaving Europe?"

"In about eight months, we think."

"You not know that neither?"

"No."

"Where your permanent address?"

"We already told you, we don't have one, but here is our daughter's address."

"I need driver's license."

"No problem."

"This says you live in Mary's Land."

"Yes, we used to live there before we left."

"What about apartment address?"

"That's our daughter's."

"What your cell phone number?"

"Here you go."

"You British?"

"No, we're American. You have our passports."

"But if you Americans, why you have UK phone number?"

"Because the cheapest cell phone plan is from the UK."

"But you say you American and live in America?"

"Yes, but—"

"You have UK address?"

"No!"

"I must call your mobile to see it works."

"Fine."

Are we really that unusual? I wonder. And then it hits me: I guess we are, in fact. We're totally untethered from a residence or jobs, and just as it took us a while to come to terms with the concept, it's hard for others to grasp it right away as well. The call from our blazingly coiffed agent rings through, Joe has calmed, and we get our car, although I'm sure the rental agent is still puzzled about our story.

A BRIEF RESPITE FROM ROME

After two weeks in Rome, we decide to explore the Italian countryside a bit before returning to the city for a month. We head northeast, deep into Umbria, to the off-the-beaten-track town of Norcia. At the base of the snow-topped peaks of the Monti Sibillini and protected behind a circuit of fourteenth-century walls, Norcia is famous for its wild boar and black truffles, and Italy's best lentils. It's also home to the stately Palazzo Seneca in the heart of the village, a sixteenth-century residence restored as a hotel. The Palazzo features two gargantuan stone fireplaces whose blazes radiate a warmth we appreciate as we chase the frosty mountain air with cups of hot tea and biscotti.

We dine in the rustic taverna across the street. Our stick-to-your-ribs Umbrian meal includes lentil stew, pasta with truffles, wild-boar sausage, crusty bread, and a bottle of hearty local red. We spend barely enough time in Norcia to explore all it has to offer, but we do learn that Saint Benedict, its famous native son, was born here in 480 AD and founded its still-functioning Benedictine monastery. We say goodbye to Norcia and pass by the hill towns of Spoleto, Assisi, and Perugia on the three-hour ride northwest to Florence.

The highlight of a visit to the capital of Tuscany is an audience with Michelangelo's *David*, standing tall, proud, and defiant in the atrium of the Accademia Gallery, designed and built just for him. It seems at any moment he might turn his head, lower his arm, and step down off his pedestal, still towering above the crowds. How is it possible that from a flawed block of marble, Michelangelo created this sculpture so pulsing with vitality? We appreciate David's chiseled perfection for as long as time allows, and while we could stay for hours more, Botticelli's *The Birth of Venus* and *Primavera*, as well as the other treasures in the Uffizi, beckon.

Shelving trepidation about the height of Brunelleschi's engineering marvel, we climb the 460-plus spiraled steps to the top of Florence's duomo sitting atop the colorful cathedral, standing watch over the city. We're rewarded with magnificent views of the low-lying city, nestled in a cup of hills dotted with spiky pines and horizontally layered cypress. The serrated silhouette of the ridges in the distance is distinctly Florentine and gives the landscape its special charm. After the dizzying descent, I fight the urge to swipe my finger against the green, white, and pink marble confection of the cathedral's walls to see if its creamy exterior frosting tastes as good as it looks.

We make our visit brief, having been to Florence before and anxious to settle down. "Won't it be nice to forget all the travel details, at least for a while?" I ask Joe.

"You can say that again—I can't wait to take a break from being a nomad and park ourselves in one place," he admits, as we battle morning traffic back to Rome. The apartment we've rented for four weeks awaits, and we're eager to stock the fridge with yogurt, cheese, and salami, stick a liter of limoncello in the freezer, and hole up for the Roman winter.

HIBERNATION TIME

It's such a luxury to be awakened by the sun, not an alarm clock, knowing there's absolutely nothing we *must* do. After thirty-three years of a baby's cry, a child jumping in our bed, or a buzzer to start our mornings, we've finally gotten used to being reprobates with loose agendas. But we take our languid days to a new level in our relaxing apartment in Rome. We follow nature by hibernating in our warm refuge, where we take things slowly, resting up for exploits yet to come.

We spend many a day rising late; having a leisurely breakfast in our laid-back studio; listening at noon to what we've started calling *Afternoon Edition* on NPR; catching up on e-mails, blogging, and our journals; finishing the novels we resolved to read while abroad; and then sipping cups of hot afternoon tea. We also spend many hours of these days planning our itinerary and reserving trains and hotels for the peripatetic weeks in southern Italy that will follow Rome.

When we imagined our year away, we glossed over the winter months, knowing we would be in Italy but not focusing on the reality of the cold. Now that we're here under a reluctant sun and in the company of an unusual frigid snap, we decide simply to hunker down. Our most difficult daily decision is whether to eat in or go out. Interspersed with warm days inside are those when we don hats, scarves, and gloves to brave the chill and discover the nooks and crannies of sprawling Rome, those often overlooked by those with limited time. It's a glorious *insalata mista* of a metropolis, since it's been here for so long and offers sights from every century of the past three millennia.

Our apartment is conveniently located on Via

Flavia, not far from the American embassy on Via Veneto and just inside the city's walls. It's a spacious studio on the top floor of a five-story building with a red-tiled terrace that provides plenty of natural light and a place to hang our laundry. In an unusual twist, we reach our apartment through the lobby of the Hotel Medici and take the elevator to the privately owned residences. Different, yes, but it's nice to have twenty-four-hour security guarding the building and someone at the front desk to greet us with *buon giorno* and *ciao* as we pass by. Off the tourist track, our neighborhood is quiet and safe, since government buildings surround us. It's also filled with family-run restaurants, and we diligently try every one. Part of why we're so conscientious about marathon training is that we need to work off the hefty servings of pasta of all shapes and sizes we consume, some of which we've never had before: *spaghettoni*, *bucatini*, *cavatappi*, *tagliatelle*, *pappardelle*, and—my all-time favorite—*strozzapreti*. I'm certain just listing them broadens my hips. I satisfy any sweet cravings with an after-dinner digestif—not as luscious as the creamy tiramisu Joe enjoys, but with many fewer calories. Running in the classy Villa Borghese park nearby is a godsend for burning off all the extra carbs.

Our Roman pied-à-terre is indeed convenient and comfortable, and the Internet is rock solid, but what we actually love best about the place is Stefano, our amusingly charming landlord. Without him, the apartment would be just another worn-around-the-edges studio; with him it's like inhabiting a season of *I Love Lucy*, Italian style.

Stefano is a fiftysomething composer of movie scores who spends most of his time with his girlfriend, who lives in the apartment above us. He's tall and attractive in a rumpled kind of way, the lines of his face hiding a gentle handsomeness. He speaks quirky English with a lilting Italian accent and apologizes repeatedly for being a musician and not a very good businessman.

We got our first taste of what renting from Stefano would be like even before we checked in. He graciously agreed to store our large duffels while we traveled with our small bags to Norcia and Florence, but he needed to "request a *piccolo favore*." He'd lost his wallet that morning and asked if we could pay the balance of our rent in cash when we dropped off our luggage. "No problem," we agreed. "Happy to help." (Little did we know that in the ensuing weeks, Stefano would lose not only his wallet but his phone, TV remote, computer power cord, and keys.)

When we arrived for our month's stay, Stefano was contrite about the less-than-stellar condition of the television (it didn't work), the clothes washer (it leaked), and the refrigerator (on its last legs and barely cool). He promised to replace them all within the week.

So we make do with what's provided, including kitchen drawers stuffed with faintly sticky cutlery. Ten days pass, and although we hear all about Stefano's lost items (he borrows the portable phone from our apartment after losing his cell phone), he makes no further mention of new appliances. When we finally break the news that the old fridge has collapsed, he apologizes profusely and comes right down to take measurements for its replacement.

We head out for a day of communing with ancient Romans among the ruins, and when we return, find the freezer open and defrosting, along with a note that our food is in a fridge in a closet across the hall. Stefano hopes we don't mind that he put a load of his clothes in the leaking washer and borrowed our laundry soap.

What can we do but laugh?

The next morning, Stefano stops by to pick up his laundry and informs us that he has ordered the new fridge. "I have chosen the quickest delivery—forty-eight hours," he says, "but do not forget, this is Italy, so we really don't know when it will arrive!"

Two more days pass, and each morning Stefano knocks on our door to express how embarrassed and discouraged he is about the appliance merchant he selected. When I tell him not to worry, he coos, "Marianne, you are so gentle; thank you for being so gentle with me" (the English false friend of the Italian *gentile*, meaning "kind").

With each morning visit comes a new request. First, Stefano borrows one of our Mac power cords because, of course, he has lost his. The next morning, when we greet him, he asks to rifle through the bottom drawer of the apartment's sideboard to find an extra TV remote; his girlfriend has misplaced hers (or perhaps it was he).

"You rented my apartment for your holiday in Rome, and all you see is my face," he laments.

On the third morning, Stefano declares, "Definitely tomorrow—by then the new machines will definitely arrive." But then it snows and all of Rome stops, including the delivery truck carrying our new appliances.

After yet a few more days, there's a knock at our door late one afternoon. There stands an ebullient Stefano with a new fridge, TV, and washing machine in the hallway. We set aside our plan to eat in and leave Stefano and the long-awaited machinery by themselves while we set out to find dinner. When we return later that evening, the new television hangs on the wall and the refrigerator hums away, snugly in place. But the new washer is noisily dancing across the bathroom's tile floor and, just as we arrive, bangs against the far wall as yet another load of Stefano's laundry steadily spins in the machine.

Ah, Stefano, I think, *thanks to you, Italy continues to be a funny place that always makes us laugh. What will your knock tomorrow bring?*

SUPER BOWL SUNDAY AND SNOW

Rome hasn't seen more than a smattering of flurries in twenty-five years and has no idea what to do when four inches of snow fall. The city skids to a standstill for four days—a full day for every fluffy inch. We witness gridlock in the streets, wait for buses that never arrive, and imagine Vespas veering off the Via Veneto as they career down the winding hill. As kids do the world over, Italian children giggle while catching snowflakes on their tongues and lean out apartment windows, arms outstretched, marveling at the sight of their first real snowfall. Snowmen with olive eyes, carrot noses, and pasta smiles appear on corners next to blackboard menus on sidewalks swept by retailers (apparently no one in Rome owns a snow shovel). The Villa Borghese takes a brutal beating with upended trees and snapped limbs, cedar and giant magnolia branches bent to the ground under the unaccustomed weight.

Two days after the historic snowfall, we pull on our fleeces, our obligatory cold-weather uniforms, and head for Scholars Lounge to watch Joe's beloved New York Giants take on the New England Patriots in Super Bowl XLVI. Just off the Piazza Venezia and across the Tiber from Trastevere, home to many US university programs, Scholar's is Rome's most popular Irish sports pub for American students abroad. It serves hearty pub grub and broadcasts the world's major sporting events live. We arrive at 9:30 p.m., a full three hours before kickoff, yet manage to secure only one barstool for the two of us. Ninety percent of the capacity crowd is under twenty-five, and we're two of only a few over fifty. I haven't been in close contact with so many twenty-one-year-olds in years (nor, for that matter, in the loo with an overserved coed losing her linguini). There's palpable energy in the room, filled with Americans eagerly awaiting the start of the game and lifting their glasses with the steady cadence of a college crew team. Along with our new friends we sing "Sweet Caroline," special for us for obvious reasons. Next up is the musical highlight of the evening: all the homesick expats in Scholars, Giants and Patriots fans alike, enthusiastically belting out "The Star-Spangled Banner" with Kelly Clarkson, hands over hearts for the red, white, and blue.

The night is cheery fun, we banter with many of those crammed into Scholars around us, and our resolute support for our team is rewarded with a come-from-behind Giants win. "Great game, great people . . . terrific time," Joe declares, as the years rewind and we're back in college, slogging through slushy 4:30 a.m. Rome. We're exhausted but reveling in the G-men and their victory as we catch an early-morning bus to our apartment. We spend the next two days sleeping even later than usual, recovering from our Super Bowl all-nighter.

CHAOS, THY NAME IS ROME

After some time in the Eternal City, we recognize that rules and regulations mean little. There are police barriers no one observes; double-parked vehicles that line every street, the owners of trapped cars leaning on their horns until the offenders appear and move their vehicles; *motorini*, the omnipresent motorbikes, zipping onto sidewalks; and signs attempting to direct customers into lines that are uniformly ignored. A simple *scusi* is license to cut in line if one is elderly, since seniors are revered in Rome. They commandeer your seat on the bus before you have a chance to relinquish it, jaywalk across busy streets as traffic obediently halts in response to an outstretched arm, and make their way with *permiso* to the front of the pack that passes for a line at retailers.

Cutting through the helter-skelter of Rome can be frustrating. Pedestrians stop when and where they want, midpavement, always on a cell phone, even if they block a tight walkway as others attempt to pass. "The oblivious Romans," we've come to call them, first with annoyance and now with amusement. When we first arrived, we railed against the disarray, thinking, *Don't they see how ridiculous this all is?* But, though products of the relatively logical United States, we soon adapt. Just ten days in, we're bristling no more and instead are just going with the flow.

But even though our attitudes have adjusted, it still takes fierce concentration to simply cross the street, as cars are parked like sardines along every curb, even through crosswalks, with no wiggle room between. Squat Smart cars parked sideways squeeze into impossibly tiny spaces with rear tires snug against the curb and bumpers extending over the sidewalk. We're on a bus one afternoon when it becomes lodged across an intersection, unable to turn because cars parked illegally and askew prevent the geometry from working. We chuckle at the craziness and listen to the blaring horns behind us. The driver of one of the cars finally materializes and speeds away with no remorse, thus allowing us to pass.

Roman retailers' opening hours are flexible and subject to interpretation, no matter what the signs say, but, as in France, closing times are sacrosanct. Come lunchtime, for example, doors are barred and you're told to come back later, *per favore*, the risk of losing a sale less important than the imminent enjoyment of a meal. One afternoon, I head for the Poste Italiane to mail some postcards and arrive at 1:27 p.m. Much to my surprise, a big yellow sign on the door says CHIUSO—1:25 P.M. *Who closes at 1:25?* Apparently, this particular branch of the Poste Italiane, whose daily hours are nine in the morning to 1:25 in the afternoon.

The following day, I leave at noon to try a second time to post my mail. En route, a renegade *motorino* whizzes by on the sidewalk, so close it drives me into the ever-present plastic orange netting that ropes off so much of the Roman sidewalk (although, as Joe has observed, "No repairs ever seem to be in progress"). The netting catches my wrist button, snaps it off, and tears my sleeve. I watch my button spiral along the pavement and drop through a grate. My tattered coat sleeve dangling, I push through a throng of smoking teens shrouded in a noxious cloud outside their high school.

I arrive at the Poste, and it's mobbed with nothing resembling a line. It takes time to negotiate the melee, get my bearings, and realize I need a number to be served. When it's finally my turn, the cashier waves me away as I approach: "The next *cassa*—she'll help you."

My ear has become attuned to basic Italian, and, although puzzled about why my number has come up if my cashier's not ready, I follow his directions and patiently wait. Just as I approach the new window, an elderly woman appears from nowhere and slips in front, insistently asserting, *"Scusi, permiso."*

Just before closing, I have my long-awaited hearing with a postal clerk. I head back home, reeking of smoke, clutching my ragged sleeve. "What happened to you?" Joe asks, looking up from his iPad and, seeing my scowl, adds, "Whatever happened to going with the flow?"

One Saturday morning, we escape the madness of Rome and head out of town. We settle on Frascati, home of the eponymous white wine in the Castelli Romani, the hills southeast of the city. Arriving at the Termini, we're happy to see our train is in the station and climb aboard. We're curious why no one else is in the car, since Frascati is a popular weekend getaway. "We *are* somewhat early," I rationalize. Finally, two teenagers join us and we relax, listening to their enthusiastic chatter.

Five minutes before departure, a friend of the *ragazzi* jumps aboard and exclaims in Italian, "It's not this train; it's the one just ahead." We all grab our coats and fly down the platform past six cars to the train actually going to Frascati. There's no indication there are actually two separate trains on the track, not just one long one, and that it's the second train that's heading out. We hop on the last car just before it moves and slump back against the seats. Did we really think taking a train from the city would let us escape the chaos that is Rome?

A TRAVELOGUE OF MILES

We've run a travelogue of miles on our journey so far: on bridges over the Seine, along the Canal du Midi in southwestern France, beside the beach in Barcelona, past the cathedral in Sevilla, amid the orange groves in the Algarve, and above the Arno in Florence. Last night we watched Charlton Heston in *Ben Hur*, and today I ran around Rome's Circus Maximus. "How will we ever go back to running on a high school track with no sights to distract us?" I ask Joe. The racetrack is now just an overgrown oval in the basin between the Palatine and Aventine hills, and none of its original marble grandeur remains. But as I jog the sandy circuit, I imagine the chariot races that took place here for cheering crowds when Rome was in her glory. The days of the city's strategic importance are over, but running past their vestiges makes them hard to forget.

I log dozens of training miles under the towering *pini romani* in the Villa Borghese, passing locals walking arm in arm for their evening *passeggiata*. Leaving the gardens, I make my way down the road that hugs the park's perimeter down the hill to the Tiber. A six-mile paved trail below street level follows the river, and while Rome isn't Paris and the Tiber is not the Seine, it makes for a fascinating run. Because the streets are significantly above water level, many riverside sights are obscured from view. But the Isola Tiberina, the picturesque island of stately, ocher-toned villas that sits in the Tiber, and the Castel Sant'Angelo, the imperial mausoleum turned fortress and then papal castle, do appear briefly to spice up the route.

Our protracted Roman stay allows us time to not only run by but also visit many corners of the city and the rolling hills nearby.

☛ We explore Testaccio, a neighborhood south of the Aventine Hill and home to a colossal mound of broken olive oil amphorae. Now obscured by weeds, Monte Testaccio, with a base circumference of two-thirds of a mile and a height of 115 feet, was created by the Roman Empire to clear the city of ceramic debris. This formidable garbage heap, now surrounded by a vibrant quarter of bars and restaurants, has sat where it is for two thousand years. Estimates put the number of broken terra-cotta vessels in the mountain of fragments at over fifty million—definitive evidence that Romans have long loved their beloved golden oil.

☛ We take the bus to the decidedly postmodern EUR (Esposizione Universale Roma), a stark district well south of the city center, commissioned by Mussolini in the 1930s as a tribute to fascism. Although World War II spoiled plans for a 1942 world's fair, the sprawling residential and business complex was originally envisioned as the exhibition site. Much of *La Dolce Vita*, Federico Fellini's 1960s black-and-white cinema classic starring Marcello Mastroianni and Swedish bombshell Anita Ekberg, which we watched the night before our outing, was shot here. While on the surface the movie presents Rome as an ultramodern, sophisticated hotbed of sex, parties, and debauchery, the desolate cityscape is a spot-on allegory for the shallow existence of the film's protagonist. The austere, white slab-sided fascist architecture and the wide, geometrical street grid are particularly bleak the day we visit, as blinding sleet obscures our view. "This place is so depressing," I pronounce, "and on top of that, I'm freezing!" We seek refuge in a McDonald's to warm up with fast-food cappuccinos, as all else has closed. We bury ourselves deep under the covers that night to watch *Roman Holiday*, the polar opposite of *La Dolce Vita*, chasing away winter with the warmth of a good old-fashioned love story.

☛ We chart the literary trail to the edge of the Spanish Steps and visit the pastel Keats-Shelley House, in which the young English poet John Keats succumbed to tuberculosis in 1821. Keats is buried in Rome's Protestant Cemetery, a peaceful, verdant spot, under a simple tombstone: THIS GRAVE CONTAINS ALL THAT WAS MORTAL OF A YOUNG ENGLISH POET WHO ON HIS DEATH BED IN THE BITTERNESS OF HIS HEART AT THE MALICIOUS POWER OF HIS ENEMIES DESIRED THESE WORDS TO BE ENGRAVEN ON HIS TOMB STONE—HERE LIES ONE WHOSE NAME WAS WRIT IN WATER. The final line is all the poet wanted as his epitaph, but his friends added the clarifying text. "I never really knew much about Keats," I confess to Joe, "but I feel so bad for him, especially since we were in the room where he actually died." We resolve while lingering at his grave to read his poetry when we return home, sensing his sorrow at being convinced his writing made no literary mark whatsoever. "If only he'd known," Joe sighs.

☛ We wander up the streets of the exclusive Aventine Hill and are rewarded with two views tourists rarely see, one magnificent and one in miniature. The first is a broad vista from the Parco Savello, a tranquil garden of leafy orange trees that looks over the Tiber toward Trastevere and Vatican City beyond. The next is on a deserted hilltop square—a perfect oval view of Saint Peter's through the Aventine Keyhole Gate. What a wonderful surprise to peek through the tiny opening of the entry to Santa Maria del Priorato

and discover the celebrated basilica framed like a
Victorian cameo at the end of the alley of impeccably
trimmed trees. "Whoever created this sightline was a
genius," I marvel.

☛ We walk several miles along the rutted Appian
Way out of Rome, the most historic thoroughfare in
the world. The Via Appia Antica connected Rome
to Brindisi on the Adriatic coast, still the maritime
gateway to Greece and Egypt. We start our bumpy
hike on the original paving stones, now worn to a
shine by Roman centurions and two millennia of
use. The aura of history descends as we stroll under
majestic cypresses so characteristic of the Roman
countryside and along the age-old road flanked by
worn statues, temple fragments, and tombs.

☛ A suburban train takes us east to Villa Adriana,
Hadrian's sprawling country estate, the Roman
version of Versailles, built long before the Sun King
arrived on the scene in France. The emperor was
an architect with wanderlust who traveled to every
corner of his vast empire, from Britain (where he
built his famous wall) to Egypt, Jerusalem, and
Athens, and then returned home to embellish Rome
by commissioning the Pantheon and his grandiose
tomb (Castel Sant'Angelo). "I had no idea the guy
got around so much," Joe comments.

- - - - - - - - - - - - - - - -

After forty-four days exploring Rome, we'll soon pull up
stakes. On my last run in the Città Eterna, my breath visible
in the chilly air but my workout clothes heavy with sweat,

I pass the now-familiar rooftop vista from the edge of the Villa Borghese. I peek down the narrow *vicoli*, the residential alleyways at the base of the Spanish Steps, catching glimpses of domestic Roman life as I run by, and realize how much I'll miss this pulsing city. While its ancient sights have always fascinated me from afar, they've now gently made their way under my skin and become part of the fabric of our every day. I find it easier than ever to visualize the Pantheon, the Colosseum, the Forum, and sundry fragments of walls, columns, and friezes as they were when Rome was the center of the universe.

Back from my run, I announce to Joe, "I've always known I could live in Paris, but now I know I could live in Rome, too."

A VISIT WITH BENEDICT

Our visit to Rome would be incomplete without an audience with Pope Benedict XVI. We join him and five thousand of his closest friends for his regularly scheduled Wednesday appearance, where we watch thousands of Catholics gone wild. There's shouting and singing, dancing and cheering; there are masks and costumes, coordinating hats, and customized T-shirts.

The cavernous hall sits behind the colonnade to the left of Saint Peter's Basilica. At full capacity, it holds 6,300 visitors in little wooden chairs bolted to its gently sloping floor, but since it's midwinter, definitely Rome's off-season, the gallery is only 80 percent full. Hundreds of religious are there: priests in notched collars cheer like sports fans when they see themselves on the Vatican Jumbotron; nuns in brown, black, and royal blue garb carry on like teenagers awaiting the latest heartthrob; a French youth group led by an enthusiastic cleric standing on a chair repeatedly sings the equivalent of a fight song for *le pape*; dozens of schoolchildren in matching yellow caps, most of them licking lollipops behind missing front teeth, chatter away in Italian in the rows behind us; and international journalists with long-lensed cameras fill the skyboxes lining both sides of the great hall.

"Look at that," I say, pointing to a pair of colorful, serious Swiss guards in blousy gold-and-navy-striped uniforms who salute when I expect them to bow as a cardinal passes by.

"I guess we know who's boss around here," Joe replies.

The anticipation of the pontiff's arrival mounts to collective restlessness as the appointed start comes and goes. I attended a papal audience with Pope Paul VI as a backpacker in 1977 and describe to Joe how the bishop of Rome was carried like an emperor on an ornate tasseled throne through the masses to the stage. We—and, it appears, most others with necks craned—assume Pope Benedict will make a similar entry. Like guests at a wedding waiting on tiptoe for the bride to appear, we all turn our eyes to the back of the hall as expectation that the pope will come down the center aisle swells. My feelings about the Catholic church aside, I find myself caught up in the emotion.

Everything is late in Rome, including the papal audience, as the hour moves five, ten, and then fifteen minutes past the starting time. The crowd is fidgety, and the noise level increases to a new high. I can't help thinking that any minute the lights will go down, the music will come up, and the pope will arrive in a blaze of NBA Klieg-lit glory. Certainly, the audience of faithful would be happy with such a grand entrance. But finally, twenty minutes late, the lights come up, the blessed rock star cometh, and the crowd goes wild. From the left side of the stage, Benedict XVI, in heavy cream vestments, zucchetto cap, and ruby slippers, slowly walks—shuffles, almost—to center stage and into the papal throne.

First up are opening remarks from the Bavarian pope in Italian, French, English, German, Spanish, Portuguese, and Polish. He reads some himself, and his multilingual staff present others. "It's like a visit to the United Nations," I whisper to Joe. Next is a New Testament reading, again in seven languages, and then comes the part of the program with a bit of circus to it: the introduction of the groups in attendance from around the world. They're announced by nation, and each has its moment in the sun; some simply wave, others hoot and holler, and still others play musical tributes to the pope. A group from Verona is decked out in full Renaissance regalia—long-beaked bird masks, capes, ruffled shirts, tightly laced bodices, and bejeweled crowns. There's an entourage of Naples policemen in blue uniforms with shiny brass buttons. The sole group from the United States hails from Santa Barbara and sings to the pope in Spanish. Between announcements of the contingents, spontaneous chants of "¡Viva el papa!" and "Vive le pape!" erupt. The pope acknowledges and waves back at all of them.

The gathering is more rally than solemn assembly and resembles a commencement ceremony with friends and families cheering, ringing bells, and blowing horns as the name of their graduate is read. The event closes with a benediction, and the program ends an hour after it began.

Our papal blessing in place, we must venture out from what has become the comfortable blanket of Rome to brave new territory on the lower half of the Italian peninsula—to experience the uniquely appealing culture of Mezzogiorno. It's time to pack our bags, take the train to Naples, and prepare for some southern adventure. *Arrivederci*, Roma.

VIII. Mezzogiorno
February 2012

IS IT TRAVEL OR TRAVAIL?

MUCH OF WHAT JOE AND I REAP from travel is invisible to the eye: a deep connection to each other as we share so much that's new, an enhanced understanding of the world, a link with people beyond our shores, and a keener appreciation of home.

But, all that said, I have had days on this journey when I've so wished the minutiae and logistical details would miraculously take care of themselves. There's a reason the word "travel" comes from the French *travail* (work): travel—or, shall I say, extended travel—takes incredible effort. I'm careful never to characterize our year away as a vacation (from the Latin *vacare*, "to be empty"), because there's a fundamental difference between vacationing and traveling. "Vacation" implies getting away from it all, while "travel" entails learning about somewhere other than home. The former is meant to be easy, and the latter can be surprisingly hard.

I would never call it work, but planning a two-week getaway and continuously charting a course around Europe as modern-day nomads are hardly the same. We google away many a day relaxing while we jump from site to site, sharing what we find, shaping days to come. Frequent debates erupt about the merits of one option over another, Joe always practical, the foil to my romantic after I've found a sweet little *albergo* in the woods miles from town. He harkens back to the desolate, isolated French Lot with, "I have three little words for you: Saint-Cirq Lapopie."

And then there are our clothes. There are days when I pull on, yet again, my worn-to-a-shine hiking pants and a dingy long-sleeved tee and have urges to toss the all-too-familiar garments off a balcony into dreary winter gardens below. "Joe," I moan at my bratty best, "just for one day, why can't I be a *bella figura*, dressed to the nines, like all the gorgeous Italian women in their sunglasses and leather boots?"

And Joe, being Joe, wraps me in his arms and says, "Babe, you're beautiful no matter what you wear, but I must admit you were stunning in your black fleece at dinner last night." The gentle spring sun cannot come soon enough, not only for its therapeutic warmth, but because the higher temperatures will let me rifle through the other half of my duffel—the half with the sundress, sandals, and pastel chemises I haven't seen since last fall's balmy Valencian sun.

Thanks to our stay in Rome and copious time for research, we're set with logistics through mid-March, when we'll leave Italy for a jaunt through central Europe. Preparing for Vienna, Budapest, Prague, Berlin, and Amsterdam will come soon enough, but for now, we're happy to have plans in place and keep our fingers crossed for warm southern sun and changing into breezier clothes. No travel *travail* for now; we're on our way to southern Italy, land of relaxation and *la bella vita*. We'll save more work for *domani*.

A STUDY IN CONTRASTS

The local bus from Sorrento takes us up the north side of the peninsula, crests the ridge, and then zigzags down to the legendary Amalfi Coast. We and the American college students sitting behind us let out collective gasps as we first glimpse the deep-green pines contrasting with the clear turquoise water of Salerno Bay. The colors paint a scenic coastline dotted with the seaside houses' whites and sherbet shades. The sky is azure and the sunlight shimmers silver on the water. High above, our bus heads east and weaves in and out of deep ravines. Around every bend is a view more breathtaking than the last. It is all just as gorgeous in reality as the postcard-perfect pictures that lured us to this part of the world. The switchbacked roller-coaster motorway carved into the face of the rock is simply the paved-over trail of the 1800s that donkey carts used to pass from town to town. It's not designed for climate-controlled motor coaches yet manages to accommodate the scores of modern vehicles that hug its twists and turns. "These people are crazy," Joe notes, as daring Italian drivers attack the hairpin curves with abandon.

We pass through pastel Positano, terraced into the hillside and tumbling down a deep ravine to the water, and get off the bus in Amalfi to explore the town and have lunch. The coastal villages are much like the Cinque Terre writ large, with a more visible nod to tourism. We order *insalate miste* and delectable gnocchi with creamy tomato sauce in a small, rustic trattoria on the main street of town, set at the mouth of a chasm and surrounded by dramatic cliffs, then hop on the next bus to farther-flung, solitudinous Ravello, an undisturbed hamlet whose elegant stone dwellings perch on a cliff and have watched over the bay for hundreds of years. This lofty setting has long been a haven for artists, musicians, and writers attracted by its pedestrian-only, rabbit-warren village of stair-strewn passages. We meander through its heart, eating afternoon gelatos, gradually realizing that much of Ravello's charm is hidden behind high stone walls through which we can only glimpse the luxury of villas and private gardens.

We travel back to Sorrento and get second looks at Amalfi and Positano from the opposite direction, now in early-evening light, our camera snapping as we attempt to capture the sunset's palette as the rapidly westering sun is sucked into the sea.

Guidebooks warn travelers about Naples; one even describes the zone around its central train station as "a horror." I can't disagree with this apt characterization. What we experience as we stride purposefully from the station confirms my image of a city overrun with swarthy men with meaty hands who look like they settle disputes with weapons. We're sideswiped by hurtling *motorini* as we cross the very first street, Joe is practically tackled by a goods-that-fell-off-the-back-of-a-truck salesman aggressively pushing electronics ("Guy, you want iPads at very good prices?"), we pass heaps of uncollected garbage, the graffiti is even worse than Rome's, and a cadaverous figure with rotted corncob teeth repeatedly jabs at me with a yellow fingernail as he begs for change. Unsightly construction that appears to have stalled eviscerates the entirety of the enormous plaza facing the station. How could such a city coexist in proximity to the wonders of the Amalfi Coast, not to mention the island of Capri, extolled as two of the most beautiful spots on Earth?

The one mission for our venture into the city is to chow down on some pizza, since Naples is noted for having the best in the world. As we do so often, we shape our visit around a specific restaurant destination, and this time it's Pizza Brandi, which lays claim to inventing the basic pizza Margherita. However, finding our targeted lunch spot is not easy, because the search takes us though the city's old town, the Quartieri Spagnoli (a moniker from the sixteenth century, when Spanish garrisons that suppressed revolts from upstart Neapolitans were housed there), on whose edge Pizza Brandi waits.

"This is what Manhattan's Lower East Side must have looked like in the early 1900s," Joe observes.

"Or maybe Little Italy," I add. The neighborhood is a grid of shadowed streets with colorful laundry hanging every which way above them. Multistoried buildings rise from grimy alleyways, and black-clad *nonni* lean over iron balconies, standing watch over the quarter's comings and goings. As we drift deeper into the belly of the maze, mouthwatering, garlic-infused aromas waft from above, hinting at midday meals stewing behind shuttered windows, triggering our empty stomachs to growl. The streets are filled with children playing soccer and residents on corners catching up with neighbors, yet *motorini*, often carrying entire families (two adults, a baby wedged between them, and a dog on the foot board—none with helmets), whiz up and down the cobblestones. The police allow bikers to drive as they please, paying little attention to laws, since to do so would result in a citizens' revolt. We've read that the community is notorious for petty crime, suffers from significant unemployment, is unduly influenced by the Camorra (Naples's particular brand of organized crime), and has many residents who continue to speak the Neapolitan language. "Hold on to your backpack," Joe warns as we wander the streets close together, not fancying being targets of the *scippatori*, purse snatchers and pickpockets on wheels.

We manage to lose ourselves beyond redemption in the warren of the Quartieri *and* enlist the help of a willing teen who speaks no English to direct us to Pizza Brandi. Following his precise directions of two *destra*s and a *sinistra*, we finally arrive at our elusive lunch spot.

We can indeed confirm that what they say about Neapolitan pizza is true. It's the best we've had on our trip, and, along with a slice from a steaming, cheese-dripping, oil-leaking pie on New York's Long Island, it tops our list of best-ever pizza. Tradition says this particular restaurant garnished a pie to mimic the colors of the new Italian flag to honor the visiting Queen Margherita of Savoy in 1889: red tomato sauce, white mozzarella, and fresh green basil. The queen loved it and thus allowed her name to be given to the new culinary concoction.

Our bellies warm, filled with an entire pizza each, we brave the streets of Naples for the tawdry train station, passing growing piles of trash and arriving just before sure-to-be-perilous darkness descends.

HEAVEN ON EARTH

I've died and gone to Capri. We spend four days on this romantic island art-directed to perfection—its colors vibrant, water clear, gardens abundant, and shoreline rugged.

Our gap year has been the ultimate lesson in geography. I admit to Joe that before we started planning our visit to southern Italy, all I had was a vague notion of Capri. "It's an island somewhere in the Mediterranean, right?" I asked when he first suggested we visit. "I'm not even sure I knew it was part of Italy," I add. Once we situate it on a map three miles off the point of the Sorrentine peninsula and read that it's a "Mediterranean jewel," having drawn pleasure seekers since Roman times, we add it to our itinerary. We also discover that if we want to sound like locals, we must accent its first syllable and not the second: it's "CAP-ree" in Italian, not "ca-PREE," as we Americans say.

It's a quick ferry ride across the Bay of Naples to the island, the first of three we'll visit in succession (Sicily and Malta are next). The boat is filled with day-trippers, and we're two of only a few dragging bags. "I feel so special to be staying for a few days," I say to Joe as we approach the fabled island. Capri is small (just ten miles around) and vertical. The sea meets the shore, and then everything heads up—straight up—until you reach Capri Town. In-season, a funicular continuously shuttles quayside visitors skyward to Capri's main square, the Piazzetta, but since we're off-season interlopers, our only option is to ride the local bus up the corkscrewed road. Past the tiny, efficient bus depot, the town is pedestrian-only, so we roll our duffels up and over the crest in the middle of town and then down several blocks to the side of the island that looks south over the Tyrrhenian Sea. Painted-tile street signs in tandem with glazed ceramic maps on every corner direct us to the shaded Via Tragara, the scenic walkway that wanders east away from town and on which our hotel is located. Even before we see our room at La Certosella, a villa set high on the hill and one of the few hotels open before April, our walk through the meticulously maintained town assures us that the decision to come to Capri was wise. And once we enter our everything-white, sunny room with daintily decorated floor tiles, sheer, breezy curtains, and a broad balcony overlooking a citrus garden and the azure sea beyond, we know our visit will be special indeed.

"Is it my imagination, or is the sun shining brighter and warmer here?" I ask Joe as I step outside. Could we be glimpsing the very first signs that winter is finally giving way? On our many walks through town, I spy gnarled gray wisteria sprouting pale green growth, and buds on the branches of compact oleander trees hint at color to come. I actually stop, close my eyes, feel the warmth, and sigh: "Ah, spring." Although most of the countless flower boxes and planters remain empty, too early to be filled with new blooms, the Augustus Gardens, with incomparable views over the Marina Piccola, a tiny fishing village on the island's south side, are already adorned with early plantings: hardy purple pansies and deep-pink cyclamen. We can only speculate about the island's in-season brilliance—how gorgeous must it be then, the hedges heavy with blossoms and the trees and gardens in full color.

Despite this lesser lament, we love walking with the locals, watching workers busily patching stucco, freshening whitewash, replacing broken tiles, and stocking stores. Purveyors of all manner of luxury items from Prada, Blumarine, and Ferragamo for the soon-to-arrive beautiful people are busy slicing open stacks of boxes filled with precious inventory—the latest must-haves—delivered on motorized carts through the jumble of streets.

In contrast with the refined main town, much of Capri remains wilderness, the result of its harsh topography, and there are plenty of trails for exploring. Appeasing our hiking appetites, we do a scramble of a walk along the overlooked western coast, three miles as the crow flies but double the distance with all the ups and downs of the craggy limestone cliffs. The recently restored Sentiero dei Fortini, the Trail of the Forts, starts at the lighthouse on Capri's southwestern corner and skirts the coast to the famed Grotta Azzurra, the Blue Grotto, in the northwest. We have the remote trail to ourselves as we pass through a landscape that looks much as it did when emperors vacationed on the island two millennia ago. The footpath climbs dramatic, cactus-strewn cliffs around wild headlands jutting into the dazzling sea and then back down carved stone steps to the water, with no hint of a sandy beach en route. "Let's just take our time and savor this," says Joe, as we stop in the ruins of a Napoleonic fort to munch on sandwiches made from breakfast leftovers and gaze out to sea.

When we round the final point and head down the hill toward the Blue Grotto, we're pummeled with wind from the north that has intensified substantially since morning, whipping up whitecapped peaks across the bay. The grotto is closed because of the rough waters, but we cross our fingers that the wind will calm by morning so we can visit Capri's number-one sight before we leave.

Subside it does, so we book a ride to the grotto with wizened Gerardo in his motorboat, *Pizza Man*. Just outside the barely visible cave, claustrophobia kicks in and I wail, incredulous, "Oh my God, we're not going through that little hole, are we?" But Joe reassures me and we transfer to a rowboat that allows us, lying flat, to swoop through the two-by-two-meter entry into the mystical sapphire cave as our oarsman grabs the entry chain and pulls us in. Refracted sunlight from a hidden opening illuminates the grotto and tints the water such that all appears to shimmer with an iridescent blue light. I lean back against Joe, and we float through the eerie sanctuary in silence.

Our final Caprese pursuit is a walk around the southeastern edge of the island, and the outing does not disappoint. Lush and green, in contrast with the barren west, this corner is shaded by soaring pines, spindly cypress, and a tangle of vines. A slippery trail wanders through the rain forest microclimate, passes the towering natural stone arch, descends to the Matermania Grotto, and then winds around to the Punta Tragara and the Faraglioni, three huge limestone eggs that sit guarding the end of the Via Tragara. We look into the depths of the sea around the massive rock formations, and the pale sand underneath is a flawless canvas for its translucent aquamarine.

Just before we leave Capri, we sit on our sunny balcony to take in the view. All sound but the rustling palms and a background of birdsong has evaporated. We decide it's better we've visited the island in her natural glory and effortless luxury, rather than in the full finery of the season. Summers are overrun with the stiletto-sandaled, Bermuda-shorted jet set licking the windows of the luxury emporia. The streets would be jammed, prices would triple, and we just wouldn't fit in.

SICILIA (SEE-CHEE-LYA) BY THE SEA

Its treasure trove of ruins first drew us to the largest island in the Mediterranean, but we soon find that Sicily has much more to offer. Taormina, our home base, is a captivating hill town on the island's northeastern coast, and the Hotel Bel Soggiorno, a nineteenth-century villa with tall, arched windows and a sunny, glassed-in breakfast veranda, is perched halfway up the rise. We're thankful, yet again, for affordable off-season rates of well below $100 a night, and we're given, we're told, "the most requested room at the inn."

We open the door to the tiny corner room, and I gush, "Joe, look at our view—we can see Mount Etna!" There are fourteen-foot ceilings and two French doors, each with its own mini-balcony.

"We really scored with this one," Joe crows, as we take in the volcano in the distance. Mount Etna is active and broods majestically yet ominously over much of Sicily, lazily blowing smoke rings to remind you she's there. It's difficult to forget the power inside her snowcapped cone, its peak blown off long ago, leaving a yawning, uneven gap below in which lava continues to boil. "I guess our plans to hike to the top weren't very realistic," I sigh, as we consider the snowy winds swirling around the summit.

We experience two shades of evening at the Bel Soggiorno: one a premature precursor, when the sun dips below Mount Etna, and the second producing indisputable darkness as the orb sinks past the horizon. We make the steep ascent into town for dinner on several evenings, tackling the stairs slowly to ensure we don't arrive bathed in sweat. Seafood dominates Sicilian cuisine, and we eat our share: swordfish and tuna, mussels and clams, anchovies and shrimp, cuttlefish and prawns. Sicily embraces being surrounded by the sea, and I so enjoy repeating in Italian what has become my mantra for our stay, the melodious vowels rolling around my mouth: *la bella Sicilia al mare, la bella Sicilia al mare.*

SICILY, THEN AND NOW

Filippo, the elegant gentleman in a silk maroon vest and crisp white shirt who brings us our breakfast of frothy cappuccinos and buttery *cornetti* on the veranda at the Bel Soggiorno, inquires, "Do you mind if I ask: Are you on your honeymoon?"

I giggle and reply, looking across at Joe, "Well, no, actually. We've been married for thirty years. Why do you ask?"

"I saw you laughing when you arrived yesterday and holding hands this morning in the garden. The only time I see that is with newlyweds," he states.

"You're an observant man," says Joe. "You're very good at spotting happy couples."

Filippo is a wealth of knowledge about Sicily. He asks us our plans for the days ahead and shares recommendations about what to see and, most important, where to eat. "I was born and raised on this island," he tells us with a teasing smile, after finding out we're traveling for a year. "You're now here on Sicily—why would you go anywhere else?" Acknowledging the wisdom of his question, we're puzzled about how to reply.

Roman ruins, in large part derivative of the masterpieces of their Hellenistic predecessors, intrigue me, but it's the architecture of the Greeks that ignites my imagination. Sicily has its share of outstanding Greek ruins, so, anxious for a preview of what we'll see in Greece, we head straight for Agrigento's renowned Valle dei Templi.

My captivation with Greek architecture may stem from my ready ability to picture myself strolling the temples with Caroline, the two of us lithe and bronzed (I appear as I like in my imagination), with flowers in our hair, in diaphanous, draped Grecian gowns and golden leather sandals, blithely discussing philosophy (or, more likely, the latest fashion). But the true reason, I'm sure, is that I had a wonderful classical art and architecture professor in college. She was passionate about her subject and coaxed the past alive for me in a way that bred understanding and appreciation of—and a lifelong fascination with—Greece. I read the writings of Aeschylus, Sophocles, Euripides, and Aristophanes and have reread my favorites over the years (*Antigone*, *Electra*, and, of course, *Lysistrata*). I would so love to transport myself back to the glory days of Greek theater to witness performances of the great works in open-air theaters. And perhaps early on a summer morning, I would join lively conversations between Socrates and his acolytes about the meaning of life and the critical issues of the day.

We rent a car for two days, but Sicily's distances are significant, and we manage only to scratch the surface of the large island. The ruins at Agrigento, Siracusa, and Taormina make our list; Segesta and Selinunte will wait for another day. The three-hour drive to the Greek temples at Agrigento's Valle dei Templi takes us across the island's center, up and over hilly black lava outcroppings, reminders of the island's volcanic beginnings. We pass signs for the town of Corleone and imagine Al Pacino's Michael taking refuge there before we descend on the autostrada toward the southwestern coast.

So unlike the white limestone Parthenon and Acropolis, Agrigento's beauties are warm honey sandstone. First spied from afar, they appear to be miniature cardboard models, but as we approach, their monumentality becomes clear. The great row of golden-hued structures sits on an elevated ridge below the modern city's plateau. The seven Doric temples of this Sicilian acropolis are some of the largest and best preserved outside Greece. They were constructed when Agrigento was the Greek colony of Akragas in the sixth century BC, before it eventually became one of the greatest cities of the Mediterranean world. Surrounded by groves of almond trees in pale pink bloom during our visit (yet another harbinger of the approaching spring), the temples look out over the sea and an immensity of Sicilian blue sky. Wind-bent cypresses line the approach trail, and miniature brown lizards lead us up the stepped path, drily skittering into nooks and crannies in the rough stone wall as we approach the crest.

The first temple, that of Juno, rises majestically above us, with the others in file behind it down the hill, including the remarkably preserved Temple of Concordia. Carthage invaded in 406 BC, Agrigento was set aflame, and signs of the fires that ravaged the temples are still visible, since sandstone turns red when heated. "That's incredible," Joe comments—"forensic evidence from twenty-four hundred years ago."

Next along our walk is a twisted, thick-trunked olive tree, still thriving, bearing fruit, and reported to be over one thousand years old. We finally reach the Valle dei Templi's largest structure: the mighty temple of Olympian Zeus. Had its construction been completed, it would have been the biggest temple ever built—the size of a regulation soccer field. Earthquakes and stone robbers reduced the structure to rubble, but there remains an enormous Doric capital in the pile. And there, like Gulliver lying prone among the Lilliputians, is one of the temple's unique elements: a featureless and badly eroded twenty-five-foot stone telamon—a carved architectural support in the form of a man, fast asleep on his back in the dust.

On visits to excavated sites such as this one, the enduring and the ephemeral compete for our attention. We envision the citizens of Akragas, their ghosts frozen in time, ambling through houses with well-preserved mosaic entries and training in the public gymnasium. These are the human, everyday details that bring archaeological sites to life and make visiting them so poignant. Whether sitting on the foundation stones of the Forum or on a grand ceremonial altar, we feel insignificant and reflect on the fleeting nature of individual lives. What were they like, these countless generations of inhabitants of this metropolis so enchanting but long ago abandoned? Their lives ended, but the remnants of what they built remain, and the permanence of the land, as always, prevails.

Not inclined simply to retrace our steps from Agrigento back to Taormina, we opt for a different route home with new Sicilian vistas along the coast. Once again in the driver's seat, Joe admits, "Every time I get behind the wheel in this country, I have to readjust. I don't think I'll ever really get used to the craziness of the roads."

"You're doing great," I reassure him, but little do we know what lies just ahead.

Sicilians take the art of tailgating to a new level, practically kissing the corner of our bumper before swerving to pass and then giving us another close encounter as they cut back in. The byway takes us southeast and reveals a less attractive, industrial side of the island. In a jarring disparity like so many we've encountered on our trip, after relishing the glories of Agrigento, we come upon Gela, possibly the ugliest town I've ever seen. "This is where the Americans landed on Sicily on their march to Rome in World War Two," Joe informs me. The coast is dominated by oil-refinery sprawl and poured-concrete buildings; gray, gulag-like, utilitarian constructions with no aesthetic relief line the streets, many of them unfinished and inhabited by squatters. The dystopian town is a mess of busted neon signs, an invasion of weeds, and unsightly wires and antennae that hang and sprout from every surface. Its built appearance is that of a ghost town, yet the streets buzz with activity.

Vehicles are everywhere: *motorini*, cars, and ramshackle vans double-park along the road and on sidewalks. The streets, none with lane markings, are like NASCAR speedways: a driving free-for-all where rules of the road are optional and traffic signs irrelevant. The two official lanes of traffic manage to make their way past each other, but cars going every which way along the periphery use a makeshift lane far to our left, on the opposite shoulder. I pronounce, "This is insane. If you don't like the road, just make a new lane of your own. If someone's in your way, just drive around on the sidewalk—who cares about the pedestrians!"

Joe mumbles his mantra, trying to convince himself, as a rebel driver yet again cuts him off, "Chaos—it's cultural; it's how they do things here." We survive the bedlam and make it through Gela, losing neither a bumper nor our sanity, but quickly veer into the hills to escape the crowded coast. We reach Taormina by sunset and watch *The Godfather* that evening, immersing ourselves in the on-screen history lesson about the intricacies of Sicilian family pride.

The following day, we drive south past Mount Etna and Catania, Sicily's capital, to Siracusa. We fill our morning exploring the semicircular open Greek Theater in the archeological park, hewn directly from the hillside in the fifth century BC; the *latomìe*, stone quarries, of which the most famous is a vertically yawning cave called Orecchio di Dionisio (Ear of Dionysius); the crumbling Altar of Hieron II, the longest ever built; and, finally, the first-century oval Roman amphitheater, so different from its Greek neighbor and the site of violent gladiator battles and other bloody circus fare.

Our next stop is Siracusa's island, Ortygia, at the eastern end of the city, inhabited since the Bronze Age and where in 735 BC the Corinthians founded a metropolis that rivaled Athens. We walk across the squat Ponte Nuovo over the narrow channel that separates it from Sicily, take the advice of guidebooks, and simply wander the compact island. A rich variety of architectural styles has accumulated over the ages, from the Temple of Apollo to the sunny Piazza del Duomo, constructed of smooth, light sandstone, in perfect juxtaposition with the dark lanes radiating from the broad plaza. Our lunch on the island is a seafood-centric, leisurely affair under an outdoor awning overlooking the harbor.

"We have to tell Filippo we took his recommendation for lunch," I say to Joe.

"Absolutely," he replies, "and why don't we have dinner tonight at that romantic seafood place he said we should try?"

"No objections here." I smile. "I can already taste what he said was his favorite: swordfish with tomatoes, capers, and sautéed eggplant."

Our tour of Sicily ends in our Taormina backyard. A well-preserved theater, refashioned by the Romans several centuries after the Greeks built the original, sits high on the hill in the middle of town, impeccably sited to frame Mount Etna behind its stage. "It must have been hard for spectators to decide whether to watch the performance or the smoking volcano behind," I say.

We love Sicily. The up-and-down cadence of the language is pronounced, the gestures emphatic, the food delicious, and the people gracious. I'm choosing to ignore Gela and our postapocalyptic drive-through and remember only the glories. And whenever I need a gauzy pick-me-up, I'll return to my sun-kissed Sicilian fantasy, Caroline at my side, ambling through the agora at Agrigento.

GOLDEN MALTA

Not content to rest on our travel laurels having ventured as far as Sicily, we continue our southern trajectory and journey an additional fifty miles to the Republic of Malta. After several bag drags, two buses, a two-hour high-speed ferry, and an even higher-speed taxi ride to our hotel, we arrive safely in the Mediterranean island-nation known for its crystalline waters, rocky coves, arid hills, and warm weather.

The Maltese archipelago of seven islands, three of which are inhabited (Malta, Gozo, and Comino), is smack in the middle of the Mediterranean, south of Sicily, north of Libya, and east of Tunisia. For such tiny islands (the largest is just ninety-five square miles), they have an incredibly rich past and witnessed more history than I'll ever be able to digest. The country's crossroads location has long made Malta strategically important, from the time of prehistoric settlements through today. A procession of powers (the Phoenicians, Greeks, Carthaginians, Romans, Byzantines, Arabs, Normans, Spanish, Knights of Saint John, French, and British) all laid claim at one time or another, after brutal battles and ruthless sieges, and left their mark. Malta became a uniquely Mediterranean microcosm and a bridge of sorts between Europe and the Arab world. After Napoleon briefly conquered it at the turn of the nineteenth century, it spent decades under British rule, before gaining independence in 1964.

Malta's official languages are Maltese and English, the former of Semitic origin (as are Arabic and Hebrew), and many citizens also speak Italian. I naively expect the residents to speak with a British lilt, but perhaps because the UK arrived late to the game (it took possession in 1814), Maltese English is heavily accented with an eclectic mix of pronunciations: Arabic, British, Hebrew, Italian, and Northern African influences all mash together into a appealing amalgam.

Our ferry from Pozzallo arrives in Malta's capital, Valletta, well after dark. The imposing walls of the fortified harbor are so thick you can drive a car atop them and, along with the city that rises up behind, are clad in enormous slabs of taupe sandstone. Given its vulnerable position, Malta's busy port of Valletta was built and rebuilt, buttressed and bolstered, always to be on the defensive, since it's seen its share of attacks over the course of its storied millennia. I half expect to see the Knights of Malta, the renowned soldier-aristocrats, standing watch over the harbor, arms at the ready, as we disembark from the ship. We opt to stay in Saint Julian's, a bustling coastal town with cafés galore a few miles west of Valletta.

When we awaken the next morning, the view confirms that not only is Valletta a bastion of stone, but all construction along the northern coast is much the same. However, what appeared an infinite accumulation of drab beige and taupe in the dark turns to a golden-ocher glow in the sunlight. It's an ideal day to be outdoors, so we join many others to take advantage of the coastal breezes and wide waterfront walkway and do a long marathon training run. We're on a high being in the company of so many runners, but it's on Malta that I first feel twinges of pain in my hip. *Just ignore it*, I tell myself. *It'll go away*. But that night I take a double dose of aspirin as the joint continues to throb.

Hoping to see much of Malta quickly and to rest my still-painful hip, we take a hop-on/hop-off bus to visit the major sights. The all-day excursion takes us across the main island's rocky hills, terraced fields, and shoreline cliffs, as well as a few pebbly beaches. Officially Roman Catholic, Malta is filled with churches, all of whose towers prominently display twin clocks: one with the correct time, the other with an incorrect hour, in an effort to trick the devil and keep him away from the celebration of mass.

"I can't believe wily Lucifer would be so easily fooled, especially by the old double-clock trick," Joe says.

We walk through Mdina, the country's former capital, a peaceful, stylish town still sequestered behind medieval stone walls on a hill in the island's center. Every town we pass through is filled with residential buildings, each facade graced by distinctively Maltese loggias—shallow, window-lined porches that provide welcome drafts during scorching island summers. Around the northeast corner, we pass a rocky bay where Saint Paul and his ministry were reportedly shipwrecked.

On our second day in Malta, we ride a glossily painted wooden fishing boat to tour Valletta's two-mile-long harbor. While waiting to board, we order frothy Burger King cappuccinos on a sunny outdoor terrace overlooking the harbor—surprisingly, the best and biggest we've had on our trip. As seagulls swoop and scream, I recall the graffiti that quoted Charles Baudelaire's poem "Man and the Sea" and adorned the wall of the *tavola calda* where we ate lunch at the ferry port in Sicily: *"Uomo libero, amerai sempre il mare!"* "Free man, you will always love the sea!"

Malta is as far south as we'll venture until mid-April, when Chris and Caroline will make an encore gap year appearance. They'll be with us for five days in Paris for moral support at the marathon, and then we'll fly far south to our next island destination: Mykonos. In the meantime, our brief visit to Malta complete, we leave the fascinating melting pot of cultures to retrace our steps north. There are bottles of Alto Adige wine with our names on them in the mountains, and we're anxious to pop the corks. It's time to trade golden-hued Malta for the reds and whites of the Tyrol and to return to Val Gardena.

DIVESTITURE

Well into our year, we decide to significantly lighten our load. We've left a Hansel-and-Gretel trail of bits and pieces across Europe: a T-shirt here, a pair of khakis there; an extra box of Band-Aids and threadbare hiking shorts went by the wayside. But six months into it, we're inspired to do some serious trimming.

Our resolve is bolstered by a chance encounter on the train. We meet retired John and Connie from Colorado, who look and act much younger than their sixty-five years and are ten months into a five-year adventure around the world. All they carry is a backpack and small bag each. They see our preposterous duffels, chuckle, and good-naturedly chide, "You haven't exactly left it all behind." Their comment seals the deal: one of our rolling millstones will stay behind in Sicily.

We attack purging with a vengeance. If Joe can live without that pair of jeans, I can get by sans travel blazer. No need for that second sweater—I'll just wash the other more often. It's amazing what a difference our bold move makes; we're just one bag lighter but much less burdened. When we leave Paris for Greece in April, the marathon and requisite running gear behind us, our goal is to be down to two bags, in addition to our packs.

We packed four overstuffed bags for four seasons, but it's now almost March, and with much of the cold weather behind us, we divest ourselves of our warmest layers and everything we can make do without. Retracing our steps to northern Italy via Sicily, we pack one of our two large duffels with everything nonessential and leave it at the Taormina train station with a tag that reads: I'M YOURS IF YOU WANT ME.

"Simplifying is always good for the soul," I say to Joe, smiling.

SOFTLY, AS WE LEAVE YOU

We sprinted to Italy after our unsettling experiences in Morocco, and now we ease out of her warm embrace reluctantly, taking as long as possible to let go.

Rather than abandon Italy cold turkey, we treat ourselves to a second dose of skiing, stalling our departure for a few more days. The bus ride to Ortisei from the Bolzano train station confirms that we're indeed back in the Italian Tyrol. A beaming, burly-bodied woman boards the bus, royally coiffed with a crown of salt-and-pepper braids affixed such that it stands on its side, encircling her head like a halo. She sports a traditional black wool vest and long skirt, both embroidered with multicolored flowers, and black boots that lace up the middle of her shins. She and other locals chat with each other in Ladin, the language spoken in just a handful of mountain communes, and occasionally throws a comment our way, not realizing we're "outsiders." Yes, we agree, it's a good decision to return to Val Gardena, perfect for tiptoeing into Austria while still in Italy.

Our days on the slopes are spring-skiing bliss, and, miraculously, my hip bothers me not a bit, as my knees and quads do most of the work. There's a mix of languages on the slopes, but we hear not a word of English until we reach the lunch *hütte* to order a mug of beer and a glass of wine to accompany the sandwiches we packed. We marvel at the number of older folk—those past their seventieth birthday—who schuss down the trails, all accomplished skiers. On several occasions we point to fluid, controlled figures weaving down difficult terrain and discover as they zip by that they're senior citizens. "Fingers crossed, that will be us in twenty years," Joe comments.

"Wouldn't you love to come back someday with our yet-to-be-born grandchildren?" I ask, as Joe nods with a smile.

Back at the Hotel Gardena Grödnerhof, we meet Angelica, a loquacious, ginger-haired six-year-old from Rome assigned with her family to the dining room table next to ours. Angelica is a bundle of enthusiasm at every meal, chatting away with her parents in melodious Italian punctuated with dramatic hand gestures and animated expressions across her freckled face about her day, the food, and her feelings overall. She's the epitome of what we've come to love in Italy.

Joe and I speak at length on chair lifts, over drinks, and at dinner about how during our three months in Italy we learned to relax about things that drove us crazy and did our best to emulate the Italians, who are patient, forgiving, and gracious about errors. They recognize that people are human and not automatons of precision.

We assess our Italian eating experiences and tally a new reckoning on our Culinary Scorecard. Our appetites were ready when we arrived in Italy, and, as expected, the food did not disappoint. The old favorites provided familiar delight (lasagna, pizza, *pasta fagioli*, and *insalate miste*), but we developed an appreciation for new Italian tastes, too: tender, olive-oiled Roman artichokes; gnocchi swimming in creamy Sorrentina sauce; pan-fried *scamorza* cheese; *arancini* (fried rice balls with a variety of flavors inside); *pasta arrabiata* (pasta with an "angry" spicy tomato sauce); bruschetta smothered with all kinds of toppings, like olives, eggplant, and anchovies, not simply tomatoes and onions; *saltimbocca alla romana* (sautéed veal that "jumps in your mouth, Roman style") with savory sprigs of fresh sage.

For special, gourmet, celebratory meals accompanied by delectable wines, France wins the trophy—hands down. Any country that came up with the notion of combining creamy goat cheese with a crisp salad and creating a foie gras crème brûlée must be awarded the haute cuisine Cordon Bleu. However, when it comes to delicious daily fare that can be found at almost any *ristorante*, trattoria, or *tavola calda*, Italy takes the prize. We enjoyed so many meals in so many comfortable eateries up and down "the boot" and each confirmed what we read about dining in Italy: People don't dine out for a unique or different experience; they go out to eat what they're used to at home—food that is basic, delicious, and familiar, but without the long hours of shopping and cooking. The updated tally has been rendered: Italy is at the top, France nips at its heels, Morocco is next, and Spain, far behind, brings up the rear.

We halfheartedly bid arrivederci to our good friend, *il bel paese*, since Austria, central Europe, and Holland await. I guess at how the cuisine of these countries will score, but who knows—a tender, juicy Wiener schnitzel could surprise us. Italy, you were a warmhearted winter companion, and we'll always remember your kindness. *Allora, andiamo*—it's time to move on. We follow the advice of the popular Italian song of the '60s, and softly we will leave you.

IX. Heading North and East
March–April 2012

AUSTRIA AIN'T ITALY

A RUDE RESPONSE CAN SOUR OUR MOOD, but multiple mean-spirited brush-offs in a row can ruin our day.

The down duvets in our budget hostel cushion our entry to Innsbruck, but insolent, unaccommodating staff at the train station mar our exit. The one-night stopover in the alp-ringed sports town in western Austria splits the long train ride from Bolzano to Vienna in two. We while away an overcast afternoon wandering the town center and along its river ("Innsbruck" means "bridge over the River Inns") and then an evening meal in a beer hall with typical Austrian fare (schnitzel, wursts, potato salad, and red cabbage). The next morning dawns drab with chilly, soaking rain as we tackle the two blocks to the Hauptbanhof. The five-hour ride on a warm train to Vienna is a welcome prospect on such a dreary day, and just one obstacle stands in our way: our ticket vouchers.

We head to the ticket dispenser to have it spit out our vouchers. *"Nein,"* responds the kiosk, ever so definitively. Unwilling to rely on the word of a machine, we head to the information office and receive another *nein*, this time from the officious clerk. "You must print the ticket. I cannot help you."

I head to the ticket office to try my luck, but it will take much more than luck to elicit a kind word or gesture from behind that counter. When I ask the stout, stern-faced matron if she can access the ticket through her system, she retorts, "It's your ticket, not mine! *You* need to print it," appearing to take pleasure in scolding me.

"How many rude employees does it take to get us on a train in Austria?" I bark at Joe as I storm past him. We have twenty minutes and counting.

After being chastised by Clerk Ratched, I furiously try to connect at the McDonald's Internet Point, but the fresh-faced, braided girl behind the counter informs me, with no smile, "No Internet today; it is finished."

While I squander precious time under the Golden Arches, Joe locates the sole *ÖBB* (Austrian Federal Railways) employee who understands our plight. Joe must have flashed his finest take-pity-on-me look, because when I arrive, the courteous gentleman is on the phone, thanking the authorities for their approval to print our tickets. Fumble-fingered attempts to enter my password (while some people function well under pressure, I forget to breathe) and a thumb-drive transfer of the file from my Mac to their desktop finally yields the documents with minutes to spare. We race to the passage below the tracks to the final insult: the up escalator to our track is *geschlossen*—closed for repairs. Adrenaline pulsing, sweat pooling, and expletives flying, we stumble up the stairs, laden with luggage, and collapse in two steaming heaps on the train. Immediately, it jerks to a start, and, miraculously, we're on our way to Vienna.

We haven't felt such frustration since we nearly missed the flight out of Fès.

Over the course of three months in Italy, we met not one rude or disrespectful person, but in less than a day in Austria, we encountered a string of them. In the end, we agree, we are no longer in *gentile* Italy, and we'd better get used to it—*schnell*. Austria is a new country with different attitudes: a sense of order, respect for rules, and a belief that authority holds sway. But the hurt from how we've been treated lingers. I reflect on Maya Angelou and how people make us feel. My natural inclination is to kill rude people with kindness as a means to make peace, but that strategy fell flat in Innsbruck. What are the odds, I wonder, of its paying off in Vienna?

MONUMENTAL VIENNA

Vienna is nothing if not clean and orderly. But you'd better follow the rules or risk serious reprimand. Yes, Italy's *motorini* have disappeared, the chaos has calmed, and graffiti is nowhere to be found, but neither is the warmth.

Our hotel is a two-mile walk outside Vienna's famous Ringstrasse, so we're quickly schooled in the art of picking a lane on our first outing into the city center. Trolleys, buses, and cars share the broad, busy boulevards, and bicycles and pedestrians divvy the sidewalks. And, as we learned in Innsbruck, no one jaywalks, double-parks, or disobeys traffic signals in Austria. Ever. You walk when the little green man invites you to, and you stop on a dime when he turns red. Walkers stay in clearly marked pedestrian lanes and don't stray into those for bikes. Order has its place, and the contrast with Italy is stark, but the extent to which the Viennese obey the rules is astonishing. At one complicated intersection, a woman stops in her tracks, hugging her purse to her chest. She's genuinely confused because the pedestrian path ends and it isn't apparent how to proceed. She wants to be told where to walk and can't continue until she finds the stenciled guidelines on the pavement. "You think she's taking compliance a little too far?" I ask Joe.

We arrive at the ever-crowded Stephansplatz in front of Vienna's cathedral, with its iconic gold, black, and green geometrically patterned roof. A man drags behind him a black Lab that starts relieving itself on the plaza. The master continues tugging as the poor dog is forced to poop in transit. Onlookers stop and stare with mouths agape, not at the man's insensitivity but because he won't clean up the mess. One older, well-dressed gentleman in a fedora is among the astonished. After building a head of steam, he shouts, *"Scheisse fucker,"* and then repeats it even more loudly. He is outraged that the rules haven't been followed and his city has been sullied.

We pass several signs demanding that owners clean up after their pets and providing plastic bag dispensers for the unprepared. We're later startled by full-color billboards featuring an innocent dog and a guilty owner in the background, dwarfed by a colossal pile of feces steaming in the foreground. The disgusting image is accompanied by the slogan *Du hast es in der hand—bau keinen mist!* (It's in your hands—don't mess it up!) Sanitation is serious business in Vienna.

I'm sure there are nice people in Austria, but none of them work in transportation. Innsbruck's train fiasco is followed by a run-in with a Viennese trolley-ticket collector. As in so many European cities, we must validate our tickets at a franking machine before boarding. We're more than familiar with the process and take great care after buying one-day passes to determine whether they need a stamp. The tickets clearly state the date and time, so we decide no validation is necessary.

We hop on a trolley and flash our passes, but we guessed wrong about validating them. The transit official is determined to embarrass us as he scolds, grumbles, and gesticulates, finally stomping off to stamp our tickets himself. "Fine. I understand. We made a mistake," I say to Joe, anger flushing my face, "but did he have to be so damned mean about it?" The effort it takes to be civil in response to someone so abrasive is considerable, but an aggressive response is beyond my emotional ken. *Would it be so difficult to be kind to visitors not indoctrinated in your country's exacting ways?* I think.

Vienna is laden with the legacies of the once-powerful Austrian empire and Hapsburg dynasty. Monumental buildings appear around every corner, and titanic statues on massive pedestals dominate many public spaces. For the most part, all work well together with the broad green lawns that surround them. But we can't shake the sense, as we walk for miles in and out of the Ringstrasse and around the palace of Schönbrunn, that the grandeur is simply a reminder of glories gone by and an Austrian empire that will never again be such an important player on the world stage.

Much of Vienna's grandiosity leaves me cold, with a notable exception: a morning practice with the gray Lipizzaner stallions at the Spanish Riding School. Children of the '60s, Joe and I anxiously awaited *Walt Disney's Wonderful World of Color* every Sunday evening growing up. We fondly remember the program about saving the Lipizzaners during World War II, *Miracle of the White Stallions*, and it is a singular thrill to set foot in the hall where much of the movie took place. Watching the trainers in their dashing empire-style uniforms (golden-ribboned bicorn hats, brown frock coats, yellow-tinged breeches, buckskin gloves, and high leather boots) and the handsome horses with their well-groomed white coats go through their classical paces is enchanting. The long baroque riding hall, opened in 1735, is encircled by two levels of visitor galleries and lit by three enormous crystal chandeliers that sparkle above the ring, suspended by chains wrapped in rich burgundy velvet. Waltzes play while the stallions exercise in what must be the most glamorous practice ring in the world. I'm fascinated by the graceful steeds and their moves—the precise trots, athletic balances on hind legs with forelegs tucked, cross-stepping, high-stepping, and changing leads such that they appear to dance. I fall in love with and follow every move of a darling dappled gray stallion with the most appealing face, whose coat has not yet gone white. Our equestrian morning ends with a trip to the Hotel Sacher, where we stop for coffee, *apfelstrudel*, and a slice of the celebrated chocolate *Sacher-Torte*.

We head out for seventeen-mile training runs along the dogwood-dappled Danube, and while Joe handles his like the athlete he is, I run for the final time before we reach Paris. At mile six, my right hip is protesting, and by mile ten, it's screaming. I limp the remaining seven miles back to our hotel, grimacing with every painful step.

"Where've you been?" asks Joe as I hobble into our room. "I was starting to get worried."

After collapsing on the bed, I explain why I took so long, and we do a quick Internet search to determine the problem. A bad bout of bursitis is our expert diagnosis, and the only recommended prescription is rest: no more running for a month. In that instant, fearing that my hopes for completing the marathon are dashed, I can no longer hold back hot tears of disappointment. "I'd hate for you just to give up," Joe gently conveys. "Who knows how you'll feel weeks from now?" So, after a handful of aspirin and a long, healing bath, I decide I'll attempt the race and run whatever distance my body allows.

On our final day in Vienna, we take a fifty-minute train ride over the Slovakian border to Bratislava. At just forty miles apart, the capital cities of Austria and its neighbor to the east are the closest in the world. We have no expectations about what we'll find and are pleasantly surprised by Bratislava's picturesque old town, buzzing with activity. The compact cobblestone center is just right for strolling, dominated by pedestrian plazas and alleyways, dark feudal structures, pastel eighteenth-century buildings, and open-air cafés. The first thing we notice is a preponderance of tall, pretty women à la Paulina Porizkova, all with too much makeup, long legs in tight skinny jeans, and stilettos finishing the picture. Bratislava is a supermodel hotbed.

We cross paths multiple times with a motley crew of rowdy rugby players (is there any other kind?) from the UK. They're dressed for drinking and fun (certainly not to meet the aforementioned women) in outlandish, mismatched ensembles of short shorts, well-worn tees, kooky hats, and wacky hair. It's a cool fifty-five degrees, definitely not shorts-and-T-shirt weather, but beer is warming their bellies on their rugby tour to Slovakia.

We hike up the rocky hill to the white castle with four corner towers and a distinctive orange-tiled roof. It overlooks the old town and shares the skyline with ugly, gray institutional housing blocks from the Soviet era and cold communist constructions beyond. We make our way back to the main square for a late outdoor lunch of schnitzel and salad served by an accommodating Bratislavan young man and then head back to Vienna for our final night in Austria.

BERLIN: FASCINATING, BUT . . .

We breeze through Budapest and Prague, two of Eastern Europe's grand cities, because the city we're most anxious to visit is Berlin. Our arrival at the massive Berlin Hauptbahnhof makes us wonder if we've gotten off the train at the airport by mistake. The futuristic construction of metal and glass soars up around us, enclosing a multileveled atrium of escalators transporting travelers up and down its honeycomb of corridors and railway tracks. Our first impression is that Berlin is grand, sleek, and modern, and that characterization holds up throughout our five-day visit.

The reconstruction, which rose from the rubble after nearly all was leveled in the devastating bombing of World War II and then resurged postreunification, when the Berlin Wall fell, is a lesson in how a city can get back up, brush off the dust, and reinvent itself. Historic areas like the Potsdamer Platz (now a showcase of modern architecture), Pariser Platz (in front of the Brandenburg Gate and American embassy), and the storied Friedrichstrasse (site of a terrifying Cold War stand-off) have been completely rebuilt as a contemporary metropolis. It's actually a surprise to glimpse an old building in central Berlin. Even the iconic damaged steeple of the Kaiser Wilhelm Memorial Church on the fashionable Kurfürstendamm Boulevard, left in its postbombing condition as a reminder of the destruction of war, is covered in a modern sheath as it undergoes refurbishment. Unfortunately, despite the addition of a few new buildings, the sprawling Alexanderplatz, with its 1,200-foot-high East German–built TV tower and open plazas, retains its bleak Soviet appearance. Other than this notable exception, most everything that was old is new again in Berlin.

A suitably modern hotel serves as our home base, a sky-high plate-glass tower rising above the Friedrichstrasse Bahnhof. We're surrounded by familiar German names from history class and the big screen (Unter den Linden, River Spree, Spandauer Vorstadt quarter, Leipziger Strasse, and Friedrichstrasse), and it's comforting to have Starbucks around the corner for morning coffee and croissants. We indulge in German fare: *currywurst* (sausage in a warm curried ketchup, a favorite among Berliners), Sunday brunch in the trendy Prenzlauer Berg neighborhood, and lunch in the amazing food court on the top floor of the KaDeWe department store (crab salad sandwiches and fresh strawberries with whipped cream). We never make it inside one of Berlin's most famous landmarks, the enormous Reichstag, home of Germany's Bundestag parliament, since we needed to have reserved visitor spots well in advance, given that it's Easter week. But we do spend significant time out front, gazing at its imposing facade, while Joe fills me in on the building's history, including a catastrophic fire in 1933, probably set by the Nazis, who blamed it on the communists—a ploy that helped augment and solidify

Hitler's hold on power.

While I'm getting my history lesson, the skies, winter white since our arrival, suddenly darken, a blustery wind kicks up, and biting wind, hail, and sleet pelt us unexpectedly.

"Well, I hope our winter layers are keeping someone warm in Sicily," I lament, as we shiver through a walk among the bare black trees in the famous Tiergarten Park. As is the wont of early spring flora in defiance of glacial temperatures, the cherry trees are flowering and patches of daffodil and crocus color dot the lamp-lit, hail-strewn pathways.

Just east of the Tiergarten is the Holocaust Memorial, officially the "Memorial to the Murdered Jews of Europe." I see the abstract representation of a horrific cemetery, but the architect's statement describes the full city block as an "ordered system, which lost all touch with human reason." Its fitting physical placement puts the memorial within view of the Führerbunker, Hitler's final subterranean residence and site of his suicide with Eva Braun in the final days of April 1945. Destroyed after the reunification of Germany, the spot is now marked with a nondescript signpost, and the terrain is covered by an unremarkable parking lot.

I'm anxious to visit Berlin's Olympic stadium on the western edge of town, built by the Nazis for the 1936 Summer Games. As a piece of epic architecture, the structure is beautiful—a gargantuan yet graceful and geometric masterpiece of light natural stone with symmetrical columns and an interior partially below ground level. *Der führer* intended the games at his grand Olympiastadion to be the ultimate showcase for Aryan athletic prowess and racial superiority. "How fitting that

Jessie Owens sprinted to four gold medal wins here," Joe comments as we enter the arena-cum–propaganda tool.

Three days into our visit, we focus on Berlin's troubling Soviet era. Several blocks down Friedrichstrasse from our hotel is the intersection that put the street in the global spotlight. In October 1961, two months after the Berlin Wall split the city, American and Soviet tanks faced off at the Checkpoint C (Charlie) crossing gate from West to East Berlin. Both vehicles had live ammunition ready to go and orders to shoot if fired upon. The chilling stare-down ended without violence, but the Cold War had indeed begun.

The barbed wire and dividing wall at Checkpoint Charlie are long gone, and only a cobblestone trail in the pavement shows where the wall once stood, separating families and keeping those on the east a stone's throw from freedom. The soldiers standing ready with rifles cocked have been replaced by a faux guardhouse, complete with sandbags, in front of which actors dressed in military regalia charge a euro for pictures. Vendors peddle East German military paraphernalia and everyday odds and ends from the GDR in what has come to be known as *ostalgie*—nostalgia for the *ost* (east). And I think, *Really? What a strange era to inspire sentimentality and spawn its own portmanteau.*

Multiple dark chapters have unfolded in Berlin, and now that they're viewed through the lens of history, tens of millions of travelers visit every year. But though the city has once again taken its place as one of the great capitals of the world—it's dynamic, energetic, and appealing—I can't forget even for a moment its reprehensible Nazi past. While no one demands, "Show me your *paperz*," I always have the feeling someone just might.

Twenty-five miles north of Berlin sits the Sachsenhausen concentration camp. Initially built for political prisoners in the 1930s, the repugnant complex, heralded for its innovative, semicircular fan-of-barracks design, became administration headquarters for all camps and training ground for SS officers. Not originally an extermination center, Sachsenhausen did eventually execute inmates: Jews, communists, homosexuals, and Soviet prisoners of war. Thousands were killed while supposedly being measured for uniforms, with a shot in the back of the neck through a hole hidden in the wall. The addition of a gas chamber and crematory facilitated what became systematic murder.

Sachsenhausen is in the quintessentially suburban, albeit disgraced, town of Oranienburg. Residential, tree-lined streets lead to the camp entrance, and tidy homes with painted shutters and manicured gardens sit quietly beside barbed-wire barricades. When I hear that those who lived near the compound were unaware of what took place there, I'm enraged. The camp is part of town, not on distant peripheries, and those who lived in Oranienburg had to have known what went on behind the walls.

Our trip to Sachsenhausen is both a necessary and an anguishing part of our visit to Berlin. Walking through the death camp changes me, as did visiting Dachau in 1977. It rearranges my internal wiring, weakens my belief in people's essential goodness, sharpens the realization of the horrors human beings can inflict on those they hate, and diminishes my capacity for forgiveness. Economic fear may have initially fanned the flames of bigotry, but sadism took over at some point. Exploring a country with such a shameful past makes me want to curse *all* Germans, even though I know that's wrong. That kind of hateful emotion makes me uneasy and anxious to hasten our departure.

"I've been to Germany so many times," I say to Joe, "but I never, ever feel comfortable here."

"I feel the same," he replies. "I just can't warm to the place."

"I have no appreciation for the language, don't like the food, will never get used to how brusque they are, and just can't forget the history."

But we had to do it, and thus our trip included a lone stop in what is perhaps my least favorite country in Europe.

BIKES, BLUE EYES, AND CANALS

Big-city hopscotching for the past few weeks has led to many mornings when we've awoken and asked each other, "Where are we?" We finally wake up in Amsterdam (a repeat visit for me, and Joe's inaugural), where the tulips are in bloom and the city is teeming. It's a joy to be in a place at the height of its season (and the price of our Easter-week hotel room confirms this is so), since we've spent so much time in locations where attractions are closed and the place is deserted.

Our hotel is next to the always-bustling Amsterdam Centraal train station and overlooks what must be the world's largest parking lot for bicycles. We gaze over the hundreds—no, thousands—of bikes parked and packed like sardines, row after row in the multistoried facility. Most of them are rattletraps with rusted rims, duct-taped seats, patched tires, and corroded fenders—transportation tools at their most basic that get the job done, appearances aside.

The extent to which Amsterdam is bike-centric is even clearer as we wait on a street corner for the go-ahead.

There are three directional lights at each intersection, which makes walking through town dicey at times, even if you pay close attention. On one side are cars awaiting a green light, and on the other, in the ever-present bike lane, are riders awaiting their turn. While there are plenty of cars in Amsterdam, they're clearly less important than the almighty bicycle. As a pedestrian, you're more likely to be hit by a bike than a car, and on several occasions we come awfully close.

Amsterdam has more than one hundred kilometers of canals (even more than Venice). They radiate from the harbor in a concentric pattern of semicircles crossed by perpendicular spokes that carve the central city into a patchwork quilt of increasingly large, canal-bordered islands and provide its distinctive charm. Strolling beside the waterways, we see few pedestrians with the straight flaxen hair often attributed to the Dutch. Holland is, however, a festival of blue eyes—light, dark, and every shade in between.

The urge to treat ourselves to a special meal hasn't tempted us since we left Italy, but since I so need my romantic interludes with Joe, the allure of a candlelit dinner cruise on a canal boat catches my fancy. "Do you think it might be too touristy?" I ask, but Joe says, "Let's just go for it. The menu looks great, and I'm sure it'll be fine."

And indeed it is. We lose ourselves in an atmospheric two-hour meander through Amsterdam over a delightful dinner of filet mignon and free-flowing fine wine. We anticipate the imminent arrival of our children in Paris, put odds on whether I'll complete the marathon, and record the locations of cozy boîtes we glimpse from the water, anticipating future meals.

Amsterdam is filled with fabulous art and

architecture, and we visit two of my favorite galleries in the world: the stately, old-world Rijksmuseum, where we enjoy the works of the Dutch Old Masters; and the sunny, contemporary Van Gogh Museum. The latter's exhaustive collection makes me smile; the paintings are so vivid and the colors so cheerful (like my favorite, *Bedroom in Arles*) but melancholy as well, because the artist suffered such a short, tormented life. While I don't find some Dutch buildings appealing—the churches, palaces, and municipal structures—I absolutely love the slim townhomes and small shops that line the canals with peeked, crenulated rooflines and multimullioned windows. They appear filled with warm, cozy garrets and interesting office spaces in which I'd like to spend lots of time.

My cheery imaginings vanish, however, during our visit to the Anne Frank House. It's my second pilgrimage to the former warehouse and now museum in whose secret, concealed annex the young author, her family, and four others hid for two years prior to deportation to concentration camps in 1944. We move through the cramped living quarters, looking at walls on which remain Anne's celebrity-magazine clippings and the penciled lines her parents used to mark the growth of their two daughters. Sadness hits me as hard as it did thirty-five years ago; there's no statute of limitations on sorrow. But while on my last visit I recall thinking of how it must have felt to be Anne, this time I find myself in Mrs. Frank's shoes, my heart breaking as my family is wrenched apart.

Amsterdam is an experiment in progressive living and thrives on its live-and-let-live attitude. It's convenient for the purveyors of all things erotic that the city's official flag is three white *X*s on a black-and-red background. They're actually Saint Andrew's crosses, but the suggestive triplets ubiquitously exploit X-rated entertainment. Prostitution is legal, as is the sale and use of cannabis in so-called "coffee shops," and a trip to the city of laissez-faire is not complete without a mosey through the pedestrian lanes near the train station. Deep breaths in fragrant clouds of smoke outside hazy establishments have the potential to ease all manner of aches and pains, and De Wallen, the infamous red-light district, is just steps away.

Just as I'm always amused in New Orleans by the sight of midwestern parents pushing strollers and older couples clutching the hands of grandchildren walking down Bourbon Street, so it is in Amsterdam. The incongruity gets me every time: Asian tour groups snapping pictures; backpackers munching on gyro sandwiches; elegant couples arm in arm; and elderly troupes with matching visors off cruise ships. Witness the quarter in the evening, and you're in some strange other world on steroids. I tell Joe I feel like *It's a Wonderful Life*'s George Bailey, stumbling into the sleazy, neon realm of Pottersville.

We leave the conventional world of Amsterdam, cross the street, and enter the tenderloin, intellectually aware of what we're going to see—prostitutes in windows under dim red lights—but to actually witness the women on display, like mannequins, electronics, or zoo animals, is a different story. I want to avoid looking but can't help myself—it's like watching an accident about to happen: I'm unable to turn away. So many of the women look bored, are busy texting or chewing gum, and others catch men's eyes and then tap on the window. It's unnerving, depressing, and downright bizarre.

TIPTOE THROUGH THE TULIPS

We make one essential stop before we head south for our return to the City of Light, our reunion with Chris and Caroline, and the long-awaited marathon. As a student in France in 1979, I visited Holland's Keukenhof (kitchen garden) just outside the town of Lisse. It's the largest bulb-flower park in the world, and I promised myself then that I would return one day with Joe.

Flowers make me happy. I like planting them, nurturing them (I inherited my dad's penchant for gardening, or maybe I just relish my memories of the hours I spent puttering around the yard with him as a child), and being around them. I take the expression "stop and smell the roses" not just as a metaphorical suggestion to slow down but as literal counsel to sniff and touch blossoms whenever possible. And thus we head to Keukenhof, in my opinion one of the most captivating places on Earth, with its rich palette of tulips and jonquils, daffodils and hyacinths, in full spring splendor. The garden features more than seven million hand-planted bulbs that burst into a kaleidoscope of color from March to May. Memory can magnify, but such is not the case with my recollections of these gardens I first experienced over thirty years ago.

The gently rolling, perfumed landscape blanketed in swirling patterns of flowery color is as appealing as I remember. Towering beech trees filter the sunlight, and fruit trees lining the footpaths around ponds yield fragile pink blossoms that offset the swaths of ground-level brilliance. After a three-hour visit, Joe agrees that yes, Keukenhof is indeed a charming sanctuary, and though he'll never be able to distinguish a narcissus from a rose, he now believes that flowers can indeed make one smile.

X. The Paris Marathon
April 2012

APRIL IN PARIS

MY HEART FLUTTERS as if I'm about to meet a lover when our train from Amsterdam pulls into Paris. It's 10:00 p.m., so all we see are the twinkling lights of the city until our car slips under the massive triangular entry fanlight of the Gare du Nord and into the station itself. I've come to Paris countless times by plane and train, but this arrival is different. Maybe it's knowing that Chris and Caroline will soon join us, that the marathon is imminent, or that we've completed a circle around Europe with stops in so many unfamiliar places—whatever the case, coming back to Paris is like a warm embrace. As we disembark under the paned-glass ceiling characteristic of so many French rail stations and hear the familiar three-tone arrival chime and the announcement *"Le train en provenance d'Amsterdam est arrivé sur la voie huit,"* my heart is aflutter, my palms sweaty, and my face flushed. I actually tremble as we make our way, luggage in tow, toward the metro escalator. *My beloved awaits me,* I think, as I look over at Joe and he winks.

We have thirty-three hours in Paris before the kids arrive, to settle in, recharge our Passes Navigo, and stock the fridge of our rental apartment with eggs and ham for Chris; yogurts, cereal, and nuts for Caroline; and wine and cheese for us all. Joe and I are able to live very frugally when it's just the two of us, but add our children to the mix, and it's remarkable how quickly we hemorrhage money. "Let the spending begin," I declare to him. "The kids will soon be here!"

The minute we see them stride around the arrivals corner at Charles de Gaulle, we're a family again and ready for celebration. Caroline rushes at her dad with a huge bear hug, and Chris picks me up and spins around. "Maman, we're back!" he cries, as I giggle at his antics. Caroline won't let go of Joe as he gives in to the emotion of the moment.

We treat them to the rewards of restaurants that became our haunts last fall: the *steak-frites* bistro near Porte Maillot, Hemingway's La Rotonde café in Montparnasse, our favorite candlelit restaurant on the *Île* Saint-Louis, and the falafel joint on the rue des Rosiers. Chris and Caroline are as content as we are to plan our itinerary around food.

The Paris lilacs are in full bloom. From intense purple to pale lavender and white, with surprise blossoms of deep mauve mixed in, they radiate maximum fragrance and make the city more gorgeous than ever, especially in the gardens around the Eiffel Tower. My mom would have loved it—lilacs were her favorite.

We quickly morph from being Marianne and Joe, lone American travelers, to a critical mass of Americans over the course of a few days. We arrive on Tuesday, the kids join us on Thursday, our nephew studying in England for the semester arrives on Saturday morning, and four friends from the States, including my former colleague Neil, who will be my race sherpa, meet us for a premarathon, carbo-loading dinner Saturday night. Nine boisterous Americans raise the decibel level at the bistro more than a bit that evening. It's April in Paris at its best, and the time to run is here.

RACE DAY

While Joe has long enjoyed running and has two marathons under his belt, I've never thought of myself as a runner. I did several half marathons in the year before we left, with no training at all, just to see if I could, and my times and race-wrecked body confirmed my lack of preparation. But I agreed to sign up for the marathon, believing that training would ward off extra pounds as we ate our way through Europe, and until last month, the plan held firm.

While the children sleep off jet lag, we collect our race packets at the Porte de Versailles expo center, but I feel like a fraud. Here I am, with my official number and royal blue Paris Marathon tote, knowing full well I'll never finish. I haven't run in almost a month, in an attempt to heal my sore hip, and I know if my bursitis flares I won't make it even close to 26.2 miles. But my gloom temporarily evaporates as we ride the metro back to our apartment and Joe points to a passage of the English version of the race pamphlet. It smartly recommends that we "make good sleep, eat a healthful breakfast, and then bandage [our] tits to prevent chafing on race day." Joe and I can't stop laughing all the way home.

Rather than start the race cold turkey, I test my beleaguered joint with a short three miles with Caroline around the Champs de Mars and along the Seine. The excruciating pain I felt in Vienna seems to have evaporated, and I'm amazed that the jog yields not a hint of pain. I consider the possibility that maybe, just maybe, I'll be okay.

Our race-day alarm sounds at 6:00 a.m. sharp. The skies are overcast with threatening clouds, and the temperature is in the upper thirties, forecast to rise into the forties by midday. Except for the wind, which kicks up strong gusts, it's textbook marathon weather. We organized our gear the night before, safety-pinned our race numbers to our shirts, and set our GPS running watches. We take hot showers and then don multiple layers, including "throwaway clothes" that will warm us as we wait for the race to begin. Joe looks the part of the quintessential runner in his standard race attire—black compression shorts, red singlet, and white long-sleeved jersey—and his lucky visor. I, on the other hand, much more concerned about warding off the cold than about how I look, am a marathon ringer if ever there was one. My layers include black shorts, a black long-sleeved running shirt, a turquoise short-sleeved shirt, and a light blue fleece. On my head is the Paris Marathon do-rag for keeping hair out of my face. But the pièce de résistance is my disposable layer: baby-blue flannel pajamas I manage to pull on over everything else and will jettison once the starting gun sounds. My pj's have served their cold-weather purpose on our trip, and I'll no longer need them once we head south, so why not use them for one final, practical reason? I'm about to attempt a marathon, I figure, so I can wear whatever I want.

"You're my Arctic warrior—Nanook of the North," Joe says, laughing out loud at my getup.

"All I care about is that I'm warm," I reply.

We shroud ourselves in the plastic Paris Marathon sheaths from our race bags, kiss the kids goodbye, confirm the mile markers where we'll look for them, and head out the door looking like a couple of Parisian bag people. We reach the Motte-Picquet metro stop on the Boulevard de Grenelle, the train arrives, and we're whisked off to the base of the Arc de Triomphe along with tens of thousands of other runners.

The usually grand Avenue Foch is covered with plastic portable pissoirs that Joe immediately takes advantage of, lining up cheek to cheek (so to speak) with all the other gentlemen. We're thrilled to do what we could never attempt otherwise: we walk across the normally car-congested Place de l'Étoile to the Arc de Triomphe and then down the middle of the Champs-Élysées. It's 8:30 a.m., and we have fifteen minutes before the gun goes off, signaling thirty-two thousand people to run the streets of Paris. I'm shaking from the cold and considerable nerves. *What am I doing?* I ask myself, as fear of failure threatens to consume me. *Are you really attempting a marathon? You're not a runner and have a hip that could give out at any minute.*

I survey the crowd and reflect on the fact that every competitor has a reason for being there. While hopping from one foot to the other to stay warm, I meet Linda from Colorado, who has the noblest of reasons for running. She and her French husband, an air force major, naturalized American citizen, and recipient of both a Bronze Star and a Purple Heart, planned to run the marathon together when he was on leave. But their plans evaporated instantly when he was killed in Afghanistan last spring. "I'm running for us both," she shares, as Joe and I well up. We hug her and bid her *bonne chance.*

Hearing Linda's story makes my anxiety evaporate, and I embrace what I'm about to begin. My children are here cheering us on, we're together in Paris, and I'm going to savor the experience.

I shed my security blanket of protective pajamas as the starting gun sounds, and we inch up to the starting line as successive corrals of runners are released. We step over piles of discarded clothing, food wrappers, trash bags, and water bottles filled with urine. Just before the arc of blue and white balloons at the race start and next to the announcer's platform, the final opportunity for nature's call overpowers personal reticence. Men peeing on the Champs-Élysées is expected, but women joining them is a surprise. One brave woman scoots up to a plastic barrier, squats, and lets it go. She breaks the ice, because five more lily-white derrieres immediately huddle around the divider. It's just the scene we need to release any remaining tension. Joe kisses me goodbye, and we wish each other *bon courage* and start our run through Paris.

I feel like a million bucks as I jog the gentle slope of the Champs-Élysées, through the Place de la Concorde, and along the rue de Rivoli, the Tuileries on my right. The gardens soon give way to the Louvre, Châtelet, Hôtel de Ville, and Marais. All nerves have vanished; my hip is happy, and I'm in the zone, taking in the sights. Just before the Place de la Bastille is the three-mile mark, where marathon veteran Neil will join me for moral support. Right at mile three, there he is, with fresh legs and enough enthusiasm to keep me and all those around me going. I then spot the kids, trade hugs with them on the sidelines, and with renewed energy continue east toward the Bois de Vincennes.

I've always run alone. I set and adjust my pace according to how I feel, never wanting to hold others back. But having Neil at my side as my very own cheering squad is a godsend. We agree that he'll stay with me for six miles or so, in deference to my lone-runner mindset, and I'll take advantage of his selfless support for as long as I can. He grabs water bottles for me, tears off banana chunks when I need them, and encourages me with every step. We make it through the 6.5-mile stretch in the Vincennes park on the eastern flank of Paris, convenient for stopping to lighten my bladder's load au naturel.

For several miles I can speak while running, and I tell Neil about the monuments and neighborhoods we pass en route. We head back into the heart of the city and approach the critical halfway mark—an important psychological threshold, since I was convinced that by now my hip would be screaming and I'd be calling it quits. But the pain never materializes, so my troubled joint and I just keep going. My hip is fine, my legs are fine, and my lungs are holding their own, although suddenly I'm very quiet. Speaking is beyond me, so I leave that to my sherpa, who does his best to pump me up as I do my best to listen.

We continue along the Seine, and I'm able to smile and enjoy the sights: Notre Dame, la Conciergerie, and then the river side of the Louvre—some of the most beautiful architecture in Paris. By this time there's no question I need Neil for the long haul, and he agrees to stick with me to go the distance.

Mile fifteen rolls around, and I'm indulging in frequent walking breaks (many more than my training plan to run nine minutes, walk one dictates), but the kids reappear at mile sixteen with shouts of "Go, Maman!" I desperately need the encouragement and emotional lift their enthusiastic faces provide.

Soon thereafter, we're in the eerily quiet obscurity of a tunnel along the river, the one in which Princess

Diana was killed, and emerge to see the Tour Eiffel on our left—a stunning sight on any day but particularly inspiring for those at mile seventeen of a marathon. At this point I learn that sharing the name of the French Republic's symbol has advantages. The generally subdued spectators holler in response to the name printed on my race bib: "Marianne, bravo, Marianne—*vous êtes l'esprit de France!*" combined with "*Allez, allez!*"

Entering the Bois de Boulogne on the western edge of Paris is a blur, my leg muscles burning with fatigue. As I start focusing on kilometers, rather than miles, since they tick away so quickly, a silent whine inside grows to a dissonant keen, and I desperately want to scream, but it's all I can do to concentrate on putting one foot in front of the other, mostly at a race-walking pace, with occasional spurts of one-hundred-yard jogs. I repeat over and over what I heard Joe declare this morning, "Once you're in the Bois, babe, you're basically home-free."

We finally emerge from the interminable woods, and I do my best to pick up my pace. If I'm going to complete a marathon, I'm going to do it in style, I resolve. As we negotiate the cobblestone corner onto the Avenue Foch, a race official yanks Neil off the course, since he isn't wearing a number, and I'm running the last leg alone.

In any race anywhere, the finish line is beauty to behold. But the end of the Paris Marathon, the Arc de Triomphe looming in the distance, has to be the most stunning finale in the world. I dig deep to force my broken, now-trembling body to continue functioning just a bit longer. I've been running on empty for miles now and fix my stare on the dramatic sight at the end of the boulevard. The tears start to flow as reality hits me: I'm about to finish the marathon. I give it my all for the last many yards and cross the line at 5:44.

I'm in a dreamlike state of physical exhaustion. *Have I actually run the Paris Marathon?* I ask myself. I started the day convinced I would not complete the race, but here I am at the Arc de Triomphe after 26.2 miles. I lean over, hands on my knees, catch my breath, and savor the moment. Maybe I'm more of a runner than I thought.

Shaking uncontrollably from exertion and emotion, I pull the canary-yellow tee and insulating poncho provided to all finishers over my head. I grab some waters and energy drinks and head toward the exit to meet Neil. As my loyal sidekick and I make the two-block walk (totter, in my case) to our appointed meeting place on the Avenue de la Grande Armée, I tell him it's my "one and done" marathon.

Chuckling, he responds, "You've actually done two—your first *and* your last!"

"You're right about that," I affirm. "Right now, I'd rather go through labor again than run another twenty-six miles."

We enter the party atmosphere at the brasserie where our gang is waiting. For the second time in twenty minutes, I'm overcome with emotion as Joe, Chris, and Caroline jump up to greet me. I'm astounded when the rest of the diners spontaneously applaud, and I manage to give the crowd a *merci* curtsy. I'm pleased with my own effort but am also so proud of Joe, who ran a personal best of 4:15. "You're my hero," I whisper to my handsome husband.

"And you're pretty awesome yourself," Joe whispers back.

We share a sweaty hug and take a long time to let go. We split a generous serving of creamy steak tartare and salty *frites* as Joe sips his frosty beer and I a glass of ice-cold Sancerre. I sit back, relax, and beam at my husband, children, and friends after a day that ends nothing like I anticipated. I've become a marathoner, and I did it in Paris.

RACE-DAY AFTERMATH

Joe and I do the "marathon shuffle" for days postrace. We limp our way through Paris but consider our sorry gait a badge of honor nonetheless. I grasp railings for dear life whenever I can to take weight off my tender thighs. We soldier up the incline to Montmartre because the kids want to visit, but the attendant steep descent wreaks havoc on our quads. I was prepared for postmarathon pain, but I wasn't ready for it to last so long.

After three days of hobbling through Paris, the four of us escape. We need a good, long rest and can't imagine a better place to recuperate than the whitewashed Greek Isles. Lying in the sun, eating Greek salads and *saganaki*, is our simple plan for recovery. Mykonos, we are yours.

XI. The Greek Isles
April–May 2012

FROM URBAN UTOPIA TO ISLAND PARADISE

OUR WEEK IN PARIS was hectic, peppered with the arrivals of our loved ones. But now that we're in the land of *tzatsiki* and the sea, we embrace a different pace: we're very busy relaxing. We went from urban utopia to island paradise in a matter of hours, and the temperature jumped fifteen degrees.

We arrive at Mykonos's tiny airport, and I'm transported back to 1979, the first time Joe and I set foot on the island from the ferry. It was my initial taste of the Aegean, and through the cool sea breezes, Mykonos exuded the warmth and charm for which the Greek Isles are known. Its beauty captured my imagination at first sight with its particular palette of red, white, and blue: brilliant white buildings offset by shutters and furnishings in shiny royal-blue enamel and abundant arbors of magenta bougainvillea. The Myconian tricolor decor hasn't changed in thirty-three years, and we're pleasantly surprised to discover that neither has the town. Mykonos has remained the same, save the addition of an ugly concrete parking lot on reclaimed land just beyond the harbor.

One other difference is that the parade of pastel Vespas is now a fleet of four-wheeled ATVs. A few of the classic motorbikes continue to zip around the island, but the sturdier vehicles, decidedly safer and the cause of many fewer tourist mishaps, reign supreme. We rent two of the rugged four-wheelers and, two of us on each, explore as much of the hilly island as we have time for. We show the children the rustic, vine-covered guesthouse Joe and I stayed in as backpackers for $10 a night, still in business but not yet open for the season. We drive to several out-of-the-way corners, including the famous party sands of Paradise and Super Paradise beaches. Both are deserted, since it's late April, and while all is calm, there are signs that opening is imminent. While we eat our Greek salads on the taverna terrace at Paradise, workers hang supersized speakers from the rafters, polish seaside dance floors, paint myriad barstools, and varnish the undulating bar. Quiet, unassuming Mykonos becomes a party island in June and an around-the-clock, pulsing bacchanal in July and August. But in spring it's a tranquil, picturesque fishing haven with just enough people-watching, including streams of transient day-trippers off cruise ships anchored offshore, to make it interesting.

Just outside our airy room for four in our harbor-front hotel is the enchanting smell of jasmine from the profusion of perfumed yellow flowers bursting from bushes ringing the patio. From the hotel's wraparound portico, we see the hill behind the port, lined by windmills the Venetians built in the sixteenth century. I never tire of looking at Mykonos's trademark row of white cylindrical structures with pointed, straw-capped roofs and graceful wooden spokes. Caroline and I indulge in mani-pedis, our favorite personal pampering treat and one I haven't enjoyed since we left home, at a just-opened-for-the-season salon tucked down one of the town's lanes. The cherry on top of the treat is experiencing it with my daughter—a shared pleasure that leads to slipping into sandals and exposing our now-pretty toes to the Greek sunshine.

Our days on Mykonos are so different from those in Paris, but despite their differences, these are two of my favorite places in the world. I can't believe I'm lucky enough to share them back-to-back with the three people I love most.

NAXOS—ANOTHER GOODBYE

Greece is a maritime country, and its freeway of choice is the sea. We leave Mykonos for Naxos, sailing the immensity of its "wine dark" waters like Odysseus, taking in the journey with all senses alert. The ferry we board is in a totally different category from the rusty, creaky buckets of bolts we experienced in the '70s. It's brand-spanking-new, with the leather seats and lounge areas of a modern cruise ship and a smooth, fast ride that has us to Naxos in two hours, including a stop on Paros. We first glimpse the island's signature symbol, the Portara, a twenty-foot-tall marble doorway to the temple of Dionysus (or Apollo, depending on the guidebook), which sits on a hill beside Naxos Town. It's a vigilant, magic picture frame whose one side watches over the arc of the busy harbor while the other gazes out to sea. With minimal trappings of a typical tourist destination, save the dozens of inviting tavernas along the waterfront, Naxos is an island on which to experience simple, daily Greek life.

We meet all who work at and live in our sweet little blue-shuttered, family-run hotel a block from the beach and a ten-minute walk to the port. The exact relationships are never fully clear, but they all revolve around three-year-old, curly-haired Georgios, oblivious to guests as he plays with his trucks in the lobby. The various players check us in, serve us breakfast, and clean our room, and we feel more like houseguests than patrons. We become part of the clan over the course of our stay, as we smell what they cook for lunch, overhear their conversations, and share the comfy sectional in front of the big-screen TV. The hotel interiors are covered in shiny white Naxian marble from quarries nearby, which we later drive through on a trip to the rocky north shore. We have lunch by the bay in the sleepy fishing village of Apollon on the island's tip. After a full week in Greece, we're in the swing of saying *kalimera* to those we greet during the day, *kalispera* in the evening, and *kalinihta* at night, and offer quick *yassous* to those we pass on the street. Greece is indeed feeling like home.

What we cherish most about our four days on Naxos is unscheduled relaxation with our children. We have plenty of time to discuss our favorite subjects (books, movies, history, and future travel) and spend hours reclining on the beach and by the pool, reading, resting, and soaking up the sun. We eat outdoors, watch exquisite sunsets, behold clear, starry nights, and sleep late. I have alone time with each of the children—a several-mile hike along the beach with Chris and a couple of runs and shopping with Caroline. We wander the old town along the bougainvillea-strewn streets and shaded passageways spanned by thick archways that lead up to and around the Venetian castle. We then head back down via stairs dotted with pots of deep-red geraniums.

At one point, I'm arm in arm with Chris, Caroline holds my other hand, and Joe snaps a picture, freezing the image and making time stand still, as I so wish I could. Chris has long towered over me, and Caroline can now look down on me as well. As we stroll along the harbor, deciding in which of the string of tavernas to have dinner, they rub my back, pat my head, and call me Little Maman, their most apt nickname for me. When did I suddenly become so tiny in between my now-adult children?

While we meet neither Cyclops nor Hydra on Naxos (and Joe and Chris lament that we encounter no nymphs), we do face the trial of having to once again say goodbye to our progeny. Having children opens your heart to joys aplenty but also exposes you to the possibility of very real pain. There's the deep ache you feel when they hurt, especially when it's of the emotional kind; the difficulty of letting them make their own decisions and the inevitable mistakes along the way; and the realization one day that your babies are gone and standing before you are a young man and young woman with lives of their own. While letting them go is the ultimate goal of successful parenting, it's never easy to do so or to fill the chasm that remains when they finally leave home for good.

Knowing Chris and Caroline will make the trip home side by side helps lessen the loss just a bit. Worrying about your children never ends, no matter what their age, and we feel the familiar anxiety as we hug and kiss them multiple times before finally letting go at the single Naxos gate. They board the prop plane together and are whisked off to Athens for their flight home. There we stand, choking back tears, peering through the chain-link fence, waving at the plane as it takes off, as if they can actually see us.

The initial minutes after a goodbye are acutely painful, but bit by bit the sting of separation subsides.

We make a hasty retreat from "family Naxos" to embrace "couple's Santorini"—a worthy distraction if ever there was one—to assuage the sharp, short-term sadness of missing our kids so deeply.

SUNSET CAPITAL OF THE WORLD

Ancient Thira, or Santorini (Latin for "Saint Irene"), as it's now known, is a haunting island unlike no other. What remains of the dark, volcanic caldera encircles a deep cobalt lagoon, and dark chunks of the original island, in the center of which is the still-smoldering volcano, mark the arc of the circumference. Fira, Santorini's main town, spills dramatically down sheer, west-facing cliffs like a whitewashed stream, as if the gods poured it over the precipice and it dripped all the way to the sea. Donkeys ploddingly shuttle tourists from cruise ships up and down the zigzagging trail to town alongside a chair lift, which makes the trip in a fraction of the time. On the eastern side of the volcanic rim, the island slopes down, steeply at first and then gently, to a fertile seaside plain dotted with farms and vineyards, and ends in a black pebbly beach. This southernmost jewel of the Cyclades is a breathtaking, otherworldly vision in the Aegean, and the approach to the island by ferry is priceless.

We opt for a simple white-and-blue budget hotel on the sloping side of the rim, with a pristine, sparkling pool. Ever-so-kind twenty-year-old Katarina, who makes our stay most enjoyable, efficiently manages the family-owned property with aplomb. We make the vertical, couple-block trek up to the caldera each evening past hoteliers in the process of preparing for the season, filling pools, varnishing furniture, and trimming dried palm fronds.

Santorini is renowned for its sunsets. The twilight descent of the fireball of a sun into the sea is theater without rival. While Mykonos and Naxos, just miles away, are under the very same sun in the very same sky, their end-of-day canvas doesn't come close to the red-and-orange fire-and-ember show taking place every evening on Santorini. We have cocktails and dinner looking over the caldera most nights, an amazingly dreamy location to spend the final hours of the day. During one dinner, a tanned, flirty waiter speaks to me, as he does all other female diners, his hand on my shoulder and a twinkle in his eye. I tell Joe he reminds me of one of my favorite actors in his prime, and my clever dining companion promptly dubs him Richard Gyros (pronounced "Gere-os"). We're surrounded by young couples but, despite having thirty-plus years of marriage under our belts, feel right at home with the honeymooners.

I'm going to turn into a Greek salad if I'm not careful. I find it difficult to resist the mix of deep red, juicy tomatoes, crisp white cucumbers, shaved pink onions, and plump, vinegary capers topped by a generous slab of soft feta cheese. My daily diet includes at least one of these healthy concoctions a day since we arrived in Greece, and on some days, I even have one for lunch and another with dinner. I never tire of the fresh ingredients glistening with splashes of olive oil and vinegar.

We've eaten so much good food in Greece, and while we continue to order our old favorites regularly—*saganaki* (pan-seared cheese), *moussaka* (Greek lasagna made with eggplant), *tzatsiki* (garlicky yogurt with grated cucumber and herbs), *dolmades* (grape-vine leaves stuffed with moist rice), and *spanakopita* (spinach pie)—we've branched out a bit and tried *stifado* (rich, tomatoey stew with beef and pearl onions), grilled squid, fried *bakaliaro* (salt cod), and Santorinian specialties fava bean spread and cherry tomato croquettes. It's easy to patronize local family restaurants on the Greek Isles, since most eating establishments are just that. And if you peek in the kitchen, you're likely to find the *yiayia* (grandmother) dressed all in black, stirring the pot.

What was a rind of a moon when we arrived on Mykonos has waxed into a brilliant orb on Santorini. We believe this gift of nature to be yet another Greek Isles miracle, but later learn we're benefiting from a bigger, brighter "supermoon," the result of its closest encounter with Earth in many years. Being on this magical island is always an experience to cherish, but add unrivaled sunsets, an extraordinary full moon, my devoted husband, and Richard Gyros to the mix, and it's a recipe for perfection.

A DELAYED DEPARTURE

As so often happens when Greek island hopping, the ferry we hope will take us to Rhodes, our next stop, is not departing when we plan to leave. Lengthening our stay on Santorini is in no way a hardship, so we adjust our plans to catch the next ship to Rhodes. An incredible eleventh-hour Internet deal of 99 euros, including breakfast, drops us at the door of the Relais & Châteaux property, the Zannos Melathron Hotel, near the highest point on Santorini. It's the type of place that responds with a wink, when we ask when breakfast is served: "We start at eight a.m. and serve until the last guest has eaten." From the moment we arrive at the base of the pedestrian-only hilltop village of Pyrgos until we reluctantly leave forty-eight hours later, we're treated like VIPs. We're met by bellman Misha and his trusty assistant Irina the donkey, who carries our luggage and leads us up the steep hill.

Hotel manager Alexander greets us in the courtyard with warm enthusiasm and shares his intimate understanding of the property's history as he gives us a tour. A wealthy merchant built the house for his daughter as a wedding gift and soon erected another for himself just below the main building's terrace. Maître d' George presents us with flutes of bubbling champagne as we settle in. We have a delicious dinner of time-honored Greek recipes prepared with modern twists while watching yet another Santorini sunset from new heights and a fresh angle. George, an expert on the cuisine, as well as on the wines of the island, answers all our questions and educates us about all things Greek.

Thick, creamy Greek yogurt with swirls of honey and slices of fresh fruit is our healthy breakfast. And when we unwind in the breezy hotel lobby, the staff makes sure we have glasses of cold water in front of us, so very important on this dry, sunny island.

I could go on about Pyrgos, the stunning views from the hotel's many terraces, and the cool tranquility of the stone-walled accommodations, but what makes Zannos Melathron a special oasis is the sincere kindheartedness of its staff. We're steadfast Relais & Châteaux property fans and have stayed at dozens over the years. They all specialize in warm welcomes, but the hotel we find on Santorini raises the bar for friendliness and service, and we'll never forget how comfortable they made us feel.

Greek kindness is without equal. The people we've met have been passionate yet gentle, optimistic in the face of difficulty, and helpful in every way. We can count on two fingers the individuals who are not up to par with their fellow Greeks on the hospitality scale, and even those folks were hardly rude—just a bit bored, perhaps. Without fail, at the end of every meal we've been given a little something extra: a shot of ouzo, a coffee liqueur shooter topped with whipped cream, a dish of pudding, or a honey-drenched dessert. At one little place on Naxos, we were even presented with a frosty carafe brimming with wine—on the house!

But the ultimate act of customer service comes after we leave Zannos Melathron to face the reality of a 1:30 a.m. ferry to Rhodes—the only time it makes the trip from Santorini. I've never functioned well without adequate rest, and I don't relish the idea of staying up well past midnight to catch a ship. If we didn't have a berth waiting for us onboard, I never would make it.

The island's port is remote—several miles from Fira at the end of a treacherous road that winds down a cliff to the edge of the bay. We head to the harbor by 8:30 p.m. with plenty of time for a leisurely dinner at a seaside taverna. By the time the ship arrives, we'll be ready to pass out for the overnight journey. Our taxi drops us off, however, to a cruel surprise: not a single taverna along the row of a dozen has its lights on. Little did we know, our late ferry will be the next to arrive, so all commercial ventures are closed and won't open until 11:00 p.m. Hanging out for hours at a dark, deserted port with empty bellies is not part of our plan. But luck is with us, as it always seems to be in Greece, and we meet Tonis.

How forlorn we must look, lurking in the shadows, sitting on our duffels. An industrious young man in his twenties with a smiling, open face recognizes our predicament. He and several friends are having dinner in front of a taverna, but he jumps up quickly and greets us: "I'm Tonis. Can I help?" We explain our situation, and he tells us, "No problem, I'll open my restaurant for you." Tonis turns on the lights, puts us at a large table in the corner of the terrace where we can spread out with computers and books, and makes us feel at home. He brings us complimentary sausages, olives, and peanuts and then serves us Greek salads, tomato croquettes, and fava bean puree. He periodically leaves his friends to check on us, bring us a fresh carafe of wine, and chat about the failing Greek economy and the country's complicated politics.

Hours later, the port comes to life as taxis, buses, and scooters deliver ferry passengers, and we've now heard Tonis's life story. The taverna's owner, his stepfather, is a difficult taskmaster, and Tonis is saving money to open his own place one day. We pack our things to join the line in the terminal hut, and Tonis offers final gifts: generous shots of scotch and ouzo. How can we refuse such generosity? We share heartfelt hugs and farewells with our new friend, filled with renewed conviction that Greek people are the most magnanimous in the world. It's not a coincidence that the Greek word *xenos* means "foreigner" *and* "guest." To be a foreigner in Greece is to be an honored guest, rewarded with warm, collegial hospitality.

Our ride to Rhodes arrives an hour late, and I can barely see straight from fatigue and Tonis's libations. While we anxiously watch the boat back up to the concrete quay, visions of the awaiting bunk bed dancing in our foggy heads, the strains of a Greek folk song sung by a young man echo melodically in the waiting room chamber. It's two thirty in the morning as we head up the ship's steel ramp. We've loved our first three weeks in Greece and look forward to three more. If we have other delayed departures, it won't be a problem.

ISLOMANIA

What is it about islands?

British writer Lawrence Durrell used the term "islomania" in his memoir *Reflections on a Marine Venus*, about the time he spent on Rhodes after World War II. He wrote of an obsession with islands, an inexplicable enthusiasm for these chunks of land detached from the rest of the world. Since as far back as Plato's story of Atlantis, written 2,500 years ago, the allure of islands has endured as a human passion and captor of our imaginations. I once knew a man, a fellow travel-book-club member, with a manic attraction to islands. It led him to limit his travel to islands whenever he needed to get away. Durrell was also a confirmed islomane who, at every opportunity, fled to one of the many paradises in the Mediterranean. The fantasy of the island as tranquil retreat for harried, frantic souls has long been around, and it may be that the idea is as appealing as the reality. Yet there's no denying the deep physical response that emerges as the shadow on the horizon first comes into view, particularly in the half-light of dawn. What at first is indistinct soon clarifies into the detailed silhouette of a place filled with possibility, a source of fascination, inspiration, and delight. There's something about islands that taps a fundamental desire for tranquility, for space, and for solitude in a world where such are rare commodities indeed.

Am I an islomane? Without question, when it comes to the islands of Greece.

WE CAN SEE TURKEY FROM OUR BACKYARD

We land in the Dodecanese, very different islands from the whitewashed Cyclades behind us. I innocently point across the water and ask a ferry official, "Which island is that?"

"That's no island," he replies, "that's Turkey. Why, do you like this place?"

"Should we?" Joe wisely retorts.

It's not prudent when in Greece to show even passing interest in "that place" across the way, so we keep our plans for visiting to ourselves. We see Turkey's mountains in the not-far distance and soon discover that Rhodes has a visible armed military presence keeping watch across the sea. There's palpable angst among Greeks that their country's long-established adversary is in their backyard.

Temperatures have increased as we've island-hopped south. It was in the midsixties on Mykonos and the low seventies on Naxos and Santorini, and now that we're on Rhodes, it's well into the eighties. The dismal gray skies and biting winds of Berlin and Amsterdam a month ago are distant memories. After several weeks in the intense Greek sun, our hair has bleached and we've turned "brown as betel nuts," as Joe likes to say. The red-toned tan of my Mexican ancestors is evident, and even Joe, whose Irish skin is not fond of the sun, has bronzed.

When things heat up, people shed clothing. And while underdressed, overexposed tourists can sometimes make appealing attractions, on Rhodes it's an unwelcome interruption of local color. Rarely have we seen seriously overweight people in Europe, but we quickly learn that the United States does not have a monopoly on obesity; I believe our fellow citizens have met their corpulent match. There are incredible numbers of central European and Russian visitors off mammoth cruise ships anchored just past where the Colossus of Rhodes once stood in the harbor, scantily clad, exposing too much. All through the winding streets of the town's brimming-with-history walled city, we watch sun-crisped tourists, their lily-white skin singed with painful-to-look-at, severe pink burns. The bellies of shirtless men hang over and hide their belts, and women in halter tops sport rolls of midriff and maximum cleavage. Joe and I are waifs by comparison. "I think we may be the only fully clothed couple in town," I remark to him.

The hordes of international tourists are an ongoing distraction, and we note similar refrains: couples in their sixties in yellow and orange plastic Crocs; thickset couples in identical plaid shirts, mismatched print shorts, and sensible leather sandals; beefy women with substantial calves in too-short skirts, embroidered peasant blouses, and hiking sandals; scores of burly, bloated tourists glistening like seals under layers of oil on striped lounge chairs on pebbly beaches.

I'm sure there are other Americans on Rhodes, but we cross paths with not a one. In fact, Nikos, the young man from whom we rent a car, shares that we are the "first people from America" with whom he's ever done business.

We drive away from the cruise ship crowds, up and down the rugged, rocky terrain of Rhodes and into cool mountain air, to visit the island's three acropolises: one above Rhodes Town, another looking over the province of Kameiros, and the final and most famous, Lindos. All are on hilltops, but that of Lindos is the most dramatic: a natural citadel perched above the sea on a promontory of solid rock. From the heights is a spectacular view of the clear blue waters of tiny Saint Paul's Bay, where the apostle temporarily cast anchor on his voyage to Ephesus in Turkey.

Back in Rhodes Town, we visit the archeological museum. Even Joe, not a fan of such displays, is won over by the treasures housed in the medieval building. The intricate mosaic floors, black- and red-figure pottery, and graceful statues from classical, Hellenistic, and Roman times are stunning, as is the rose- and oleander-filled garden that graces the museum's courtyard.

A DAILY DETAIL HIATUS

We're feeling rather *fatigué* from incessant daily decision making and have decided that for an interlude of ten days, we'll give up control and hand the reins to others.

Absolute spontaneity while traveling is possible only when you never have to go home. And while our time is not endless and the end of our year is starting to come into view, we've had plenty of time to play with our itinerary, change course, and take serendipitous detours. We'll soon take the overnight ferry to Piraeus, the port of Athens, where we'll board a ship for a ten-day cruise.

The decision to set sail was simple. After leaving the Greek Isles, we hoped to make our way around the Peloponnese peninsula and up the eastern coast of the Adriatic to Croatia. But despite hours of scouring guides, poring over Internet sites, and dissecting travel blogs, we saw only two starkly different options: negotiate the logistical nightmare of a complicated train, bus, and car combo (no ferries service that part of the world) or hop aboard a cruise ship. We stumbled upon the 350-passenger ship *Aegean Odyssey* in our research, and it was love at first sight. The itinerary includes the places we want to see, as well as daily excursions with expert guides to the ancient sights, and onboard professors give lectures on relevant history, art, and architecture. Once we're quoted last-minute discounted fares for the cheapest cabin (Joe looks at the deck plan and determines it's a "quiet" space right next to where they drop the anchors), we commit. We'll likely be among the youngest on board, but that'll be nice for a change, since we're often the seniors in a sea of youthful backpackers. We're so looking forward to a hiatus from sweating daily details and are ready to relinquish control. For now.

XII. A Voyage to Antiquity
May 2012

ALL ABOARD

I'VE BEEN MARRIED TO A MARINE ENGINEER for over thirty years. When Joe talks about "going up ladders," I know he means climbing stairs, when he says, "starboard to," I understand the right side of our vehicle will be along the curb, and if he suggests there's "something interesting portside," I turn my head to the left. And I've often heard myself say in times of need, "I really have to go to the head."

Joe has worked with ships since he graduated from the US Merchant Marine Academy in 1978, but I never realized the depth of his love for these "engineering marvels," as he calls them, until we landed in the Greek Isles. The scores of photos he takes of cruise ships, ferries, tankers, and containers (but only rarely of the sleek sailboats, colorful dinghies, or working fishing boats) in seafaring Greece and the tender way he refers to a floating hulk as "she," smiling in admiration at "her graceful lines," attests to his lifelong fascination. He knows firsthand the complicated calculations that go into keeping these colossi afloat. We've jumped on and off ferries every few days over the course of our weeks in Greece. But now that we've boarded one of the hallowed white cruise vessels for ten days, I know we made the right decision. There's nothing that warms my heart more than seeing Joe transformed into a joyful little boy, happy in his surroundings and itching to find the engine room. It's a busman's holiday for a marine engineer and Joe is in ship heaven.

God is in the details, and on the *Aegean Odyssey*, one of the gods is Bacchus, since quality wines are served with dinner, included in our fares. Every evening after we shower off the dust of the day's archeological sites, we don our best for dinner. "You're my Bubba Gump of the black dress," Joe observes, referring to the *Forrest Gump* character's recitation of all the ways in which shrimp can be prepared. Similarly, I do my best to come up with new combinations of the same handful of clothing: my long black dress with or without a black belt, or with a gold pashmina, a purple scarf, a long black sweater, or a short white one; my short black dress with black flats, strappy sandals, a white belt, a brown belt, or a silky black tee on top. I exhaust every combo possible and wonder if anyone other than Joe notices my minimalist wardrobe.

The cruise company is Voyages to Antiquity, and we harbored a fear before boarding that it might be more appropriately called Voyages *of* Antiquity. While we're definitely on the younger side of the demographic (we're told the average passenger's age is sixty-eight), there are several couples who are our juniors, and most of the older crowd is young at heart. We meet fellow passengers as we settle in, most of them British, Canadian, and Australian—quite the Anglo crowd. As always, whenever there are people to observe, types emerge. We give them names and then watch them behave in character.

There's Austin Powers, an affable look-alike with

big teeth, a broad smile, black glasses, a '70s shag, and a twinkle in his eye; the Bulldog, his face in a permanent Grinch grimace, who finally smiles when I offer a hearty good morning on the Lido deck; the Betty Ford clone with a touch of Parkinson's who animatedly reads the daily headlines to her husband at breakfast; Miss Lonely Heart, a middle-aged woman always alone and looking terribly sad; and the Biker Canadians, who wax poetic about their extended bicycle excursions in the American West.

And then there's the nasty old woman with a constant scowl who wields her black cane like a scepter, as if to say, *Out of my way—don't mess with me.* On the second day of the cruise, we sit across from her on the tender heading to shore, and on arrival she struggles to stand. Joe kindly asks as he holds out his hand, "Are you going to make it okay?"

"Of course I'm going to make it," she snaps back. "Let's see how *you* do when you're my age."

If her scowl hasn't branded her, that response does. From now on, she's simply the Bitch. There's no other way to describe her, and time after time, for the rest of the trip, she lives up to her label. I can't help wondering what life did to make her so bloody nasty.

We're sure fellow passengers have a label for us as well. And while I'd like to think it's the Blond, Athletic Americans, it's more likely the Gap Year Marylanders in Hiking Boots or the Guy with the Wife Who Enjoys Her Wine.

While I love to fly and find airports exhilarating, they pale in comparison with the romance and promise of a voyage by sea. The salt-air smell, the ship's powerful horn each time we leave port, and the excitement of a new harbor are intoxicating. I'm indeed the wife of a marine engineer, and while my passion for all things nautical may not reach the level of Joe's, since we boarded the *Aegean Odyssey* I've definitely joined him in ship heaven.

GROWING OLD WITH GUSTO

Life is not a journey to the grave with the intention of arriving safely in a pretty and well-preserved body. But rather, to skid in broadside, thoroughly used up, totally worn out, and loudly proclaiming . . . wow, what a ride.

—MARK FROST

There's growing old gracefully, and there's growing old with gusto. Most of our shipmates aboard the *Aegean Odyssey* continue to embrace life, paying little attention to the fact that they're well into their seventies and eighties. Studies find that those over sixty-five are the happiest demographic, and many elders admit that one of their few regrets is they wish they'd been less cautious and taken more risks.

We abhor aging in the United States and do all we can to disguise it. What we should actually do is welcome the change and the freedom it affords. Rather than look in a mirror, wondering what happened to the taut muscles of our youth or trying to figure out how in the world our thighs got so jiggly, our backs so stiff, and our knees so creaky, we should concentrate on what else we want to learn and where else in the world we want to go. Much easier said than done, of course, but we need to follow in the footsteps, literally and figuratively, of Angus from Toronto and Bob from Philadelphia.

We spend time with ninety-one-year-old former engineer Angus, his khaki adventurer's hat protecting him from the fierce sun and his lilting Scottish accent belying the fact that he's lived his adult life in Canada. He has lots to share about his wife, Mary, the love of his life, whom he lost years earlier, and about his many travels, including to Antarctica the year before. He also shows us his delicate watercolors of penguins and snowscapes. His artwork is evocative, but what is even more remarkable is that he took up painting just two years before we met.

Bob from Philly, also traveling solo, is in our excursion group and at eighty-six has not tired of seeing the world. He tells us he sold a successful restaurant in Provincetown on Cape Cod thirty years ago ("You wouldn't believe how much they paid me for it," he confesses, still incredulous) and has spent much of the windfall on his voyages. No longer steady on his feet, Bob needs an assisting arm or firm grasp from a mate to negotiate the uneven stairs of medieval towns and rock-strewn ruins where there are few helpful handrails. But he just keeps going, shuffling one foot in front of the other, and always arrives on time.

PORTS OF CALL

Taking a cruise is sightseeing with a stopwatch. You swoop in and see as much as you can in the time allotted, and then it's back on board for yet another meal on the Marco Polo deck.

The *Aegean Odyssey* arrives as scheduled in each new port with the reliability of a Swiss watch. But, as with a windshield tour, you dip your toe into a place and then quickly pull it out, because once again it's time to go. There's never time to interact with the locals, explore aimlessly, or unwind at a café, watching resident life pass by. We contribute little to the local economy other than stipends for our guides, attraction fees, and the purchase of an occasional postcard. The pièce de résistance of ship travel, the need to unpack only once, is dampened by the realization that you have just slices of days in fascinating places where you'd love to stay a week.

Misgivings about a floating expedition aside, the ship takes us where we want to go—no muss, no fuss. Our ports of call are magical locales, some of which I've long wanted to visit and others I'd never heard of. We stop in Nafplio, Greece, a pretty town on the Peloponnese peninsula, gateway to the ruins of Mycenae and home to Agamemnon, leader of the Greeks in the Trojan War. Monemvasia, a squat peninsula off the southeastern tip of the Peloponnese at the base of a Gibraltar-like rock, is a village of cobblestone lanes of bougainvillea-covered ocher houses and charming stone architecture cut into the cliff. It long reigned as a key port in the Byzantine, Venetian, and Ottoman empires but is now simply a rocky sliver of postantiquity Greece.

When we find ourselves lost in the constricted village maze, a local woman with whom we share not a word of common language sees our plight, leads us through the ends of alleys and up and down stairs, and points us in the right direction. But before releasing us, she invites us in to see her property, of which she is clearly proud: a renovated monastery turned boutique hotel. "Can't we stay for a while?" I ask Joe, feeling the inn's magnetism and imagining dinner there under glittery skies. But our ship is calling, and we must pull ourselves away from this openhearted village, its back to modernity and its tawny face to the sea.

I've long wanted to visit Olympia. As we dock at Katakolon, its unassuming seaside port, I can't wait for our morning among the ruins, communing with the spirits of ancient Greeks who flocked there every four years to celebrate Zeus's sacred games. Olympia includes a stadium and hippodrome (the marble starting and finishing blocks are still in place), a *palaestra*, or wrestling school, and a gymnasium (from the Greek for "nude"), where competitors trained for a month. The complex was also a shrine and thus boasts temples, altars, and votive offerings for worshipping the gods. The most celebrated temple is that of Zeus, inside of which is a monumental statue of the father of all gods in ivory and gold. Next to Zeus's temple is the Heraeum, dedicated to his wife, Hera, which includes the victors' podium. I lose myself in reverie, imagining the games of physical glory; I can hear the crowds cheering and see the oiled, bronzed musculature of the athletes in action.

We next sail to Ithaca, island home of Odysseus and Penelope, off Greece's western coast, green and lush, with an inviting natural harbor. But Aeolus, keeper of the winds, flaunts his might, making it impossible to disembark. The next port of call is Corfu, the first Greek island Joe and I set foot on in 1979. It's wrapped in the most dramatic coves and hidden inlets, and the combination of green pines, blue waters, and white cottages is simply, chromatically perfect. But much has changed in thirty-plus years, the town's maze of streets now overrun with tacky tourist shops all selling the same tchotchkes. The main square facing the old port, on which as backpackers we once stayed in a cheap, walk-up boarding house with sawdust pillows, has fallen into disrepair, since most activity has migrated around the headland to a chic, colonnaded quarter. As we sail from Corfu, we hold out hope that the rest of the island has remained as pristine as we remember. After six weeks in the land of Pericles, I'm filled with a tristesse similar to what I felt when we left Italy. Waving farewell to Greece is like saying goodbye to yet another dear friend.

As we approach the Albanian port city of Sarandë, it's clear we're no longer in Greece. Communist-era apartment-block housing, stupefyingly ugly and only half completed, looks like it could collapse tomorrow. The entire seaport needs a good coat of paint and a legion of street sweepers. But a few miles from the city, via a rattletrap road that practically shakes our teeth loose, lies the remarkable site of Butrint, a Greek city and then Roman colony surrounded by a lagoon. Few have heard of this clandestine repository of ruins in southwestern Albania because it was behind the Iron Curtain in this dirt-poor country, so word never got out about the archeological treasure hidden beneath soaring eucalyptus and home to throngs of singing frogs.

Our guide, Maria, is frank about her country's economic difficulties. "We have a long way to go to get even close to where tourism is in Greece and Croatia," she confesses; "we just need lots of foreign investment." She's a kind soul with an industrious spirit; if she is representative of her compatriots, Albania will steadily progress toward a better future.

We make several stops in Croatia, the first at Dubrovnik, noted as one of the world's ten best walled cities. After brief visits to Split, where Roman emperor Diocletian and Croatian native son built his retirement palace, and Zadar, a buzzing university town, we're on our way back to Italy.

We lean over the *Aegean Odyssey*'s upper-deck railing for arrival in Venice from the Adriatic—a breathtaking approach by sea in the dawn haze. The city slowly awakens and takes on a rosy hue as our ship silently makes its way alongside fishing boats, ferries, water taxis, and vaporettos. We're anxious to explore the recesses of la Serenissima (the Most Serene Republic of Venice, its formal name), beyond the madding, camera-toting crowds of Saint Mark's Square and the overrun Rialto Bridge.

As our Adriatic cruise nears its end, we're conflicted about going ashore. The sense of accomplishment we enjoy when traveling independently is nonexistent when we're escorted from place to place, but it was all so easy. "I so needed this break from daily details," Joe admits, and I agree, adding that the itinerary was just what we wanted: a survey of Peloponnesian and Adriatic ports.

When my spirit lags and I'm feeling sentimental, I see our year as a series of goodbyes: to places to which we've grown attached, people we've met, countries we've come to love, and our visiting children. But then I perk up and remember there are new adventures and possibilities ahead. When we clomp down the *Aegean Odyssey*'s metal gangway, rolling our duffels into the real world of Venice feels like being dropped off at college after a respite at home. We're elated to be back on our own but already miss, just a bit, the rhythm and ease of shipboard life.

XIII. From Venice to Turkey
June 2012

LA SERENISSIMA

WE'LL BE IN VENICE FOR SIX DAYS, and it feels so much longer than previous visits, when we had only a couple of overnights. Having already visited the major sights, we can now stroll leisurely, absorbing the details of tranquil, deserted squares, the Jewish quarter, the public gardens, far-flung streets, and the glass-blowing island of Murano. We luxuriate in soaking in the Venice of our imaginations: a city locked in its glorious past, a place apart from the fast-paced, modern terra firma across the lagoon.

Venice has no classical foundation of its own—no Greek nor Roman antiquities of which to boast or on which to build. Its original settlers fled to the uninhabited marshy delta in the Adriatic to escape plundering Germanic and Hun invaders in the sixth century. The new city rose from the wetlands and, despite the fact that it fostered its own distinct personality, believed it important to create the illusion of links to Christianity's beginnings. Starting from scratch, Venetians resorted to plundering priceless treasures from others to establish their own bona fides. In the ninth century, the new democracy showed chutzpah by stealing the bones of Saint Mark from Egypt, thereby proclaiming its own religious stature. Clever marauders, those Venetians.

The so-called canals of Venice are actually not canals at all. La Serenissima is a cluster of over one hundred islets separated by fortified passages initially created by desilting the dividing waterways to allow boats to pass. Each muddy channel evolved over the centuries as individual islands developed independently, much like a puzzle whose pieces fit together but whose resulting image makes no sense because different artists painted each segment without consulting others. The streets on one island don't correspond to those across the way, and apparent arteries unexpectedly stop at a dead end or at a canal with no means to cross. City planning was not a priority as Venice grew, which is why few streets actually link across canals and the overall street pattern has neither rhyme nor reason.

Hordes of day-trippers temporarily swell Venice's midday population to 120,000, twice its number of residents. The gelato-wielding crowds crawling the city's streets are so dense one morning that exiting the tight alley of our bed and breakfast is like merging onto choked lanes of the Long Island Expressway. We jostle for an opening, jump out decisively, and join the flow, along with the feral cats that abound in Venice. They appear well fed, and shopkeepers and restaurateurs help support their presence, since "cats are better than rats," our landlord tells us.

On our last full day in Venice, we're having breakfast in our satin-walled, yellow-brocade room, listening to gondoliers crooning *"Volare"* from the canal around the corner, when an earthquake hits. Some minor rocking and rolling with windows jingling, sirens wailing, and dogs barking alerts us to the temblor. We check in with the front desk to make sure all is okay and then, after the *signore* reassures us that Venice is safe because it "bounces in the water" during earthquakes, continue with our day. Our plans include some aimless wandering, followed by a heady dose of culture: an afternoon at the Gallerie dell'Accademia art museum, an early dinner, and a night at the opera.

While neither of us is an opera aficionado, I do like hearing familiar arias. Joe, on the other hand, needs more than gentle prodding to attend Puccini's *La Bohème* in la Fenice, the famous Venice opera house. When I tell him we can get nosebleed seats for just 25 euros, he acquiesces but teases me mercilessly about "making" him go. As the 7:00 p.m. performance approaches, he ratchets up his taunting such that I want the show to begin just to silence him. I finally snap. "Stop! I'll go by myself and give your ticket to someone who'll appreciate it. Go get yourself a beer!" I say, and march on ahead.

We arrive well before showtime but find the square in front of the opera house packed with the buzz of disappointed ticket holders; the show has been canceled due to damage inside the theater from the morning's earthquake. I stand incredulous in the evening shadows, with tears of disappointment clouding my vision. But Joe, always the jokester, has to poke fun further, so he jumps in the air with a celebratory fist pump and an enthusiastic "yes!"

- - - - - - - - - - - - - - - -

Leaving Venice is like retreating from Technicolor Disney World to the monochromatic swamps of central

Florida. One minute we're in a vaporetto cruising the Grand Canal, the world's comeliest aquatic boulevard, past romantic salmon, apricot, and tawny buildings with flower-spilling window boxes, and the next we've been disgorged onto the dusty, colorless Piazzale Roma, Venice's unsightly transportation hub on the edge of town. We board a bus and are quickly propelled along the causeway to the mainland. Land is plentiful on the other side of the lagoon, and used-car lots, office complexes, and housing projects dominate. And just like that, we're back to reality, having traded la Serenissima for black-and-white suburban sprawl.

HOW GREEN WAS MY SLOVENIA

What I'll remember most about the little Republic of Slovenia is the color green, hundreds of neatly stacked woodpiles, dense pine forests, and a spotlessly clean country. I had no expectations when we decided to visit, only that Joe told me after he went to its capital city of Ljubljana on a business trip in 2004 that the town is a little gem. The five days we spend in Slovenia confirm that his characterization applies not only to the capital but to the rest of the country as well. The young nation of just over two million people emerged from its years as part of Yugoslavia relatively unscathed, was the first former communist country to join the Eurozone, and is well on its way to a solid tourist trade.

We head east into Slovenia from Italy. Our first stop is the Hotel Kendov Dvorec, a Relais & Châteaux manor hidden in the mountains in the evergreen-rich village of Spodnja Idrija, to celebrate our thirty-first wedding anniversary. The property is rustic, friendly, and quiet—

just what we need after the hustle and bustle of Venice—and we have a romantic dinner of Slovenian specialties in the candlelit dining room.

Next is spectacular Lake Bled in the Julian Alp foothills near the Austrian border. I'm definitely a beach girl when it comes to relaxing by the water, but this fairy-tale lake invites us to put up our feet and stay awhile. It changes my mind, at least for a few days, about my favorite waterside setting. Lake Bled is a glistening jewel, pure and simple. Swans float on its emerald waters, and gondolier-style oarsmen row canopied boats that shuttle visitors to the lake's signature centerpiece, Bled Island. The Church of the Assumption's pretty white steeple with its pointed gray tip, its image reflected in the green waters, beckons couples from around the world to tie the knot on the tiny island. In fact, our hotel is filled with the friends and family of a British couple getting married this weekend. To appreciate the setting from every angle, we walk the four-mile route around its perimeter and then up to red-roofed Bled Castle, built atop a white limestone cliff that rises dramatically over the crystalline lake, providing a bird's-eye view of the surrounding countryside.

We leave this rural area for an overnight stay in Ljubljana, one of Europe's newest capitals. As we approach from the north on the motorway, we pass rows of shamefully ugly apartment blocks, vestiges of the bygone communist era. But while not visually attractive, all is as clean and tidy as the countryside. The prefab concrete housing quickly morphs into the pleasant medieval architecture of Old Ljubljana, a prosperous neighborhood buzzing with theaters, museums, and galleries. There is no shortage of restaurants, bars, and clubs kept hopping by a significant student population. The Ljubljanica River bisects the heart of the city, and its embankments are magnets for activity, including promenades of myriad baby strollers. We cross the Triple Bridge, its three arms reserved for pedestrians, walk through the old town, take the funicular to the twelfth-century castle that watches over the city, and end our day with dinner at a chic outdoor café.

Our final Slovenian destination takes us back into the countryside, this time outside Lipica, home of the original Lipizzaner stud farm. We witnessed these mighty steeds in Vienna and are surprised to discover that most had their beginnings in Slovenia. From the moment we glimpse the horses, my heart melts and I'm once again a little girl in pigtails, my nose pressed to the fence, watching the weeks-old foals with knobby knees and spindly legs frolicking in fields with their mothers. We stroke the velvet noses of the mature, muscled stallions in the stables, including Kanizo, an equine beauty presented as a royal gift to Queen Elizabeth on a state visit. When we ask the price of a horse, we're told, "Let's just say that rich people buy horses and really rich people buy Lipizzaners."

ISTANBUL: FIRST IMPRESSIONS

Our flight to Istanbul takes us over the northern Greek coastline. The peninsula southeast of Thessaloniki, its three slender fingers reaching into the northern Aegean, is clearly visible below. Our plane plunges into thick cloud cover, and when we emerge thirty minutes later, the terrain has completely changed. Geometrical green and brown fields are now haphazardly shaped parcels in a rainbow of colors, like the artwork of a kindergartener who scribbled freehand and then colored in the resulting shapes. Visions of an unsettling Fès-like experience to come interrupt our anticipation, despite the fact that all reports indicate Turkey will not be another Morocco. We wonder what we'll find in the country's largest metropolis, which dates back to 3,000 BC and has been known over the centuries as Istanbul, Constantinople, Byzantium, and the New Rome. It's the world's only transcontinental metropolis: one-third of the population lives to the east in Asian Anatolia, but its commercial and historic center is to the west—in Europe—along with the bulk of its residents.

Arriving in ninety-degree heat, we appear to have flown in from the Arctic. We wear multiple layers of our heaviest clothing in a successful bid to avoid extra baggage-weight fees on EasyJet. Joe sticks out in his sport jacket fitted snuggly over bulky upper layers, but my sartorial excess of tights under baggy sweats, hiking boots, several shirts, a fleece, and a pashmina around my neck is hardly out of place. The sun is shining and the airport terminal stifling, but everywhere are women whose clothing conceals any hint of exposed flesh. The moment I disembark, the sweating starts in earnest and I can't imagine donning this many layers as a matter of course. The variety of female attire in the terminal runs from close-fitting miniskirts and tank tops to full black burkas with narrow eye slits. *Welcome to the mix that is Turkey,* I muse. More the norm are dozens of women in loose, colorful headscarves and belted, floor-length, beige London Fogs—cum-burkas. I imagine the rivulets of perspiration running beneath them, but of course any evidence of this indignity is safely hidden from view.

The drive from Atatürk airport into old-town Istanbul is via broad boulevards lined by dense beds of purple petunias, red geraniums, and yellow marigolds along closely mowed lawns worthy of an affluent American suburb. We pass scores of tankers and cargo ships lying low in the hazy distance on the Sea of Marmara, patiently waiting to pass through the Bosporus Strait. Along the waterside promenade are men running in gym shorts and women power-walking in long skirts with covered heads.

Istanbul straddles the seventeen-mile Bosporus, one of the world's busiest waterways, which connects the Sea of Marmara to the Black Sea and separates the city's old sections from the new. It's a sea of humanity—almost fourteen million people—teeming with activity. Our shuttle battles tram lines, cars, motorbikes, trucks, bicycles, and handcarts through the city's crazy road system built, rebuilt, and reworked over centuries. Drivers ignore the universal octagonal red signs commanding DUR in white capitals, and gargantuan tinted-windowed tourist coaches squeeze through lanes ill equipped to handle the complications of contemporary traffic. They risk snapping off side mirrors and scraping enamel paint jobs. Istanbul makes unruly Rome seem like a buttoned-down English city by comparison. We approach our hotel via a rat's nest of dusty streets that wind up and down the hilly Sultanahmet quarter of the old town.

Our accommodations are of the modern tourist variety. Efficient yet welcoming, the Lady Diana Hotel (the owner was a fan of the late princess) is surrounded by blocks of old wooden structures, many with broken windows and appearing as if termites have gotten the best of them. *Hmm,* I project, *this is going to be interesting.* The Lady Di is conveniently situated not far from the Golden Horn, the broad natural harbor off the Bosporus in the center of a rectangle formed by the city's top sights.

After eight hours in Istanbul, its past resplendent and its present complicated, Joe and I are already on sensory overload. The city is ancient and modern, conservative and freewheeling, cramped and sprawling, filthy and spotless, young and old, deafening and serene. Overall, it's congested, just like I imagined, but grittier and noisier. It's definitely not Morocco, since we've been hassled not once, but we're not sure what we've gotten ourselves into, and we remain tentative about what we'll find and how we'll react. Still, because we've been told that much of Istanbul's allure is hidden and must be discovered, we're optimistic about the days ahead and anxious to explore this European city with an Islamic overlay.

BREAKFAST WITH A SIDE OF HUMAN RIGHTS

Our first morning in Istanbul dawns under hazy sun and high clouds; it's going to be a hot one. We don our jeans and T-shirts and head upstairs to the rooftop terrace with broad views of the Blue Mosque and Hagia Sophia for a Turkish breakfast buffet. The multitabled spread includes the usual suspects: yogurts, fruits, cereals, boiled eggs, cheeses, breads, jams, and a few surprises, like halva, tomatoes, cucumbers, and olives, and the Turkish version of bagels with cream cheese schmears.

Next to the coffee urns, I spy a wine cart on wheels displaying a variety of vintages tucked next to the coffee urns. The young man servicing the buffet tells me, "In the evening, the breakfast room turns into a bar, and yes, wine and beer are served." When I ask about the availability of spirits in Istanbul and Turkey overall, he assures me that while some establishments abstain for religious reasons, many others cater to wine lovers like me. *Phew*, I think, and breathe a sigh of relief—I'm starting to warm to this place.

We grab our customary morning plates and claim a

table by the 360-degree window. I take a spoonful of yogurt and look up, instantly losing my appetite. An upsetting family scene is in progress two tables away. A man sporting casual Western clothes—a green striped hoodie, jeans, and Nikes—and an adorable little girl in a flowered sundress are enthusiastically downing their hashbrowns and scrambled eggs. Across the table, a woman in a black, face-concealing burka attempts to eat her own breakfast, and I recall the woman I saw in Granada. I watch, astonished, as she deftly lifts the heavy fold of veil and surreptitiously slips a forkful of eggs between her lips, as if to be observed eating is a depravity. Just as swiftly, she drops the black cloth so her masticating mouth is once again hidden. Her husband and daughter revel in their morning meal while she struggles with every bite.

On our first day in Turkey, we witnessed fathers doting on their daughters, adorable, creamy-skinned cherubs with soft blond ringlets and olive-skinned beauties with silky, dark manes. A misguided theology will compel many families in a few short years to subjugate these carefree, spontaneous young girls by hiding them under shrouds the minute they reach puberty. The burka will make these girls less than individuals—nameless and faceless—and inhibit social interaction. Is this future of anonymity, of being covered and smothered, what they want for their daughters? Every time I see women so attired, I have the urge to sit them down and suggest that if they want anonymity, they should grab some Jackie O. sunglasses, slip on a shapeless muumuu, and don a floppy hat. Thus, women could go about their business in public, unnoticed and undistinguished, but not communicate subservience and oppression. It'll be up to younger generations connecting in person and online with others not limited by their religion to envision possibilities and carve out independent lives separate from fathers and husbands. And there will be young men who want their women independent, not just shrouded trophies battling to finish their breakfasts.

We drain our coffee cups, pack up our things, and head for the stairs. As I glance back for a final look at the draped woman, I see she has pulled a BlackBerry from beneath the folds. I suddenly have hope for her daughter.

ISTANBUL: THE SIGHTS

First on our agenda is a casual luncheon cruise on the Bosporus, heading for the Black Sea. The day is sweltering, but, our boat ride underway, the Bosporus breeze lowers the temperatures, and we enjoy a tasty paper-plated lunch of kebabs and rice. We're kept company by dozens of dolphins, which play in our wake on the broad, critical waterway that slices through Istanbul. After cruising north past sumptuous palaces followed by wooden mansions and the Selimiye Barracks (where Florence Nightingale worked during the Crimean War), we disembark in the harbor of a nondescript fishing village, climb the steep hill behind it, and gaze over the vast, storied Black Sea. All at once it hits me: we're on the eastern shore of the Bosporus, and our gap year has taken us not only to Europe and Africa but now to Asia as well. Seeing Europe is an adventure, but going to these two continents has added elements of intrigue and, I'll admit it, a bit of fear. We're stretching the boundaries of our travel comfort zone, and so perhaps we're braver than we thought.

The following day, having not done adequate Istanbul homework to venture forth effectively on our own, we join a small tour group to take in the city's highlights. We find ourselves part of a remarkable cultural stew: a French-speaking woman from Quebec who runs a relief organization in Nairobi, Kenya, and her sixteen-year-old daughter; her husband, originally from Saskatchewan, who heads up a refugee agency in Khartoum, Sudan; a woman from Bangalore, India, in town for a regional meeting of the World Economic Forum; and a young Filipino couple who work in Dubai. We're an impromptu set of international visitors ready to see Istanbul.

Sightseers know the Sultan Ahmed Mosque, built in the 1600s, as the Blue Mosque, so named for its exquisite interior blue tiles. With its six minarets and cascading domes, it's a magnificent piece of architecture. We pass the ablution fountains, I drape the requisite scarf over my head, and we slip off our shoes before stepping barefoot onto the plush Turkish carpet. Despite the crowds, the cavernous chamber is hushed and the muted morning light streaming through pastel stained-glass windows enhances the space's tranquility. Every available surface is embellished with hand-painted blue, green, and red tiles in graceful, flowery patterns, none with human or animal images, since Islam equates prayer in front of such with idol worship. I find the mosques we've visited more peaceful and conducive to contemplation than the many churches we've seen. They're lofty, light-filled places of prayer devoid of distracting statues of Saint Sebastian punctured by arrows, frescoes of bleeding, beheaded martyrs, or dark paintings of souls condemned to the fires of eternal damnation.

Our next stop is neighboring Topkapi Palace, sprawling residence of Ottoman sultans, their families, and their concubines and the bejeweled, golden-hilted dagger made famous by the caper film *Topkapi*. Much of the palace's enclosed space is dedicated to priceless treasures and Islamic artifacts on velvet cushions behind thick vitrines. Just as we saw in Croatia, where myriad macabre Catholic relics are displayed—shards of saints' bones and clips of their nails in gold coffers in the shape of arms and feet—so the sacred relics of Islam's holy messengers are presented. A hair of Mohammed's beard, a tooth, his sword, and his cloak are similarly preserved in gilded and argentine receptacles. I wonder, as I did in Croatia, about the authenticity of these artifacts: Who vouches for the provenance of such things? The sultan robes on display are close replicas of the priests' vestments in Dubrovnik: royal regalia of gilded thread and the finest embroidery. Is it any wonder citizens and royalty alike became wary of "bedecked like kings" clergy? In Croatia, each room of the convent treasury was vigilantly guarded by a genial, habited nun who, we were told, would have no problem pouncing on us should we attempt to take pictures or lay a finger on any treasures. In Topkapi Palace, armed guards from the Turkish military replace the smiling sisters, but I'm not sure with whom I'd rather tangle.

What compels people to buy funny hats and ridiculous shirts on vacation and wear them as if they were attractive? Over the course of our travels we've seen so many tourists, especially bands of merry men off cruise ships, in silly-looking sailor caps and black-and-white-striped sailor shirts or cheap straw Panamas with coordinating ribbons. They wear their new apparel enthusiastically, but I'm certain that once home, they toss it all on piles of previously discarded attire from other excursions. I imagine their lucky offspring picking with glee through heaps of cast-off bonnets and chemises as they prepare for Halloween and other dress-up occasions.

On our Topkapi tour, I spot a troupe of several dozen women, faces weathered, draped to the floor in black and sporting navy-and-white baseball caps atop their headscarves. *Well, that's a unique look,* I think, and though I'm happy to see the women out and about, ask Joe, given their hats, "Do you think they could be off one of those cruise ships in the Bosporus?" Our guide informs us that they're actually peasant women from rural Turkey on their first trip to see the top cultural and religious sights of Istanbul, compliments of a charitable foundation. *Wow,* I think, *their baseball caps are not silly at all,* and I'm certain that once they've returned to their farms, the women will continue to wear them proudly.

Around the corner from the palace, monumental Hagia Sophia (Holy Wisdom) rises at the end of what was a Roman hippodrome. In the reverse of what took place in Córdoba, where the victorious Catholic monarchs mutilated the mosque by dropping a basilica into its heart, the triumphant Ottoman Empire defaced the cathedral by turning it into a mosque. In both cases, the buildings would have been better left alone, but, alas, such is not the behavior of conquerors. The echoing interior is a massive example of Byzantine architecture and was the world's largest cathedral for nearly one thousand years, until Sevilla's cathedral finally dwarfed it.

Lying beneath Istanbul are hundreds of cisterns that stored water for emperors from the city's days as

Constantinople. We leave the streets' blistering hundred-degree temperatures to descend to the cool depths of the grandest of them all: the Basilica Cistern. Sometimes called the Sunken Palace because that's just what it appears to be, the cistern covers two subterranean acres and includes processions of 336 marble columns. Illuminated by atmospheric lighting, we walk along raised wooden platforms, watch slowly moving, ghostly carp silently guarding the waters, and hear the *drip-drip-drip* of moisture from the vaulted ceiling. A welcome relief from the heat, the cistern is an eerie and entirely unexpected stop on our guided itinerary.

There are more than three thousand shops in Istanbul's celebrated Grand Bazaar. While merchants are anxious to make a sale, shoppers are not subjected to undue pressure à la Morocco. Retailers ask if we'd like to see some handcrafted belts or shawls or carpets but then smile and allow us to carry on when we shake our heads and say, "No, thanks." The covered marketplace is quite modern, and while many of the stalls are tiny niches overflowing with merchandise, others are large, bright showrooms with plenty of space for displaying their wares.

Our stay in Istanbul ends with our airport van driver, a young man who, when we tell him we're American, enthusiastically tells us, "I've always wanted to visit the US—and I really want to go to Dallas." He's a huge fan of the late-'70s television show of the same name and wants to see ranches and horses and wear cowboy boots and a cowboy hat like J. R. Ewing. We wish him well as he drops us at the terminal and then head for our flight to Cappadocia—Turkey's particular version of the American West.

THE WILD WEST, TURKEY STYLE

Our morning flight from Istanbul on Turkish Airlines arrives in central Anatolia at the tidy, modern Nevşehir airport on a vast, arid plain ringed by distant mountains. We've landed in the middle of nowhere. The transfer van takes us across lowlands to the east, where there's nothing to see for miles until the green of vineyards appears.

"Look, grapes!" I exclaim. "There must be wine."

Joe, ever the optimist, replies without a beat, "Or jelly."

We eventually reach a two-lane country road, where we slow behind horse-drawn produce carts and pass farmers tilling plots with mule-drawn wooden rudders. Like in the rustic scene of a Millet painting, sturdy, sunburned farming women in heavy babushkas and long woolen skirts wield hoes in scorched fields. Are these rural scenes we witness actually taking place in the twenty-first century?

Continuing our drive through more sprawling, nondescript terrain, we at long last reach the flat-topped mesas and sinuous valleys we first spied on the horizon. In an approach reminiscent of the unremarkable drive toward the south rim of the Grand Canyon, with the scraggly olive trees of Turkey standing in for Arizona's parched scrub, the earth suddenly opens up and an extraordinary landscape miraculously appears. We've reached the heart of Cappadocia, and there they are, greeting us: forests of dreamy, delicate fairy chimneys, unique rock formations sprouting across acres of moonscaped terrain tucked between curvy, sandstone cliff faces. The thin stone columns, some like elongated tepees and others textbook phallic formations, are the vestiges of volcanic eruptions whose lava flows the elements sculpted over millennia into strange, lofty creations. Four thousand years ago, Hittites chiseled homes into the gigantic anthills that look as though they might crumble to the touch but are actually hardened, solid cones. The original inhabitants paved the way for future residents: Byzantine Christians seeking refuge from persecution, first by pagan Romans and then by marauding Muslims, cave-dwelling hippies in the 1960s, and now patrons of today's chic boutique hotels. Gazing at the structures in their surreal setting, I expect oversize desert insects to crawl from the pointed tops. Surely the creator of *The Flintstones* took a trip to Cappadocia for visual and atmospheric inspiration, because here we are, smack in the middle of the Turkish town of Bedrock. I fight the urge to break into the TV show's theme song. "I'm so glad you insisted we come to Cappadocia," Joe says. "I had no idea this place even existed."

Our accommodations in the bustling frontier town of Göreme, smack in the middle of Turkey, are in one of the cave dwellings turned inns. The accommodating Kelebek Hotel is up a cobblestone road set high along a ridge, dug dramatically into volcanic rock. It's an all-stone property with rock-hewn archways and cozy panoramic porches covered with soft Turkish carpets and strewn with overstuffed pillows. We spend two relaxing evenings on the unique loggias and experience the troglodyte lifestyle, sipping crisp Cappadocian white wine and gazing over the otherworldly valley.

We hike the scenic Red Canyon just outside Göreme and, the following day, the distant Ihlara Valley. Dwellings called pigeon houses—traditionally used to collect bird droppings for fertilizer—carved directly into the walls of the canyon riddle the sheer rock faces. The remnants of eleventh-century monastic settlements and one-room, vaulted-ceilinged chapels from the time Christians hid and practiced their faith in difficult-to-discover gorges are cut into the bases of cliffs and line the green valley. Simple but effective stone wheels that easily roll into place as a last line of defense against attackers peek out beside the entryways. Our valley hike ends with a simple outdoor lunch at a brookside restaurant that includes bowls of white lentil potage, eggplant-and-tomato stew, and plain yogurt drizzled with honey for dessert.

Beneath Cappadocia's landscape, so desolate it seems not of this earth, is an intricate network of cave cities in which local Christians hid from ever-present hostility. They went underground, in a literal sense. Each of the subterranean systems housed up to ten thousand people, and the largest yet discovered are ten levels deep, with tight passageways connecting floors like so many hamster burrows. We stoop and squeeze through tight tunnels, fighting back waves of claustrophobia, and see smoke-blackened kitchens, handy indentations for storing spices, undulating ventilation shafts, and chambers near the top for housing farm animals. They are extraordinary labyrinths dug in response to frightening times, and we gratefully breathe the fresh air when at long last we resurface.

Cappadocia is the Wild West, Turkey style, its landscape and spirit so evoking Arizona and Utah. There are towering buttes and squat mesas, horses, dust, and the unmistakable feel of a border town. As we sip cold drinks in a shaded saloon, I have a powerful urge to saddle up and head for the hills.

EPHESIAN REVELATIONS
Our final Turkish destination is Ephesus, along the Aegean coast.

We arrive at our hotel in a beach resort town outside Ephesus just in time for dinner. As genuine and serene as the Kelebek Hotel in Cappadocia was, the Hotel Tatlises is not: it's the epitome of factory tourism at its worst. Our check-in coincides with the arrival of six air-conditioned coaches, which pull up and disgorge waves of international tourists looking for sun and fun on a budget. The place is evidently successful in catering to travelers looking for bargain-basement deals. There's an enormous patio the size of a football field on which meals are served, and we join the crowds for the never-ending dinner buffet once we learn our evening meal is included in our room rate. We enjoy decent Turkish food but suffer bad '80s music (who can appreciate stuffed grape leaves and baklava listening to a Muzak version of "Get Outta My Dreams and into My Car"?) while sitting on stained, white-on-white, faux-satin slipcovered banquet chairs. We feel as if we're at a wedding with no bride, no groom, and not a soul we know.

Our one unfortunate night of impersonal, mass-produced travel behind us, we proceed to the archeological site. We discover that the ancient Greek city and then prosperous Roman metropolis in the first century BC had a population of over 250,000, which made it one of the largest cities on the Mediterranean. Once we arrive, without warning, I have an epiphany. Ephesus . . . Ephesians . . . Saint Paul . . . Saint Paul's letters to the Ephesians . . . Now I know where we are! I've connected the language derivation dots.

We visit the Virgin Mary's House at Meryan Ana Evi, a Roman Catholic shrine on Mount Koressos, which overlooks what remains of Ephesus. The house was discovered in the 1800s when archeologists followed the visions of a Roman Catholic nun. Ever since, a steady flow of pilgrims has filed through the two-room stone dwelling and chapel in the belief that the mother of Jesus was taken there by Saint John and lived with him until her assumption into heaven. It's a sweet little house and a touching story, but I don't believe this particular vision quest.

The temperatures intensify, progressing to the dry, white heat of the Mediterranean midday that washes all color to dull greens and grays. We see the remains of Ephesus: temples, public baths, the amphitheater, fountains, brothels, public toilets (a fascinating side-by-side marble bleacher system with no privacy and running water drainage canals underneath—just pay your fee, lift your toga, and relieve yourself in comfort next to your neighbor), and the magnificent Celsus library. The building's interior and all it housed were destroyed by fire after a devastating earthquake in 262 AD, and only the colossal, reconstructed facade remains.

XIV. The Hills Are Alive
June 2012

YOU CAN GO BACK AGAIN

THERE HAVE BEEN WEEKS in my life about which I can recall not one particular detail. But the memory of the day I hiked from Grindelwald, Switzerland, to the Kleine Scheidegg pass in 1977 is as vivid as the blue sky under which I made the fourteen-mile round-trip trek. It was my first real hike ever. I know what I wore (clunky shoes that stood in for hiking boots, blue knee socks, cotton navy shorts, and a collared, flowered blouse I'd made), what I ate (yogurt, cheese, and a hunk of bread), what I heard (the bleating of goats and clanking of cowbells), what I saw (dramatic snow-covered peaks), and, most of all, how I felt (exhilarated). Lederhosen-wearing von Trapp—like families passed me along the way, and I swore then and there that hiking treks would become part of my future family's getaways. I spent a mere ten hours in the Grindelwald valley in 1977, yet the memory is indelible. When Joe and I undertake the very same hike as a duo, I'm elated to find that the often-distorting lens of nostalgia neither magnified the location's beauty nor exaggerated the thrill of accomplishment.

What a difference a day makes. Sweltering in upper-nineties heat when we left chaotic Turkey, we're now shivering in the cold drizzle of pastoral Switzerland. The blistering sun of the Mediterranean and recurring calls to prayer are behind us—no more olives, no more eggplant, no more soft pita, and no more southern warmth. We're in the land of crusty bread, cheese, muesli, and brisk but polite demeanors. Flying from and to countries not part of the European Union means suffering through interminable lines after arriving in Basel and the dour officials at passport control. Is a genetic inability to smile a job requirement for becoming a border control officer—especially in Switzerland? (Although we encountered them just once, the passport officials in Turkey managed to sneak in unsanctioned grins as they inspected our paperwork.)

After an uneventful train ride to Interlaken, we transfer to the red, wooden-benched cog railway that carries us up to Grindelwald in thick fog and mood-dampening rain. A pair of twentysomething backpackers disembark with us, and I wonder if their soon-to-be-made memories in the surrounding mountains will be as enduring as mine. Will they return years in the future, as I have, to relive them?

Beni, extreme sports aficionado and owner of the Hotel Lauberhorn, and his equally enthusiastic-about-the-outdoors wife, Connie, pick us up at the tourist office in their van and drive us a mile out of town to our home for the next eight days. The conditions are dismal and the cloud cover so thick that nary an alp is in sight. We're exhausted after our long day of travel and dismayed by the weather, so we skip dinner, crash, and sleep like babies.

The sun wakes us the next morning, and we nearly

fall out of bed when we roll over and see the spectacular north face of the Eiger staring at us through sliding glass doors. This magnificent peak was hidden on our arrival but now fills the view from our chalet dorm. Until this startling moment, the sightlines over Mount Etna from our room in the Hotel Bel Soggiorno in Sicily topped our list of most appealing views, but the snow-topped Eiger peering into our bedroom bumps the Hotel Lauberhorn into the top slot.

There is little time for relaxation in Grindelwald. Our hosts are off to hang-glide for the day, and we're determined to hike in earnest to prepare for next week's Tour du Mont Blanc. Today's the day for reconstituting my Kleine Scheidegg hike of yore, the centerpiece of our visit to Switzerland. Trekking poles in hand, we make our way down to the base of the valley, cross the bridge over the chalky green river that thunders below, and start the relentless four-thousand-foot climb up, up, and then farther up toward the snow line.

From the tiniest blossom to the rugged vistas of the encircling mountains, our ascent to the Kleine Scheidegg is "wow" hiking at its best. An abundance of Alpine wildflower fields with a riot of color—yellow buttercups, purple asters, pink campions, and blue gentians— embellish the way. How does nature paint the landscape so perfectly, I question, with just the right mix of pastel and intense shades? We follow the trail through meadows and pine forests, across rocky streams and over stiles. The footpath crosses farm after farm, and the only sounds are the deep clangs of huge Swiss bells on the necks of munching cows and the wind chime—like tinkles of teeny bells dangling from bearded goats. Unlike an entirely orchestrated pastiche at Disney World's Epcot Center, this mountain paradise is genuine, with all the sights, sounds, and earthy smells that come with the reality of Switzerland. At long last, and when my burning lungs are about to give up, patches of snow and the glacier's edge from which frigid streams sprout cross our path, signaling our approach to the final vertical mile. The hike is billed as a four-hour trek, but we make it to the Kleine Scheidegg ridge about a half hour earlier than expected. We're at the snow line, looking straight up at the big-boy triumvirate, all commanding attention as they march in a row: the Eiger (13,025 feet), the Mönch (13,448 feet), and the Jungfrau (13,642 feet). Wow.

Basking in nature, where I completely unplug and take the outdoors in, allowing its power to nourish me, opens me to the present the way nothing else can. I'm always surprised at the ideas that bubble up during a long hike, and when I share the experience with Joe, it deepens our connection.

"I know it's hard to talk about," I say, "but where do you think we should look for an apartment when we get back?"

Joe immediately responds, "Bethesda," and I'm so pleased, because it's exactly the Washington suburb I've been thinking about, even though we haven't wanted to talk about leaving Europe yet, because it makes our departure at the end of the summer real.

"And what do you think about flying directly to Florida to visit your parents before we head back to Maryland?" I propose. Joe agrees, and, since I've opened the door to visualizing some details about our return, we continue brainstorming about being back in the real world.

Such are my thoughts and our conversation as we devour wursts and *rösti* potatoes on the terrace overlooking the western-facing side of the pass, across the chasm to the village of Mürren, suspended precipitously on a mountain terrace. After an extended lunch break, we relace our boots and reluctantly start the descent back to Grindelwald. We take in the mountains' majesty in reverse, this time looking over the peaks to the northeast. Practically crawling when we return to the Hotel Lauberhorn, we debate which was more difficult: going up or coming down. The ascent was a killer for our aerobic capacity, but the descent wreaked havoc on our knees and turned our thighs to Jell-O. While I was hardly in great shape in 1977, I was, after all, just a kid, with twenty-one-year-old lungs and twenty-one-year-old muscles, and no matter what shape I'm in now, my body parts are fifty-six years old, with plenty of wear and tear. We feel every single step we took, and I say to Joe, "I can't imagine why anyone would ever want to do anything but sleep."

ALPINE MOUNTAIN HIGH

The day after our hike, we call home and are greeted with my dad's familiar refrain: "So, where in the world are you today?" We tell him we're high in the mountains of Switzerland, and he responds, "It's awfully expensive there, no?" Sticking to a budget in Switzerland is a fool's errand—the Swiss franc (Switzerland doesn't use the euro), valued during our trip at just over a dollar, is stronger than ever, and prices are jaw-droppingly high—but we decide simply to eat and drink less and go with the exchange-rate flow, rather than obsess about expenditures and ruin our stay. Because access to many of the best hiking trails is facilitated by an initial ascent in a cable car, we purchase six-day unlimited passes for the price of a hotel room for two weeks in Greece.

Though we are more than comfortable traversing mountains on gondolas and chair lifts for skiing, doing so across the green summer countryside is a new experience. As in winter, we depart each morning, trusty trail map in hand, chart our course, and then hike from the top of one lift across rutted terrain to the base of the next. Our scenic lift rides take us to the mountain villages of Wengen, Mürren, and Lauterbrunnen, where endless trails are always within sight of waterfalls and earshot of the thunder of summer avalanches.

We take a dramatic hike along the edge of a ravine overlooking the glacier below. After an hour's ascent, we feel the wind whip up and then suddenly still. Thunder rumbles in the distance; we turn on a dime in an abrupt about-face. The rain is torrential within minutes, and, having not donned foul-weather gear when we set out under morning sunshine, we're soaked by the drenching squall. Water runs down our legs into our hiking boots, turning our socks into sodden sponges. We squish and squeak as we slosh our way back to the trailhead, and just as we make it into the gondola hut, lightning flashes above. We're relieved, but it teaches us an enduring lesson—when humans are dealing with the outdoors, Mother Nature always wins.

The flagship excursion of a trip to Grindelwald is the ascent to the Jungfraujoch, the permanently snowed-in saddle between the Mönch and Jungfrau peaks. We skip a few more meals to pay the supplement for this remarkable train ride. The cog railway from the Kleine Scheidegg climbs rapidly before plunging into the solid rock mountain face and continues for seven long miles inside the Eiger and Mönch, eventually reaching the highest train station in Europe.

It's pitch dark in the tunnel, but when we emerge, the light dazzles, blinding sun reflecting off every snow-covered surface. We slip on our sunglasses and, once our eyesight is restored, realize we're not alone; it appears that all of India, Pakistan, and Japan is with us at twelve thousand feet. As we learned from Beni and Connie, Switzerland is the country pictured most often in Bollywood blockbusters and has become the stuff of vacation dreams for many. Indian directors in the 1960s and '70s often shot their work there, finding the lush green meadows and snowcapped peaks inspired backdrops for love and romance. Specially packaged excursions shuttle entire families to the Bernese Oberland region for the complete movie experience, including lunch at the "Bollywood" restaurant at the top of the Jungfraujoch. Similarly, the area is a popular destination for packaged tours from Japan for those who want to make the pilgrimage to the mountains they know from the children's classic *Heidi* and the beloved *Sound of Music*. One Japanese woman tells me, "They market the romance of Switzerland wherever you go. TV ads talk about the clean Swiss air, and travel agent windows are filled with pictures of snowy mountains and edelweiss."

In an effort to flee the stifling crowds at the Jungfraujoch station and view the magnificent vistas in solitude, we hike for an hour across the glacial snowfield to the Mönchsjoch mountain hut. Despite the brilliant sun, once we set off across the icy plateau, winds whip through the pass and the temperature drops into the forties. "I guess I shouldn't have worn my hiking shorts," Joe laments, shivering. Much-appreciated, belly-warming soup and hot tea help thaw our chilly selves, and we head back across the snow to Bollywood central and the elevator that takes us to the panoramic Sphinx weather tower. We are indeed on top of the world.

After eight days in Switzerland, we hate to leave, but our wallets have thinned, and my beloved France, still in the Alps, is the next destination calling us.

ON LANGUAGE

Is it possible to overstate the importance of language in forging friendships across borders? I don't think so.

The trip from Grindelwald to Chamonix, France, requires five trains and one bus. As the crow flies, the distance isn't far, but crossing the Alps can be a multilegged, many-houred proposition. On one of the trains, a Japanese couple take their places across from a Swiss gentleman in the seats next to ours. While helping them with their luggage, the gentleman initiates a conversation in Japanese. The look of pure, unadulterated joy on the couple's faces lights up the train. They're on their own, far from home, and the serendipity of selecting seats next to someone who speaks their mother tongue is priceless. Animated conversation among the fast friends continues, the Swiss gentleman pointing out features of the surrounding peaks as our train proceeds down the valley. They laugh, heads nodding and smiles widening, and my heart warms as I imagine the talk turning to families, travel, and Japan. When the train slows for the native son's stop, they exchange cards and, hands at their sides, quickly bow goodbye.

During our stay in Grindelwald, we met a couple from Dresden, in the former East Germany, who spoke passable English. They told us that nowadays, all children learn English from an early age, but they didn't take it up until adults; Russian was the requirement when they were growing up. Subjugators demand that the subjugated learn their language in a decisive power play.

Language is a delicate art. We've been amused on occasion by the quirky use of English by some of the people we encounter. I overheard an Italian traveler in Rome triumphantly exclaim, "The bull has entered into the china store," and our guide in Dubrovnik, after she asked us if we were familiar with an anecdote she shared about her city, inquired, "Is that bell not ringing?" Such endearing errors highlight the subtle nature of language and translation but shouldn't inhibit us from giving another tongue our best effort. Learning foreign languages has always helped me listen to English more carefully and pay closer attention to expressions that might be difficult for non-native speakers.

Speaking of languages, we'll soon be back in the land of the quintessential romance language—my beloved French. I may at times speak it like a bull that's entered into the china store, but *le français* has always helped keep my bell ringing.

OUR RETURN TO THE PROMISED LAND

I have an existential moment that comes without warning soon after we arrive in France—a flash of clarity so pure that my life races in front of me and I'm in harmony with all.

We disembark in Chamonix, alfresco mecca extraordinaire, after a full day of travel. The quintessential sports town is the Moab or Vail or Tahoe of France. Every other retail space houses an outdoor outfitter—North Face, Marmot, Columbia, Quechua—and most of those walking through town are dressed for mountain pursuits.

For our first meal back in the Promised Land, we find a little chalet restaurant whose menu is filled with mouthwateringly familiar choices. There are a dozen items on the menu I could select—*poulet a la crème avec champignons, la salade forestière,* and *la raclette à l'ancienne*—but I settle on a few of my favorites: *soupe à l'oignon, une salade de chèvre chaud,* and *un pichet* of crisp Haute-Savoie white wine. As the waitress comes to take our order, the wistful strains of Joni Mitchell's classic "Both Sides Now" fill the room. The friendly French of our *serveuse,* the comfortable ease with which we respond, and the backdrop of the timeless lyrics fill me with a serenity that whispers, *All that's happened in your life has brought you to this very moment.* While I've had my share of disappointments, anxieties, and struggles, what flicker in this instant are the triumphs and the joys, the love and the contentment, of my life. The accretion of every step I've ever taken and every decision I've ever made has led me to sitting across from Joe, having this rustic French dinner in Chamonix. If I'd changed any detail of my life along the way, this particular crystalline moment might not be happening. Perhaps it's the optimist in me, perhaps it's simply that I relish my life, or perhaps it's that my now-mature self looks back and remembers only the good things about clouds, love, and life. For me, right now, I'm back in France, my very own paradise, for the balance of our year, and all is right in my world.

TMB: THE OVERVIEW

The Tour du Mont Blanc, affectionately known to its devotees as the TMB, is one of the world's classic long-distance footpaths and is a capstone event on our itinerary. Experiencing the Alpine wilderness in the presence of the dramatic ice-capped peaks is the proverbial icing on our sabbatical-year cake. In seven days, we'll hike seventy-five miles around Mont Blanc, the highest point in the Alps at 15,770 feet, undertake elevation gains and losses of over 36,000 feet, cross through three countries with six companions, and complete one magnificent hike. We signed up for the hike before we left the States, having read about it in a hiking magazine years before. The writer did a good job of communicating his enthusiasm for not only the physical beauty of the TMB but also the excitement of the challenge and the thrill of doing it with a partner. Joe and I love undertaking personal challenges, as well as discovering new places, just the two of us. It's like having secrets no one else knows and that only we share. Once we read about it, we knew the TMB would be one of those shared experiences.

The circular route goes from village to village, ascending through flower-filled meadows and up precipitous, barren mountain passes. It winds its way through vertiginous, scree-strewn elevations and descends through quaint hamlets into green valleys overlooked by intimidating glaciers in France, Italy, and Switzerland. The trail begins in the Chamonix Valley and traces its way through its international neighbors—the Val Ferret in Italy and the Trient Valley in Switzerland.

The complete 105-mile TMB requires a ten-day commitment. We'll undertake a slightly abbreviated version by doing the "less interesting" legs, those that follow paved roads, in support vans. We'll walk from France to Italy, on into Switzerland, and then back to France, progressing from one rustic mountain refuge to the next. I find a wealth of information about the Mont Blanc loop on the Internet and have Kev Reynolds's *The Tour of Mont Blanc*, the de facto bible on this classic hike. Because the fair-weather season is so brief, the mountain refuges (some of which cannot be reserved) fill up quickly in summer. I read reports of hikers at the end of a long day of trekking fifteen-plus miles being stranded with no place to stay in sometimes-below-freezing night temperatures. This possibility, combined with fickle mountain weather, sealed the deal. We've opted for a guided TMB excursion with an adventure outfitter, Boundless Journeys.

Our TMB program is inaugurated at l'Oustalet, our comfortably rustic Chamonix inn, with drinks on the back lawn. Our tall, handsome French guide and outdoorsman who looks the part, Eric, meets us with the understated enthusiasm we'll come to expect from him. As our fellow hikers materialize one by one, we size each other up to see where we fall on the relative fitness scale. In the days leading up to the excursion, I was anxious. Will our companions for a week of intense trekking be older or younger? Will they be less or more in shape? Will we see their hard-body physiques and realize we're in over our hiking heads?

As it turns out, our abilities, while not identical, are compatible, and, somewhat more important, our senses of humor are in sync. The fuzzy silhouettes of fellow hikers we imagined have now materialized as real people: a twentysomething Australian couple; a research librarian and her New York real estate husband; an attorney from Rhode Island; and Eric, our guide, a Chamonix native. It looks like the weeklong adventure will be not only physical but social as well for our affable ensemble of eight.

TMB: THE HIKE

The morning of the mountain adventure we dreamed about for so long finally dawns. Despite how excited I am, I do my best not to sound too chirpy when we meet up with our group in the breakfast room—I don't want them thinking I'm not serious about what we're about to undertake. Our Grindelwald training hikes under our belts, well-broken-in boots supporting our feet, and trekking poles at the ready, we're reasonably confident as we start the ascent of what is billed as our "TMB practice hike." But the romantic images of gentle bucolic inclines through Alpine meadows are now very real rocky ascents rising defiantly in front of us, daring us to climb.

A cable car deposits us beyond the tree line in the shadow of a bread-knife range of peaks on the northern side of the Chamonix Valley. This inaugural time together allows Eric to assess our hiking abilities and helps us learn to trust his close personal relationship with the terrain. It doesn't take long before we hang on his every word and take as gospel everything he says. If Eric predicts it will cool off, we soon feel a chilly breeze. If he suggests taking pictures from a certain promontory and we listen, we're assured of photos with the absolute best backdrops. When Eric tells us to don foul-weather cover, it will start spritzing, guaranteed.

From the valley's northern slope, we look across the rooftops of Chamonix far below to the pristine white dome of Mont Blanc rising on the southern side. We have an incredible view of the big guy, the imposing mass that anchors the corners of France, Switzerland, and Italy fifteen thousand feet in the sky. Our orientation day is graced by visits from sturdy ibex, wild goats with enormous backward-curving horns standing watch on rocky ledges. As they do in early summer, one adolescent is dutifully scratching off his long white winter cover against the stiff, bristly branches of scrub bushes, allowing his short, sandy summer coat to appear. We also spy the more elusive, graceful, and wiry chamois, an entirely different species of goat-antelope careering down a steep, rock-strewn slope. Alpine marmots—adorable, oversize ground squirrels—are our constant companions, always on the lookout beside their holes and sounding repeated whistling alarms whenever we approach.

We're humbled by our first day's exercise and talk excitedly about the days ahead with our companions over dinner.

Our hike starts high above the village of Les Houches, where a cable car drops us in a flower-filled mountain meadow at the foot of a glacier. A vaporous mist puts the Chamonix Valley below into soft focus, and we head up and around the mountain and then through the Col du Tricot toward our first night's destination.

A hiking trifecta graces our first day. We feel the frosty spray of a mountain torrent and gushing waterfall; pass over a swollen, raging river on a bobbing suspension bridge; and witness a gossamer rainbow after gentle rain. Our picnic lunch in a green pasture studded with daisies is cut short by drizzle, but the sun soon returns and we pack away our slickers for the rest of the day. The scenery is reminiscent of Colorado, from the shaded trail through fragrant pines and groves of rustling aspens to the snowcapped vistas across the valley. Seven hours after starting, we reach our destination village nestled beside a noisy stream with just enough time for much-needed showers before dinner. Our day had plenty of literal ups and downs, but the difficulty level was manageable. *I can do this,* I think; *I'm definitely ready for more.*

As we come to expect each evening after dinner, our muscles protest getting up from the table after having relaxed and then tightened during our meal. The ascent to our room is a painful reminder of the miles we covered that day. On this first night, our room is three flights up, and each step is successively more difficult. Eric warned that the weather report for the following day, reputed to be one of the most difficult legs of the TMB, is less than propitious and that we should make sure we're prepared. Like obedient schoolchildren, we lay out our waterproof foul-weather layers, down some extra-strength Tylenol, and collapse into the tumble of duvets.

Eric is right, as always. About everything. The next leg of the hike is wet, cold, strenuous, and long. The morning dawned under light cloud cover, but by early afternoon, we're making our way through gentle mist that turns to opaque fog as we reach the snow line. At one point midascent up steep, interminable slick rock, my overworked lungs burn a hole in my chest, and I ask myself as I bend over, yet again, to fully catch my breath, *Did we actually pay to put ourselves through this agony?* The terrain changes from rocky to muddy to an increasingly thick cover of slushy snow over the course of just several hundred yards. Cold rain and scalpel-sharp winds soon follow, and the mist is so thick by now that we can see only the heels of fellow hikers' boots in front of us. If ever we were crazy enough to think we could tackle the TMB independently, such delusional pretentions evaporate in the obscurity. The incline remains steep, and all is eerily silent, save the slushy sounds of one boot being planted in front of the other in the prints Eric cut ahead of us in the snow. The fog thickens further as the rain pelts our slickers and soaks our pants. From the tail end of our string of hikers comes the plaintive query: "Have we reached Nepal yet?" The timing for a giggle is opportune, since the hiking hero in me is fading, succumbing to the elements in lonely frustration. Joe and I haven't exchanged a word in hours, and I'm chilled to the bone, foul-weather paraphernalia notwithstanding. The backs of my heels have blistered despite significant applications of moleskin, and my pinkies are now simply two chafed hot spots. I will myself to continue every step of the way as we draw closer to the elusive pass.

The fog is such that had we been on our own, we surely would have missed the trail markers and been hopelessly lost—a dangerous proposition at over eight thousand feet. Even my ordinarily reliable sense of direction would have failed us. But just as my last reserves of will are waning and my spirits are about to hit rock bottom, the Refuge de la Croix du Bonhomme miraculously appears out of the mist at the pass. The rustic wooden hut with a central potbellied stove is the oasis I visualized over these cold, wet hours, and a mug of hot tea never tasted so good. The refuge is filled with the cheerful energy of grateful, shivering hikers sipping steaming beverages, resting in various stages of undress on long wooden benches, outer layers drying on clotheslines overhead. The atmosphere is festive, the room humid, and the windows fogged; no one is anxious to head back into the elements.

After we've spent an hour warming ourselves with a couple of doses of brew, Eric rounds us up and announces that the weather has cleared. We pile on still-damp layers for the sharp descent to l'Auberge de la Nova. The fog has indeed lifted, the rain has slowed to a drizzle, and soon after we leave the hut, patches of blue sky appear and the valley below becomes visible. Initially thrilled to be finally heading down, I'm soon lamenting the direction change as my knees scream in pain. I was worried that the hike would reignite my premarathon hip pain but never imagined that my knees would cause me problems. Keeping them intact and successfully negotiating the slick, muddy trails down the slope amid melting snow patches requires serious assistance from my trekking poles. So lean on them I do as I make the balance of the trip down among grazing cows.

We reach a hamlet of old stone buildings, and to our spent bodies it's paradise. Our simple hiker's inn with one toilet and one shower shared by the dozen guests on our floor is as comfortable as a five-star resort. It provides a hearty dinner and a functional bed—all we need.

Subsequent days take us from Les Chapieux, France, to Courmayeur, Italy, and on to Finhaut, Switzerland. While hiking becomes slightly less difficult (is it because the weather is perfect, or could it be that we're getting used to the daily exertion, the tempo of our steps, and the catastrophes that are our feet?), it never gets easy. As precarious as the day's weather on the climb to the Croix du Bonhomme pass was, the balance of our days on the TMB are scrumptious: skittering cotton-candy clouds in a pure blue sky, and just enough cool breeze to moderate the sun.

Each morning we awaken to the familiar *tick-tick-tick* of trekking poles as hikers getting an early start pass our open windows. I spend my first few waking moments wishing I could bypass the day's daunting climb, but my dogged spirit prevails (either that or I'm too embarrassed to say, "Today I'll take the shuttle"). We acclimate to the rhythm of our days: on the trail by 9:00 a.m. and at our destination by late afternoon. Mornings start with relentless, lung-searing, uphill climbs, until we're beyond the canopy of trees to the stunning view from a barren *col*, and we anticipate the promise of lush scenery over the crest, in the middle of which we'll have a picnic lunch. We fill our water bottles and CamelBak bladders with pure glacier output from rushing streams and have our midday repasts in the company of whistling marmots, shrieking swifts, and squeaking, diving pipits, spooky cracks of glaciers in the distance. We then embark on the welcome dip into a new valley, always in the presence of the sleeping Mont Blanc giant, losing all the elevation we gained that morning.

One day, while trudging through a cow-filled pasture on our way up to that day's pass, we stop at a dairy farm to watch sharp, grassy-flavored Beaufort cheese being made. The cows are milked in the pasture as they munch away, and then the milk is brought to the dairy and dumped into a gargantuan copper pot. From inside the damp cheese shed, whose nutty, moldy aroma is most pleasant, Eric buys a sizable chunk from a gargantuan cheese wheel, and we demolish it as part of our lunch. He always surprises us with new local specialties, but I draw the line at *lardo*, an Aosta Valley charcuterie made of fatback cured with herbs. I pass on the Italian delicacy, which looks like a pasty white fruit roll-up made of pure Crisco shortening.

We cross mountain glens splendidly carpeted with wildflowers: gentian violets, a lovely lavender-colored variety of Queen Anne's lace, alpine crocuses, wild thyme, tiny marguerite daisies, and magnificent lupine. A dozen chamois sprint over a glacial snowfield, one by one nimbly negotiating the slippery slope with grace and speed. We trek through polite Swiss villages of chalets with Arcadian charm and window boxes spilling over with abundant pink and red geraniums. I stop often to look around and snap mental photos to preserve the images for as long as I can.

The panoramic vistas that come into view as we pass back into France from Switzerland are some of the prettiest of the hike, and we glimpse the village of Le Tour, our journey's end, in miniature in the distance. I ask Eric, "Are you enjoying the commute home after your business trip in the Alps?" When he smiles and nods, I observe, "It certainly beats being stuck in a Washington, DC, traffic jam."

We spend our final afternoon on the TMB descending through above-the-tree-line meadows and then delicate aspen woods. At times the aerobic ascents just about killed me, but I now experience little trouble heading down—as long as my reliable trekking poles support me. On the other hand, a couple of fellow hikers are like mountain goats, going up without effort but finding the extended descents more difficult. In fact, halfway down to Le Tour, one of our comrades takes the gondola down to the finish line, rather than further destroy already-ravaged knees. Joe, as usual, emerges unscathed. And while every big and little muscle in my body aches and it will take my roughened heels and blistered, callused, chewed-up feet months to recover, the only lingering injury I sustain is some painful sun poisoning on my lower lip.

At the end of each day, we were dirty as dogs and tired as babies, and this trek was the hardest physical challenge I've ever done, the marathon included. But it scares me to think that tomorrow we'll no longer be on the trail. Being outdoors in the presence of unbridled, unspoiled nature is a humbling experience and reminds us of just how insignificant we are compared with the wild. We're guests passing through—part of the plan but not in charge, try as we might. We must acquiesce to nature and not the other way around, because, as Eric likes to remind us, the mountains will always be better competitors.

DEPRESSION SETS IN

At times it feels the past ten months have been one long serial checkout. We're forever unpacking, repacking, and saying goodbye to places to which we've grown attached. On the road again or back on the rails, we wave goodbye, promising to return.

So it is with leaving Chamonix, the Alps, and the companions with whom we shared the TMB. The eight of us bonded like children at summer camp, and so the departure is difficult. Much like the day after a long-planned wedding, we welcome the opportunity to relax and reflect, but the after-party letdown and inevitable disappointment that the event is over leave us feeling flat. Our fellow hikers depart the next morning, but we have more time to spare and give ourselves an extra day in the mountains before we board a train. The day is cool and rainy, exacerbating the doldrums, and we spend most of it in our hotel room, massaging sore muscles and reminiscing about the hike. "I'm so sad it's over," I sigh to Joe, and I can see from his face that he feels the same. For much of the day we're quiet, overcome with melancholia, and I'm close to tears. Added to post-TMB longing is the fact that leaving Chamonix and heading for Provence means we're entering the final phase of our journey. "Are there really only two months left in our year?" Joe asks, shaking his head.

The gloom continues into the evening, and so we do what comes naturally when we're in the dumps: we head out to eat. Our final dinner in Chamonix is at La Moraine, the very same restaurant where Joe and I had a quiet, memorable Thanksgiving dinner (*poulet Vallée d'Auge*—chicken with apples, cream sauce, and Calvados) in 1978, when I was a student. He visited me in France, and we took the train to the Alps to celebrate the American holiday weekend.

We easily find the cozy chalet restaurant thirty-four years later, ignore the rain outside, and chase away the blues by planning our upcoming weeks in the sun-drenched van Gogh landscape of Provence. Safely back in our hotel, we watch the European soccer championship between Italy and Spain, and Joe suggests that perhaps the country that wins (Italy is the eventual victor) will have the privilege of declaring bankruptcy first. It's a good sign—our sense of humor is back.

XV. Provençal Paradise
July–August 2012

SENSING PROVENCE

SOFTENING OUR ALPINE DEPARTURE is a shift of my thoughts from the chilly mountain air to the warmth of Provence. By the time our train leaves the mountains, the rain has stopped, and once we board the TGV for Avignon, the Provençal sun has taken over. We pick up our rental car, dump our warm layers in the backseat, and, spirits revived, head deep into the south of France.

We have two weeks to wander the countryside before we settle into Aix-en-Provence, where we've rented an apartment and I'll take a monthlong French course to sharpen my conversational skills and brush up on current lingo. Details for the TMB impeded our planning of what would come next, and we have few specifics in place. We consider making it up as we go along, but there are too many must-dos on our list to leave discovering Provence to whim. The area is rich in potential for outdoor activities, and we'll take advantage of what's available—*en profiter bien*, as the French like to say.

Over the course of visits in years gone by, the south of France got under my skin. Paris aside, Provence is by far my favorite corner of the hexagon. It's a veritable feast for the senses, starting with sound. I sit and search the Internet in the shade of a plane tree with a buzzing background chorus of *les cigales* (cicadas). The insects' whir leads some to earplugs and is said to drive others mad, but it helps me sit back, absorb the sounds of summer, and map out our stay here.

This is also the most pleasantly fragrant place we've visited. Lavender, always one of my favorite flowers for its soothing fragrance and healing essential oil, has become a familiar symbol of the area. Its tiny clustered blossoms, also a favorite of butterflies and bees, dot farmhouse gardens, add their gentle purple color to municipal floral displays, and spread in parallel rows of redolent blooms across acres of farms. Café culture is alive and well in Provence, so in addition to lavender, ubiquitous is the scent of coffee in the coolness of green awnings, another defining feature of Provence. Afternoon shade is a necessity as the sun blazes, and it can be found easily thanks to the proliferation of sheltered cafés, all of them filled with locals sipping demitasses of strong, pungent coffee.

The tastes of Provence are so different from those we savored in the mountains. The hard, nutty cow cheeses are now soft, herbal goat varieties, and preserved hams and beef have morphed into fresh vegetables and seafood. Butter has disappeared, since all is cooked and dressed in olive oil, and oversize capers and soft, ripe olives yield salty, vinegary mouthfuls. I always prefer a bowl brimming with such briny tidbits to one filled with ice cream, so Provence and my palate are fast friends.

Although we have yet to face it, the fierce touch of *le mistral* always threatens. The locals continually refer to the almighty cold wind that whips south down the valleys of the Rhône and Durance rivers for days at a time, even in summer, battering everything in its wake. Since this visit to Provence will be extended, we're sure to experience it in the coming weeks.

I take a break from my computer and walk for hours through the countryside surrounding the rural château northwest of Avignon to which we've treated ourselves for the first two days so we can relax and plan our route. The surroundings are parched, much like Arizona, and the rocky hills in the distance remind me of Tucson's mountains. I pass through lush orchards of fig, pear, plum, and peach trees, their branches heavy with not-yet-ripened fruit, and cross miles of vineyards with tiny, hard green grapes tucked beneath wide, flat leaves. In two more months they'll be fat, juicy, and ready for harvest— *just as we're readying to leave,* I think. Alongside the vineyards, boundless fields of sunflowers, *les tournesols* (literally "turning to the sun"), extend to the horizon. The wide yellow blooms are fully developed and appear bashful in the afternoon light, shying away from the blinding sun down toward the shadowed brown earth. When the flowers are still in their growth phase, their faces follow the sun as it moves across the sky. But once they mature, the burning orb is too hot even for them, and they turn away.

I look up at the sky, the deepest azure imaginable and completely free of clouds, close my eyes, feel the sun on my face, and savor the sensations of Provence.

EXPLORING PROVENCE

The Luberon Valley is our favorite spot in Provence. It's comfortably familiar, not just because we read Peter Mayle's *A Year in Provence*, but because the landscape, the architecture, and the flora touch us. Even as first-time visitors, we felt as if we'd been here before.

It's nearly impossible to get last-minute lodging in the Luberon in July, but after repeated attempts, we secure a room at le Roy Soleil in Ménerbes. The amiable *mas*, a traditional Provençal farmhouse turned hotel, is nestled among the vineyards at the foot of the picturesque hill town. Our garret room looks over the bougainvillea-encircled, umbrella-covered terrace that serves as the summer dining room. The smell of coffee wafting up to our window and the tinkling of breakfast silverware awaken us each morning, and we doze off at night to the murmur of whispered dinner conversations below. On our first evening, we join the other guests on the patio and dine on a meal of Provençal specialties served with healthy helpings of olives and fresh vegetables. Joe feasts on lamb with crispy rice and asparagus, and I have langoustines with fava beans. Eighty percent of the wine produced in the region is rosé, and so our usual order of *un pichet* of white turns into a fruity pink selection—a local varietal chilled in a stylish, pastel plastic ice bag (all the rage in France).

As we consistently eat too much food and drink too much wine, we also persist in taking long walks, running when we can, and seeking out interesting hikes in an attempt to continue to fit in our clothes. We follow intriguing signs that take us to le Colorado Provençal de Rustrel in the northeast corner of the valley. The colorful park is the site of an abandoned ocher quarry, and the miles of trails take us past red, gold, tawny, and pure white cliffs and wind-sculpted spire formations set against deep-blue skies. We hike for two hours, marvel at the natural palette, work up an appetite, and then find a café in the village of Rustrel.

We visit the Luberon's top sights—the hilltop towns

of Gordes and Lacoste (where the Marquis de Sade once lived in his château), Bonnieux and Ménerbes, Lourmarin and Roussillon (a beautiful golden village), as well as those in regions farther afield. We canoe under the Pont du Gard, paddling our way south on the Gardon River until we pass beneath the graceful and almost-intact three-level Roman aqueduct bridge. We have lunch at the Café de Nuit in Arles, the subject of van Gogh's *Café Terrace at Night*. It's always been a favorite—in fact, I carried a journal with the image on its cover through college—but I now feel an eternal emotional bond with the artist and this painting.

Years ago, I read an article about a young Belgian couple who opened a fine-dining restaurant in the sleepy town of Eygalières in the heart of Provence. I saved the clipping, and so we have a romantic dinner under the stars on the veranda at Maison Bru. In addition to the delectable appetizer of poached egg with truffle butter, what I'll always remember is spying the sous-chef slipping into the garden, snipping some fresh herbs, and heading back to the kitchen.

There's a most unusual gallery in Les Baux-de-Provence. Under the bauxite hill town are les Carrières de Lumières—the Quarries of Lights. The geometrical walls of the cavernous interior spaces are filled with projections of van Gogh and Gauguin paintings, accompanied by fitting inspirational music. It sounds kitschy, but it works; the large-scale reproductions make you feel as if you're inside the paintings themselves in the cool of the quarries.

We venture out on additional exploratory jaunts after breakfast, and every place we visit stirs up new questions about art, architecture, history, and language. We study our guidebooks and do Internet searches to try to answer our questions, but there's never enough time to learn all we want to know. About van Gogh and Gauguin. About Provence. About France, Europe, and all the places we've visited. Even with a full year to ourselves, dedicated to nothing but seeing, experiencing, and learning, we just never, ever have enough time to complete our education.

Late in the afternoons, we return to our hotel to lounge by the pool, lie in the sun, and brown like roasts on recliners. The air is so arid that five minutes after we take a dip, our bathing suits have dried as if we'd never gotten wet, so back into the pool we go. How quickly what we long for can change.

"Do you believe we were shivering in the Chamonix rain just ten days ago?" I ask Joe as he towels the sweat from his brow.

"Yeah," he agrees, "we could use some of that cool right now, because this heat is just too much of a good thing."

STAYING PUT IN AIX

Our itinerant days of meandering the south of France are over. It's time to settle down with a satisfying, stay-put month in Aix-en-Provence. The moment we arrive, we know we belong here. There's a particular brand of the relaxed Provençal spirit in town, affirmed by the sign we see posted on a local bus: NE SOYEZ PAS PRESSÉ, ICI ON SE HÂTE LENTEMENT. (Don't be in a hurry; we speed up slowly around here.) Our arrival coincides with the July 14 Bastille Day weekend, so, having missed the Fourth of July at home, we pretend the holiday fireworks will be to honor America's birthday.

A dynamic, livable town, Aix lies twenty miles north of Marseille. It's been continually inhabited since its founding in 123 BC by the Romans, who luxuriated in the thermal waters that continue to flow and provide modern-day hydrotherapy benefits at the Sextius Baths spa. The hub of Aixois activity is the Cours Mirabeau, one of the most stylish avenues in the world. It starts at the grand Fontaine de la Rotonde and runs to the stone statue of le Roi René, a favorite leaning post for tourist snapshots. It's the Champs-Élysées of the south, with a small-town vibe and none of Paris's hustle-bustle and conceit. The broad boulevard is bordered by elegant eighteenth-century *hôtels particuliers*, shaded by double rows of soaring plane trees, dotted with fountains, and lined with chic cafés that spill onto its sidewalks. The most famous eatery along the Cours is the Deux Garçons, built in 1792, whose most famous patrons were native sons Paul Cézanne and Émile Zola in the late 1800s. The boulevard traces the line of what was the city wall and splits the town in two: the new town, the Quartier Mazarin, with its classical, grid-patterned streets to the south, and the old town, its irregular streets twisting to the north.

The place we call home for our month in Aix is a third-floor walk-up in the Quartier Mazarin, just a couple of blocks off the Cours Mirabeau. Our one-bedroom apartment is airy, modern, and filled with natural light. While not air-conditioned, it has an industrial-strength fan that chases away the midday heat and allows for comfortable sleeping. The weather in Aix is consistent: sunny and hot. On occasion, the day dawns with a light cover of clouds, but the sun soon reminds the interlopers of whose territory this is, and by 9:00 a.m., all clears to an impossibly blue sky.

Every day in Aix, there's at least one open-air market: on the Place Richelme, on the Place des Prêcheurs, and along the Cours Mirabeau. Purveyors of everything from fresh fruit, cheese, and vegetables to honey, sausage, tapenades, and olives to linens, sandals, lavender soap, and hand-crafted jewelry sell their wares. The displays deserve a fresh gander each time we pass by, just in case some new treasure presents itself. We inevitably come away with a bag of fresh goodies to stock our fridge.

On one particularly memorable Sunday, local producers of Coteaux d'Aix-en-Provence wines offer tastings all afternoon along the Cours. The vintners sell their nectars with an irresistible proposition: buy your wineglass for 3 euros (or bring your own) and go from winery to winery, tasting the offerings from twenty-five vineyards for free. It's a blissful Aix afternoon and a perfect excuse for a midday nap.

A WIDE-EYED SCHOOLGIRL

I was born in the wrong country. There must have been some mistake. Then again, if I'd been born in the hexagon, my passion for all things French wouldn't exist. I'd have been raised with the language's romantic euphony, and the fluid succession of words would be part of my everyday world. Some other tongue and faraway culture would have caught my fancy—so perhaps, just perhaps, it's fortuitous my birthplace was Fort Wayne, Indiana, and not Paris.

Passions are essential to a happy life. When we care about something, it shrinks the world to a human scale, breaking it into wieldy pieces to love and nurture. My passion for French shapes my world, yet why I love this lyrical language so dearly is an essential mystery I'll never fully understand.

I love being a student of French, no matter my age, but on the first day of my conversation class at IS Aix-en-Provence, I'm predictably nervous, as I've been on day one of every school year of my life. I lay out my clothes the night before and imagine first days of school gone by: my freshly ironed plaid uniform, crisp white blouse, just-purchased navy knee socks with tags still attached, and newly polished oxfords. I pack a snack, just as I did in grammar school, and I'm ready to go. My giddy younger self emerges the moment I cross the classroom threshold, polished floorboards creaking, where I am once again a wide-eyed schoolgirl eagerly poised over a blank composition book, pencil sharpened and my ardor for the subject on my sleeve.

My class of ten includes students from Australia, Finland, the Netherlands, Spain, and Sweden, none of us a youngster and all on an educational vacation in summertime Aix. I introduce myself and stumble on the choice of tense. Do I use the present or the future tense of "to be"? Do I affirm *I am* a French teacher, or do I demur and say *I'll soon be* a French teacher? I opt for the former, *Je suis prof de français.* It bolsters my confidence with a frisson of pride.

My *prof* is Céline—gorgeous, funny, and particularly warm. I so wish I could be like her—*une jolie française* who speaks lovely French. As I walk home from class, it hits me, as it has so often before: yes, I am a newly minted French teacher, but no matter how I try, no matter how I practice, no matter how fiercely I study, I'll never be French. I'll never be *française.* I'll never sound like Céline. I'll forever be on the outside looking in, my face and palms pressed against the linguistic glass. I plunge into a microflash of depression. But I proceed across town, under soaring sycamores, content to have a passion I can call my very own.

The French often truncate words by dropping the final syllables and adding an "o." *Apéro*, McDo, and *resto* (aperitif, McDonald's, and restaurant) have long been staples of my French vocabulary, but thanks to my classes, I add abbreviations to my repertoire: *accro* (hooked on), *les actus* (the news), *un ado* (an adolescent), *bio* (organic), *un dico* (a dictionary), *perso* (personal), and, my favorite, Sarko (Nicolas Sarkozy). Each week in class, we prepare presentations about *les actus*, and I do one on social media. *Twitter* and *blogger* have now entered the daily lexicon as regular "-er" verbs. We learn the quirky French term for "walkie-talkie" (*talkie-walkie*), that the expression *vachement bien* (amazingly good), which was very popular thirty years ago, is much less in vogue nowadays, and that it is *très chic* to say *super* (pronounced "sue pair"— accent on the "sue"), especially if you're a woman. The café was *super-bon*; your dress is *super-chic*; he looks *super*. I also frequently use, "sympa" — short for sympathetique (nice). I imagine the French language police, the Académie Française, must be *super-fâché* (very angry) about all the new Franglais.

- - - - - - - - - - - - - - -

Indeed, much has changed in France over the past thirty-five years. There's a new generation with kinder attitudes, more customer-service orientation, and lots of English spoken, so unlike the France of days gone by. Everyone wants to speak English, but I want to speak French. I'm bolstered by Joe, who always encourages, "Make them speak French, babe," so we have uneven, lopsided exchanges:

"Good evening, madame."
"Bonsoir, monsieur."

"Would you like an aperitif?"

"Oui, je prends un kir, s'il vous plaît."

"Very good. And you, sir?"

"Un kir aussi, merci."

It's initially disconcerting, but they eventually get the point and give us what we want. We really do appreciate the attempt to be accommodating and their eagerness to practice our language. If only Americans would exhibit the same passion for learning new tongues.

A NIGHT AT THE OPERA

Attending a performance under summer stars in the ancient Roman theater in Orange, France, is at the top of my bucket list. I'm well aware the experience hasn't made Joe's list, especially because it's opera, but he agrees to be my date, knowing how disappointed I was by the cancellation in Venice.

Le Théâtre Antique d'Orange, considered among the finest and best-preserved remains of the Roman Empire in Europe, is a semicircular stone auditorium that seats nine thousand. It's home to the internationally acclaimed summer festival les Chorégies d'Orange, an hour's drive north of Aix, in the Rhône valley. The theater's audience faces north, and the original stage wall, its back to the notorious *mistral*, remains intact, providing performances with outstanding acoustics and protection from the whipping wind. Performing-arts festivals have been held at the Théâtre Antique since the middle of the 1800s, but in 1969, les Chorégies became exclusively opera, leaving theatrical works to migrate to Avignon.

Our long-awaited outing begins well. It's a typically sweltering evening in Provence, and even the shadows of a sinking sun bring little relief. It's with great gusto that we gulp down liberal goblets of the refreshing house aperitif at the outdoor café where we dine: grapefruit juice and rosé wine over ice. Perfect for a preopera summer night.

We take our seats in the theater, amazed that we're sitting on the very same stones Roman derrieres graced two thousand years ago. The sun sets, the performance begins; the orchestra is brilliant and the setting spectacular.

Let's review my gap year history with live opera and the continuation of my misadventures in Orange.

1. **December 2011**: We attempt to get tickets in Milan for *Don Giovanni* at la Scala. It's opening night and they laugh.

2. **May 2012**: We have tickets for *La Bohème* at la Fenice in Venice. There's an earthquake, the theater is damaged, and the performance is canceled.

3. **July 2012**: We attend *Turandot* at the massive Roman amphitheater in Orange. It's a moving performance, but in the third act, the leading man's voice gives out, he's unable to finish the signature aria—long my favorite—"*Nessun Dorma*," and I'm crushed.

I declare defeat. I'm able to cross this item off my list; live opera under the stars in a Roman theater: check. But I grumble to Joe as we file from the theater with the other disappointed patrons, "From now on, I'm settling for opera on my iPod."

STALKING CÉZANNE

The artists I've studied are those I've come to love, and such is the case with Paul Cézanne. I always found his ocher-toned paintings of Provençal landscapes and depictions of Mont Sainte-Victoire pleasing. But now that I've lived in his town, visited the seminal spots of his life, and walked in his footsteps, I feel as if we've forged a close personal bond.

Cézanne was Provençal through and through and, above all, a son of Aix. He was passionately attached to his hometown, in particular its perpetual play of vivid light on the countryside, which so influenced his art. Cézanne's work evolved over the years until it was perched on the precipice of cubism and abstraction at his death; thus, many deem him the father of modern painting.

Our quest for the true Cézanne begins at the Jas de Bouffan, the home west of town where he lived with his parents in the late 1800s. The verdant property with its straight, sycamore-lined approach is secreted behind high stone walls and an equally imposing iron gate. The rectangular manor house is where Cézanne completed his first paintings in the high-ceilinged dining room turned artist's studio, using its walls as experimental canvases.

Next on our journey in the steps of Cézanne are the Bibémus quarries, on a rocky plateau east of Aix, where he spent significant time as a teen. It was while walking under towering pines with his friend Émile Zola (yes, *that* Zola) that he discovered his inner painter. The sandstone quarries were worked until the mid-1800s, but when Cézanne and his chum came upon them, they were abandoned and overgrown. The mustard- and molasses-colored rock retains the angular shapes cut by quarry laborers in sharp contrast with the soft green and brown lines of nature. Cézanne was drawn to the distinction, and the drive to depict it on canvas consumed him.

We follow the artist's route on the fragrant pine needle–cushioned forest paths through the quarries to the stone hut with a red wooden door where he safeguarded his artwork and spent nights. It's from a vantage point near the hut that Cézanne viewed and painted, obsessively, the dramatic, 3,300-foot Mont Sainte-Victoire against the Provençal sky. The famous mountain dominates the artist's work, and nearly one hundred of his paintings feature the rugged, gray stone peak.

We make the hour-long hike down the ridge from the plateau to the shaded town of Le Tholonet, one of Cézanne's favorite retreats. The village has two cafés, a *pétanque* pit, an abundance of trees, and a château that Cézanne painted. We choose le Relais *Cézanne* for lunch and while away the afternoon on its cool terrace.

The artist's studio halfway up the Lauves Hill north of Aix, which he customized for the practice of his art and to which he walked from the Jas de Bouffan every morning of the final four years of his life, is infused with Cézanne's presence. The high-ceilinged central room he designed, with a huge picture window that bathes the room in natural light, has been left as it was when the artist was alive. His furniture, still-life objects, painting chemises, palettes, brushes, tools, overcoat, hat, and cane are as they were when he died in 1906.

We end our pilgrimage in the Saint-Pierre cemetery on a hill at the edge of town: the artist's unassuming final resting place. Cézanne was born in Aix and died in Aix and is the town's favorite native son. And during my time in his fair city, I've become an ardent Aixois, just like he was. Our wanderings among the places most important to him leave me with an understanding of the man and the work that drove him. "I almost feel like I knew him personally, you know?" I say to Joe as we leave the cemetery. He nods his head and wholeheartedly agrees.

A DAY IN OUR LIFE IN AIX

The wealth of Aix is plentiful and varied: a warm ambience and relaxed culture, delicious food, vibrant cafés, sophisticated restaurants, an abundant natural environment, exquisite art, sophisticated buildings, interesting museums, Roman ruins, and thousands of years of history. But the script of our every day remains sweet and simple: it allows for routine and repetition, the mark of residing, rather than just passing through, and my daily go-to-school routine helps connect us to the community.

Every morning at five forty-five, the chartreuse-uniformed workman hosing down the rue Frédéric Mistral, three floors below the bedroom window of our pied-à-terre, awakens us. He power-washes the street, leaving it scrubbed and ready for waves of day-tripping visitors to soon swarm the town. Five minutes later, the church bells chime, calling the faithful to morning mass, and I stumble out of bed while Joe sleeps in.

I brew the coffee, open the living room window, and push open heavy wooden shutters. Incessant birdsong greets me in the soft light of morning. I grab a yogurt from the fridge, add cream to my coffee, sit at the kitchen table, and review my homework. I read what's à la une—in the headlines—of L'Express online, find an interesting story I can share in class, carefully read it several times, and scribble brief summary notes.

By seven thirty, the buzz of the *motocyclettes* whizzing by on the street below is constant, marking the arousal of the waking city. I lean out the window and see that the bold Provençal sun has risen, creating sharp shadows on the yellow walls and blue-gray shutters of the building *juste en face*, on the opposite side of the street. By eight, Joe joins me for breakfast, and we review our plans for the day.

At 8:40, I swing on my backpack and Joe walks me to school. It's a picturesque, unhurried stroll, and while we occasionally vary our route, we most often head straight across the Cours Mirabeau, through the Passage Agard, which cuts through the row of *hôtels particuliers*, and into the square of the Palais de Justice. We weave our way through the open-air market, inhaling and ogling the irresistible offerings. We turn right on the rue Portalis, which takes us to the Cours des Arts et *Métiers*, where I spend my mornings in class. The school is in a two-story building with tall, thick-paned windows, small, cozy classrooms, and planked wooden floors. Classes start at nine, and for the next three and a half hours I converse with my teacher and classmates, reveling in being the luckiest person in the world as I continue my French education.

On his way home, Joe lingers in the markets and buys fresh produce from the list we've prepared, plus whatever else appeals. He then gets his daily exercise by running through Aix, sticking to shaded parks, including la Promenade de la Torse, along the southeastern flank of town.

At twelve thirty I say *à demain* to school and walk home, my head filled with new vocabulary and expressions I'm anxious to try on the locals. I amble down pedestrian lanes and stop at our regular *boulangerie* to pick up *une fournée*, our new favorite variety of French bread. While all baguettes are delicious, this particular loaf is made from whole-wheat flour, has an especially crunchy crust, and is deliciously yeasty inside. Warm *fournée* tucked under my arm, I turn left down the rue Frédéric Mistral and ring the bell on our apartment building's doorstep, and Joe buzzes me in.

We make lunch from whatever hand-wrapped goodies Joe has brought home this day and dine on fresh Provençal fare as we fill in each other on our mornings.

Our afternoon itineraries vary, and if I have no school excursion, they include taking in a museum, discovering a new park, watching the local men play *pétanque*, or looking for interesting restaurants. We pass the luscious displays of fruit tarts and cream-filled pastries in pâtisserie windows, all so gorgeous to the eye. July is the month for clothing sales—*les soldes*—in France, but since I have no room in my suitcase and few euros left in my wallet, I settle for *lèche-vitrine* (window shopping). I'm so ready to burn my clothes, having worn the same things for eleven months, that I can barely even look at them, much less put them on, but shopping must wait until we're once again employed.

By late afternoon, it's time to slow our pace. We stop on the Cours Mirabeau for a cold drink and watch the parade of passersby. While I love the look of the brightly colored drinks the French enjoy over ice in summer (mineral water tinted with mint and grenadine syrups), I have no desire to partake. We stick to sipping Perriers to pass the time before dinner. The days are long, remaining light until 10:00 p.m., so eating at eight feels premature, even for early diners like us.

"I love that there's never a rush while eating out in France," I often remark to Joe. "Once we sit down, we own our table and no one ever rushes us to leave."

He adds, "And they never give you the bill until you ask for it. How civilized."

We eat dinner leisurely, accompanied by heartfelt conversation about the children, current events, and rebuilding our lives back home, always under the stars.

We stroll home hand in hand during *l'heure bleue*, that romantic French expression for twilight, the time between day and night when it's not yet dark but no longer light. The daily tourists have disappeared, and the town is back in the hands of the locals and its very-lucky temporary residents. The *marché nocturne*—the evening market—is in full swing, but we've done our shopping for the day and will save our purchases for the morning. We turn on the *télé* and watch an hour of *les JO—les Jeux Olympiques*—broadcast live from London. Yet again we hear the energized announcer pronounce Michael Phelps, with a thick French accent, "*un champion exceptionnel!*"

And thus the sun sets on another day of our life in Aix. I watch the aerial evening dance of the swallows over the roofs across the street, taking a moment to listen to the thin strains of their cries, before I secure the shutters, fall into bed, and close my eyes on one more day in paradise.

FIELD TRIPPING

On any given day in Aix, we have myriad choices of what to do. We take fabulous field trips with my classmates, attend presentations, and venture out on our own. Perhaps because remaining sedentary in a corner *boîte* is so tempting, we valiantly fight the urge, get up and out, and then reward ourselves later with café relaxation.

Aix is graced with a Relais & Châteaux property, the

Villa Gallici, on a hill on the edge of town, secreted behind thick hedges of cypress and oleander. One afternoon, we lunch there on a sycamore-shaded terrace at a glass-topped table in thick-cushioned patio chairs overlooking a chic swimming pool. Enjoying the afternoon through the gentle haze of a bottle of Bandol rosé, we're fascinated by the image of a waiter in a tuxedo delivering delectable chicken salads on a silver tray to a willowy woman in an itsy-bitsy burgundy bikini lounging under a matching pool umbrella with her young son.

We go on a weekend school outing to the Mediterranean coastal towns of La Ciotat and Cassis. Our bus is packed with international students ready for a day at the shore. The first stop is La Ciotat's Saturday-morning market along the harbor, where we shop for fresh lunch provisions. Market people are happy people—we have yet to meet a surly seller behind an open-air stand. *"Des olives pour votre pique-nique, monsieur?"* one bronzed vendor asks Joe, who eagerly nods and walks on with a small bag filled with green, garlic-infused nuggets. We have a hard time saying no to any of the offerings and buy tapenades, a baguette, chunks of cheese, slices of ham, sun-dried tomatoes, and juicy white peaches, eager for the picnic we soon devour at our second stop, the local beach. The day is the usual sun and azure skies, and we lunch on a rocky embankment in the cool shade of seaside cedars. We move on to the charming town of Cassis, where we catch a boat to explore les Calanques, steep-walled limestone coves with translucent water that perforate the Mediterranean shoreline east of Marseille.

One afternoon, we venture into Marseille itself, a thirty-minute bus ride south of Aix. Founded in 600 BC, the oldest town in France, it's now the second-largest city in the country (although residents of Lyon often challenge this claim). We have an early seafood dinner along the lines of yachts and fishing boats of the *vieux port*, and, having watched *The French Connection* a few nights before, I comment, "This area isn't half as gritty as I imagined. Where are the drug traffickers and organized crime?"

"Seems a lot has changed since the 1960s," Joe replies.

Despite the sea breezes, the day is extremely hot, lethargy prevails, and we find ourselves purchasing the most touristy tickets of our year. We take the miniature baby-blue train that wanders the city and goes to the top of a limestone peak with a panoramic view over town. As we approach the summit, the electronically generated (and, apparently, translated) French commentary announces we're arriving at Notre-Dame de la Garde, famous for its thirty-foot-high gilded Madonna and Child atop the steeple. So far, so good, except that the English translation that follows suggests that we "look up to see the golden Virgin and her kid." We must be the only English speakers aboard, because we're the only ones laughing.

I'm so proud of Joe, quite the adventurer when it comes to accompanying me and paying close attention at afternoon, school-sponsored, all-in-French epicurean presentations. As he likes to remind me, when the subject is food and wine, his comprehension is amazingly good. The first is a wine *dégustation*. Our master wine educator brings five bottles for us to sample after a brilliant lecture on the history of wine and the finer points of drinking it. We've been to many wine tastings over the years and at each one learn something. One of the fascinating new tidbits the *prof* imparts is that the reason vineyards developed along rivers and the sea was not because grapevines need irrigating. Rather, because most of the ancients traveled by water, they communicated with those along the way about viticulture; thus was the word disseminated. It started in eastern Turkey and spread from there.

When there's wine, cheese is sure to follow, so our next *dégustation* is of the dairy variety at the home of a local Aixois woman—a gracious hostess who loves opening her doors to international students. We sample every one of the cheeses, at least thirty local varieties—all sheep and goat cheeses, since there are no cows in Provence (it's much too hot to grow grass for them). We try everything from bland, watery *fromage frais* to the buttery, runny, stinky sort. Each taste is accompanied by a slice of crusty bread and either some homemade olive, pesto, or sun-dried tomato spread or a touch of thick homemade jam—and, of course, a healthy swig of full-bodied red wine.

Next up on our tasting circuit is olive oils. As olive lovers, we've always liked the rich, unctuous oil—fish and vegetables cooked in it and pasta and bread dripping with it—but we never knew much about where it came from or how it's produced. Thanks to our *sympa, prof,* a passionate olive oil aficionado, we're now much wiser. He pulls Joe and me aside after class to make sure we know how he loves welcoming foreigners to France, especially kind-hearted Americans (*"J'aime bien les américains—vous êtes si généreux,"* he confides), and hearing them speak French. He's fascinated by our love for his country and language, and we do our best to be worthy diplomats and gracious students.

On our last full day in Aix, we sign on for a final weekend field trip with a couple dozen fellow students. We first stop at Riez, a former Roman settlement that's now a bustling market town, for lunch supplies. Our bus proceeds to the striking Gorges du Verdon, a deep, compact chasm at the bottom of which rushes chalky turquoise water headed for the man-made Lac de Sainte-Croix. Time doesn't allow for more than a cursory walk beside the lake, but we make a mental note to return one day for a substantial hike in the gorge.

Just as my trips when I was young left me with lists of places to which we've returned, I now have a new catalog of possibilities for the future, because surely this isn't our last visit to Europe. A visit to the pilgrimage town of Moustiers-Sainte-Marie, built into a rocky cliff and famous for its *faïence* ceramics, tops off the day trip. After ascending and then coming back down the dramatic stairway to its Notre Dame church, we say goodbye to the vertical village, as we'll reluctantly say goodbye to Aix the following day. It leaves me feeling terribly *triste*. In fact, I've been feeling melancholy since I closed the door on my last French class the day before and had to say goodbye to the school and teachers I so adored. Packing up our month in Aix this evening is going to take an additional toll on my already wistful state.

My forehead pressed against the sun-warmed bus window on our two-hour ride back to town, I watch the endless rows of lavender as we pass along the back roads of Provence. The weary plants have lost their royal purple luster, their tiny blooms faded to a tired, August gray. I relate to their end-of-season torpor: less than two weeks remain of our gap year, and I wonder how we'll muster the energy to move toward what comes next, now that we've realized our dream. It's our last full day in Aix-en-Provence. Tomorrow we head north toward Paris for the final two weeks of our year.

I resolve on that long, hot bus ride back to Aix to simply focus on coming back to the lavender. Provence will always be there, and yes, I will always come back. For more field trips. For more wine, more cheese, more olive oil. And certainly for more of the lavender.

XVI. We'll Always Have Paris
August 2012

HEADING NORTH

I FEEL A STINGING RUSH OF AFFECTION for Aix as we leave and head north, waving goodbye to the fields of sunflowers flanking the highway. We pass by their heavy, bowing heads, which, just like the lavender, are done for the season, their broad round faces tired and brown. And so begins the recitation of our on-the-road "lasts": we pick up our last rental car; we see our last sunflowers; we pay our last toll; we stop at our last rest stop; we exit our last autoroute. There will be countless more in the coming days, and each time we check one off, it takes a little more out of me.

A mere five hours on the road and we arrive in a different world. Thick clouds have moved in; it's dreary and raining. We're in Burgundy, home of many famous wines, but already I miss the southern sun. France fits into America's second-largest state with a few stray Texan angles poking out, but the geographical variety of the hexagon outdoes the Lone Star State, hands down. Every corner has its own special treasures, and we've loved getting to know so many. But the stops we've planned for the five days on our way up to Paris will be completely new to us:

Burgundy, Lorraine, and Picardy.

I think about the string of valedictions behind us, and it reminds me of the things we've left strewn in our wake. All along the way, every time we repacked, we did what we could to lighten our heavy load. In Amsterdam, I finally convinced Joe to say goodbye to the rarely used, clumsy golf umbrella he lugged along for eight months (I called it Albie, short for Albatross). And there are T-shirts, shorts, socks, jeans, sweaters, and scarves—in bus depots, train stations, tourist offices, and hotel rooms, on park benches and trains. We generated a trail of laundry we no longer needed or that we could no longer bear to wear from France to Turkey and, of course, abandoned the packed duffel in Sicily. I always anticipated the possibility, with both embarrassment and more than a little amusement, that we would see someone on a train or in line at a museum wearing one of Joe's discarded sweaters or my oversize sweatpants.

Our arrival at the incomparable pink and green–shuttered Bernard Loiseau country auberge in tiny Saulieu, smack in the middle of vineyard-rich Burgundy, snaps me out of my soulful reverie. It's time to face forward and appreciate present pleasures. For years I hoped to one day visit the legendary inn, lovingly built around the three-starred Michelin restaurant as its centerpiece, despite the fact that the property is burdened with a tragic past.

I read some years ago about its chef-owner, Bernard Loiseau, a deeply troubled, driven, perfectionist husband and father of three. In 2003, at age fifty-two, in the depths of depression, he committed suicide after putting in a full day's work in the kitchen amid rumors that his restaurant would soon lose one of its Michelin stars. He'd worked tirelessly for seventeen years to earn his bona fides yet was seriously in debt and had grown increasingly despondent. His aggrieved widow took over the business, which not only survived but prospered under her direction. The ironic chapter of the sad story is that the restaurant never lost a star and, in the hands of a new executive chef, has thrived.

We spend two nights at the Relais Bernard Loiseau and relish our first-ever three-star meal. The elegantly rustic dining room is warmly decorated and dimly lit and looks over a leafy garden courtyard. The food does not disappoint. We surrender to the sheer joy of eating and savor every dish, gourmandise, and *mignardise* purposefully placed in front of us. Each mouthful is sublime with subtle flavors, the service is faultless, the atmosphere is relaxed and unhurried, and there's nary a pretension. The radiance of our dinner in Burgundy eases our ache for the sun.

THE FINAL APPROACH TO PARIS

We spend our final itinerant days before returning to Paris wandering the country roads of Burgundy and then Lorraine and Picardy, through one little French town after another. Every one has grown up around its very own *hôtel de ville*, and each town hall is proudly adorned with civic pride and window boxes trailing summer flowers. Bold red, white, and blue RF shields (for "République Française") are prominent, and on either side fly the French *tricouleur* and the local flag. Also fixtures in each village center, no matter how small, are two memorials inscribed with the names of all its men who died in the First and Second World Wars. It's a shock to see so many names, especially for World War I, in hamlets whose entire populations couldn't be more than a few dozen.

On our way out of Burgundy, we roll over the fertile hills of Chablis under a fleetingly sunny sky and make our way toward the city of Verdun. The clear light reflecting off golden wheat fields and green vineyards soon gives way to overcast skies and portends somber scenes of war ahead. We talk less than usual, both of us subdued and pensive. Thinking about our inevitable return to the United States, we're content in the close-companioned silence that feels comfortable only in the most familiar relationships.

We arrive in Lorraine to face the World War I killing fields. Visiting the sites of war is not my favorite pastime, but it's of great interest to Joe, and it's hard to resist all he's taught me over the course of our battlefield pilgrimages. We follow la Voie Sacrée (the Sacred Way) into Verdun, the one route that provided access into the beleaguered center during the almost-yearlong battle for the city. All others were controlled by German firepower. Multiple monuments, graveyards, and war sites line the road, and after multiple stops we find ourselves at Fort Douaumont, in the hills northeast of town.

Captured by the Germans in the early days of the Battle of Verdun, it remains a dangerous place. Signs along the pathways read: DEAR FRIENDS AND PILGRIMS, FOR YOUR OWN SAFETY AND OUT OF RESPECT FOR THOSE WHO FOUGHT AND DIED IN VERDUN, PLEASE KEEP TO THE FOOTPATHS . . . THE WEAPONS OF WAR CAN STILL KILL! A short drive from the fort and the still-live minefields, the Douaumont Ossuary overlooks a French military cemetery and houses the remains of 130,000 unidentified soldiers who lost their lives in battle.

World War I was especially brutal, and the scale of

destruction and human slaughter of the war intended to end all wars was unprecedented. While the trenches and mine craters have been softened by time and the greening forces of nature have reclaimed much of the landscape, the scars remain nonetheless. We continue traveling west in warm drizzle down country lanes, behind plodding farm vehicles. Huge white dairy cows graze on age-old farms whose mossy stone buildings appear to have been there since the Middle Ages. While there was no direct fighting on these farmlands, I can only imagine the devastation experienced by those who lived there. So many millions were killed in World War I, and for what?

It's been a sobering, gray road trip. The sun is still hidden, and a humidity we haven't sensed since we left home presses on us. "We'd better get used to it," I tell Joe, and he shakes his head wistfully, unable to respond. We're only eight days from heading back to the States and the closing weeks of summer in Washington, where the mid-Atlantic trifecta—heat, haze, and humidity—awaits. We see the lights of Paris on the horizon and count on them to lift our subdued spirits.

PARIS: THE LAST, HOT HURRAH

We return to the studio we rented for our first month in Paris for these last days and listen to the familiar sounds in the building: the couple chatting next door, the cougher upstairs, and the opening and closing of the heavy front door. When we arrived twelve months ago, the weather was cool, with fall in the air, but we're now in the thick of the sticky, hot summer. Everything and everyone is in slow motion because of the heat—over one hundred humid degrees in a city where air-conditioning is hardly de rigueur. The weather is such that even as we sit quietly in the shade on a bench near the Eiffel Tower, we're bathed in sweat. As perspiration drips down our temples, puddles on our upper lips, and drops onto our thighs, we consider joining the teens jumping into gushing fountains for relief. Indeed, we've come full circle in returning to Paris, having cycled through the seasons of Europe. We reluctantly go about unpacking our bags for the final time on our trip. When it comes time to stuff everything back in, we'll be preparing for the flight back home.

Paris is a ghost town. We arrive on a Thursday afternoon, and the calm is palpable. "Are you sure it's not Sunday?" I ask Joe, as all is quiet along the banks of the Seine. But then the next day dawns, and even at the height of what should be the morning rush, Paris continues to sleep. It's our first time in the city in the second half of summer, and although I've heard how deserted the place is in August, witnessing it is strange indeed. I half expect tumbleweeds to roll down the Boulevard Saint-Germain past les Deux Magots. I always delight in the surface sparkle of colors set against the never-ending French vanilla of Parisian buildings, but even the local pigments are muted in August's indolence. The locals have abandoned Paris for the mountains and the shore and left their fair city in the hands of the tourists; anyone we pass is not speaking French.

The slow pace of August in Paris mirrors the tempo of the waning days of our year. We're in sore need of some unscheduled downtime to mentally and emotionally prepare for our return home. Thus, as has become our habit so often over the past twelve months, our days in Paris are shaped by internal rhythms, not haste or timetables. We awaken each day with no agenda and eschew temporal exactitude for serendipity—a luxury we're keenly aware will vanish in the real world. It's our last gasp of spontaneity for some time.

Every Monday morning, I mark the new week by replenishing my vitamin caddy. It's now pillbox countdown time, our final week ticking by, and I feel so profoundly the inevitable passage of time as I drop the tablets into their daily slots for the final time in Europe. So few pills remain. So few days linger. Our flight leaves Friday, and here it is Monday.

We embark on some final, gentle exploring of neighborhoods unknown and find ourselves in northeastern Paris on the banks of the Canal Saint-Martin. There's an energy along the channel, much like that found in quarters all over the world where young people flock, play instruments outdoors, and converse. Quirky boutiques and trendy cafés line both sides of the waterway, and iron footbridges cross from side to side. We stop for dinner in an industrial space turned funky bistro serving Indian fare. I'm sure the other patrons—young, hip, and international—wonder about the fifty-six-year-old interlopers in their midst.

With just two more days and a wake-up left to our gap year, and desperate for the relief of some genuine air-conditioning, we decide to indulge in a capstone lunch at a fine restaurant. But doing such is no easy task, since almost all are closed in August: Lasserre, Taillevent, le Pré Catelan, and others. I envision all the finest chefs of Paris in starched toques, sipping umbrella drinks at tiki bars along the Côte d'Azur.

And then Joe suggests, "How about Jules Verne on the Eiffel Tower?"

All associations with the doomed engagement of Tom Cruise and Katie Holmes aside, our meal is *magnifique*. We have no expectations other than a beautiful view, but not only is the panorama priceless, but the food, the service, and the wine at this Alain Ducasse restaurant make for a wonderful memory. I sip my Sancerre in a thin-lipped, long-stemmed wineglass and reflect on the times over the months when we lacked fine crystal goblets or even a simple tumbler and settled for nightcaps in plastic cups. And here we are, lunching on the second level of the Eiffel Tower. We've certainly mastered the art of turning on a dime from budget-traveler basics to the finest Europe has to offer.

We do a final tally for our Culinary Scorecard and agree on all but the winner. Greece and Turkey are tied for third, with Morocco in fourth place and all others falling well behind. While Joe sticks with Italy, I return to my beloved France and put it in the top slot, having enjoyed the simple garlic- and olive-infused Provençal classics all summer.

As we prepare to leave Paris, Joe and I talk about the thousands of couples who have made it their own since we left last fall. And with the conviction that only true love can deliver, we know in our hearts that no one else's attachment to the city is quite like ours and never will be.

ON RETURNING HOME

The gap year fantasy had been with me for as long as I can remember—in my mind's eye for over thirty years. The vision first took shape when I returned from studying abroad, clarified somewhat, and began to merit its very own manila file folder as it remained in my heart while I became a young mother, career-ladder climber, and dual-college-tuition payer. It then blossomed into a concrete plan with spreadsheets, maps, and piles of references as I matured into a middle-aged empty nester. My *idée fixe* of a year in Europe with Joe sustained me through many a professional trial, boring weekend, sticky Washington summer, and fleeting two-week vacation. I distinctly recall Joe's holding my hand, leaning over as our jet took off in 2001 for our twentieth-anniversary trip to France, and saying, "Just imagine we have one-way tickets and we're leaving for a full year abroad. How exciting will that be?"

I've been in a lump-throated daze for the past week, a heavy-chested sadness overtaking me. I find myself asking, *What will get me over future hurdles now that my vision has been realized? What escapist imaginings will consume my idle hours? Will life be harder now that we're members of the exclusive "those whose dreams have actually come true" club?* Here we are in Paris, concluding our long-awaited year abroad, poised for a ceremonial burning of clothes: Joe's black sport coat, worn to the point of translucence; my limp green hiking pants, devoid of life; and white T-shirts stained, gray, and ragged from too many ineffective sink washings. *Then again,* I think, *I've caught myself longing now and then for the comfort of the familiar. Perhaps, just perhaps, it's time to go home, time to allow routine back into our lives, time to find a place to nest.*

We'll soon be back to the frenzied daily grind, in the clutches of the Washington Beltway bourgeoisie, subject to the incessant drumbeat of our modern world. I envision the stresses lurking just beyond the horizon back in the States, ready to pounce the moment we arrive. We're resolute, however, about resisting the pressures and remaining dispassionate about the day-to-day exigencies of life in the nation's capital.

Thirty-one years after Joe and I set up house together, I consider what a gift we've been handed: to start our lives anew. As world-weary travelers now, we'll actually take pleasure in settling down and rooting in the familiar. We'll lose ourselves in new routines, untested and pregnant with possibility. Yes, we'll begin again, with no idea of where we'll work or live. We'll reinvent our lives, our surroundings, and ourselves and play a fresh hand of cards. Life doesn't get much luckier than that.

I'll miss being surrounded by languages other than our own every day, and French most of all. I'll suffer through withdrawal, like an addict going cold turkey, as I distance myself from the pleasure that is France, the pleasure that is Europe, the pleasure that is traveling.

Will we experience reverse culture shock on returning to the United States? Will the frenetic pace of American life take us aback? Will we ask, *Why are these people walking so fast? How is it that we understand everything said and don't frantically search for words to make ourselves clear? Why do toilets flush with handles on the side and not buttons on the top?* And, last but not least, *Why are these portions so huge?*

After being foreigners for so long, we're certain to continue feeling like strangers despite being back on home turf. We'll have to get used to seeing signs in English and adjust to the visual parade of the morbidly obese, chronically loud, and badly tattooed. And while I do love my country and our life in America, I fear that in an acclimating fit of pique I may one day scream at fellow citizens, "Why can't you be more like Europeans?"

Is there a new person emerging from her exploits across Europe as she wipes off the dust of magical places? Perhaps I won't know the answer until we're back in the melee and dealing with the quotidian details. But I've experienced some revelations while we're away, chief among them reinforcement of the virtues of simplicity and kindness. There were times while traveling when we had an acute need for a kind gesture—just a little one. And when it materialized in the form of a clerk's smile or a pedestrian who helped direct us, it made all the difference in the world. I want my days to be filled with kind gestures—both those I offer and those I receive. At this time in my life, I'm not interested in being with people I don't care for, who aren't thoughtful, and with whom I'm embarrassed to sit in a restaurant because of how they treat the staff. The most important thing in life is to be kind, and I find I now have no tolerance for anyone who isn't.

On the eve of our departure, if someone knocked on our door and told us we must stay another few months, smiles would immediately overwrite our leave-taking frowns. A few more months among the wonders of Europe would suit us just fine. But knowing we'll soon be back in the United States, seeing our children, friends, and family, is not a bad thing either. Going home is hard when you love where you've been, but being in the same country as our kids will make our hard landing somewhat softer. It's been difficult on Chris and Caroline to have us so far away, and while we're used to living apart, the wide Atlantic Ocean was a very real gulf that made our separation more acute.

It's difficult to admit, but perhaps my contentment pendulum has swung back to longing for a comfortable home base and the desire to settle down—to move to a place we can call our own, where we can unpack, knowing that in a few days we'll not have to repack yet again, and where we can become reacquainted with the familiarities we left behind.

But I know myself well, and the cozy complaisance of life in the familiar will last only so long. My craving for novelty will once again wrestle with my need for security. On some undetermined evening in the not-too-distant future, over a glass of wine in the dark corner of a local bistro, my always-persistent wanderlust will poke through the fabric of our daily lives, and I'll declare to Joe my need for adventure, movement, and discovery. And the determined planning for more travel will begin yet again.

LE DÉPART

Alfred Hitchcock observed, "Drama is life with the boring bits left out," a sentiment that might well apply to long-term travel. Viewed from the sidelines, it's kaleidoscopic, sophisticated, and always in Technicolor, every minute of every day. But the reality is that an extended journey is just life, after all, with days filled with laundry, food shopping, bill paying, and other ordinary tasks. There are ups and downs; there is excitement and ennui. Our year included bouts of tedium, exhaustion, and longing for our children, who thankfully managed to stay healthy and reasonably happy during our absence. Only once, in the deserted French village of Caunes-Minervois, did we ever consider cutting our trip short to head home.

The unveiling of our gap year aftermath, of our reassimilation to what will be the rest of our life, is about to begin. The day of our departure from the escapades of the Old World for the possibilities of the New has arrived. We've done what we can to make our time in Europe last as long as possible—to appreciate every minute and create vivid memories—but the inexorable flow of time is impossible to stanch. It seems like forever and yet only yesterday since we left the United States and landed in France.

On our final morning, I repeat for the last time what has become my travel-day ritual. I slip on my uniform of comfort (boyfriend jeans, black tee, and hiking sandals), bid au revoir to our rented studio, and take to the road. Dragging our bags behind us, we pass Parisians performing their early-morning rituals: sweeping brasserie floors, polishing shop windows, posting *plats du jour*, and unstacking the burgundy and yellow plastic-webbed chairs of sidewalk cafés. It's painful to think of the orchestration of daily life in Paris continuing on without us. I want to cry, but somehow I don't. We walk by our favorite neighborhood *boulangerie*, resisting the urge to stop, as we have so often before, for fresh, buttery croissants and yeasty baguettes. Breakfast at the airport will have to do.

As we roll up the escalator to the Motte-Picquet metro platform, a busker serenades us on an accordion below, a fitting morning elegy for the conclusion of our year. It hits me like an arrow from a tightly strung bow: it's really over. We're leaving Paris, saying goodbye to France; our adventure has come to a close. My tears finally spill over.

Life on the road was not always glamorous; traveling does indeed have its difficulties. There were days of skinned knees, both literal and figurative, on the cobbled streets of Europe. Over the past year, we could have cross-examined ourselves daily about whether taking a year off was testament to our madness or a tribute to our pluck.

But in reality, we always knew it was the right thing to do at this point in our lives and never questioned our decision. Was our journey the answer to our long-standing dream of living in Europe to absorb it deep in our souls? The answer is yes—a resounding, heartfelt yes. We've run maniacally from the logic of self-satisfied people of privilege who, because they've been blessed, believe they deserve it. We simply feel happy that we made our dream come true, lucky to have been able to take a gap year from regular life, and fortunate to have had calm waters at home, such that our sabbatical was without interruption.

I didn't know then what I'd learn in the months to come. We'd continue to be lucky and happy as well. I would find a job teaching French at a suburban middle school and Joe a position in the Washington Navy Yard, building ships. We would settle into a cozy apartment for two in Bethesda, Maryland, around the corner from an authentic French bistro at which we would become regulars, drinking Sancerre alongside café fare, pretending we're still in Paris.

As we lift off from Orly, I recall the young, newly married Filipino couple we met in Turkey who sought our travel advice. "Is two weeks enough time to see Europe?" they innocently asked.

"Oh my," we replied. "We'll be here for a year, and we'll barely scratch the surface."

Our plane soars upward, and the individual sights of Paris and its suburbs quickly blend into the mosaic of rural France below. It's a gentle palette of outlined shapes—the soft greens, tans, and browns of the countryside—until at last we disappear in the clouds. Our twelve months are over, and we're halfheartedly heading home.

"So, what do you think, Gap Year Girl—is there another adventure like this in our future?" Joe asks.

I snuggle close and without hesitation reply, "I wouldn't rule it out."

ACKNOWLEDGMENTS

FIRST AND FOREMOST, thanks to Chris and Caroline, without whose encouragement, visits, and weekly calls from the States we never could have stayed away for a year; to Annie, editor extraordinaire, whose gentle touch made all the difference; to Lisa at *Bethesda* magazine and Brooke at She Writes Press, for taking a chance on me; to my parents, who always let me ride my bike clear across town to the library, and to my mom, who always encouraged me to write; to Al, for always understanding, and Noreen, for always being there; to my faithful readers, who followed our trip every step of the way, including Mary Anne, Spencer, Nancy, and Cathy, as well as my brothers and sisters; to Davida, dear friend, fellow writer, and technology advisor; to Neil, who willed me across the marathon finish line; to all those we met along the way, including Anton and Cecilia, Mathias, Hugo and Cinzia Bernardi, Sherry, Céline, Juliette, Aarti, Caroline, Alexander, Tonis, George, Filippo, and Stefano; to our intrepid fellow TMB hikers: Eric, Laura, Mike, Robby, Brooke, and Bruce; and finally to Joe, who always believes in me and without whom traveling would be just a series of stops.

ABOUT THE AUTHOR

~

PHOTO CREDIT: J. CHARLES

MARIANNE BOHR, freelance writer and editor, married her high school sweetheart and travel partner. With their two grown children, she follows her own advice and travels at every opportunity. Marianne lives outside Washington, DC, where, after decades in publishing, she followed her Francophile muse to teach middle school French. *Gap Year Girl* is her first book.

SELECTED TITLES FROM SHE WRITES PRESS

She Writes Press is an independent publishing company founded to serve women writers everywhere. Visit us at www.shewritespress.com.

Daring to Date Again: A Memoir by Ann Anderson Evans. $16.95, 978-1-63152-909-2. A hilarious, no-holds-barred memoir about a legal secretary turned professor who dives back into the dating pool headfirst after twelve years of celibacy.

Renewable: One Woman's Search for Simplicity, Faithfulness, and Hope by Eileen Flanagan. $16.95, 978-1-63152-968-9. At age forty-nine, Eileen Flanagan had an aching feeling that she wasn't living up to her youthful ideals or potential, so she started trying to change the world—and in doing so, she found the courage to change her life.

Seeing Red: A Woman's Quest for Truth, Power, and the Sacred by Lone Morch. $16.95, 978-1-938314-12-4. One woman's journey over inner and outer mountains—a quest that takes her to the holy Mt. Kailas in Tibet, through a seven-year marriage, and into the arms of the fierce goddess Kali, where she discovers her powerful, feminine self.

Seasons Among the Vines: Life Lessons from the California Wine Country and Paris by Paula Moulton. $16.95, 978-1-938314-16-2. New advice on wine making, tasting, and food pairing—along with a spirited account of the author's experiences in Le Cordon Bleu's pilot wine program—make this second edition even better than the first.

This is Mexico: Tales of Culture and Other Complications by Carol M. Merchasin. $16.95, 978-1-63152-962-7. Merchasin chronicles her attempts to understand Mexico, her adopted country, through improbable situations and small moments that keep the reader moving between laughter and tears.

Peanut Butter and Naan: Stories of an American Mom in India and the Middle East that will Stick to the Roof of Your Mouth by Jennifer Magnuson. $16.95, 978-1-63152-911-5. The hilarious tale of what happened when Jennifer Magnuson moved her family of seven from Nashville to India in an effort to shake things up—and got more than she bargained for.